Reading, Writing, and Rising Up

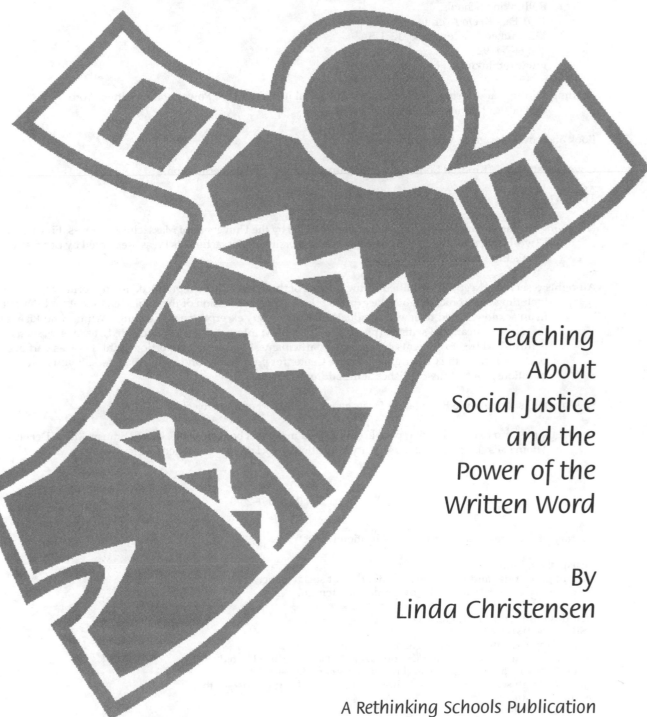

Teaching
About
Social Justice
and the
Power of the
Written Word

By
Linda Christensen

A Rethinking Schools Publication

Rethinking Schools, Ltd. is a nonprofit educational publisher of books, booklets, and a quarterly journal on school reform, with a focus on issues of equity and social justice.

To request additional copies of this book or a catalog of other publications, or to subscribe to the Rethinking Schools journal, contact:

Rethinking Schools
1001 East Keefe Avenue
Milwaukee, Wisconsin 53212 USA
800-669-4192
www.rethinkingschools.org

Book and cover design by C.C. Krohne.

Cover illustration, "Kindred Spirits" by Jane Murray Lewis. Used by permission.

Thanks to Ann Shearer for digitally optimizing photos.

"forgiving my father" by Lucille Clifton copyright © 1980 by the University of Massachusetts Press. First published in "Two-Headed Woman," published by the University of Massachusetts Press. Reprinted by permission of Curtis Brown, Ltd.

Special thanks to the Joyce Foundation for its generous support of this project.

Special thanks also to the following people who helped make this book possible: Rita S. Brause; Maria DeFelice; Thomas Favia, president, Jersey City Education Association; and Bartlett G. Hewey.

ISBN 0-942961-25-0

Library of Congress Cataloging-in-Publication Data

Christensen, Linda.
  Reading, writing, and rising up : teaching about social justice and
the power of the written word / by Linda Christensen.
     p. cm.
Includes bibliographical references (p.).
  ISBN 0-942961-25-0
  1. Reading (Secondary)—Social aspects—United States. 2.
Literature—Study and teaching (Secondary)—Social aspects—United
States. 3. Social justice—Study and teaching (Secondary)—United
States. 4. High school students—United States—Social conditions—20th
century. I. Title.
  LB1632 .C49 2000
  306.4'88'0973—dc21
                          00-010916

Reading, Writing, and Rising Up:
Teaching About Social Justice and the Power of the Written Word

A PUBLICATION OF RETHINKING SCHOOLS

Introduction

Why reading, writing, and rising up? Because during my 24 years of teaching literacy skills in the classroom, I came to understand that reading and writing are ultimately political acts.

Africans brought in chains to the United States were denied literacy because slaveholders knew it could be the pathway to liberty. As Frederick Douglass wrote in 1845, "A [slave] should know nothing but to obey his master — to do as he is told to do. Learning would spoil the best [slave] in the world. Now if you teach that [slave] how to read, there would be no keeping him. It would forever unfit him to be a slave."

Today, literacy is denied or withheld in other kinds of ways. The continued "achievement gap" between white students and students of color is further testimony to how education — especially reading and writing — continues to be a barrier to equality. In a country that has the wealth "to put whitey on the moon" as Gil Scott-Heron sang in the '70s, it is a sin that every child cannot read and write.

Without the basic tools of literacy, "rising up" can be limited to the "mute rebellion" that lands too many in prison. "In prison, 19% of adult males are illiterate and 40% are 'functionally illiterate'. . . . [O]ver 70% of prisoners in state facilities have not completed high school. If illiteracy, as some believe, is a major cause of crime, literacy provides a means to see oneself, one's life and condition, and to imagine alternatives" (Chevigny, 1999).

People who lack reading and writing skills have difficulty expressing who they are. Their words are strangled and they learn to be silent. Their lack of literacy becomes internalized self-hatred. Poet Jimmy Santiago Baca wrote in the powerful essay, "Coming into Language" from the anthology *Doing Time: 25 Years of Prison Writing* :

> *Ashamed of not understanding and fearful of asking questions, I dropped out of school in the ninth grade. . . . Most of my life I felt like a target in the crosshairs of a hunter's rifle. When strangers and outsiders questioned me I felt the hang-rope tighten around my neck and the trapdoor creak beneath my feet. There was nothing so humiliating as being unable to express myself, and my inarticulateness increased my sense of jeopardy. Behind a mask of humility, I seethed with mute rebellion. . . .*
>
> *[In prison] I met men, prisoners who read aloud to each other the works of Neruda, Paz, Sabines, Nemerov, and Hemingway. Never had I felt such freedom as in that dormitory. Listening to the words of these writers, I felt that invisible threat from without lessen — my sense of teetering on a rotting plank over swamp water where famished*

alligators clapped their horny snouts for my blood. While I listened to the words of the poets, the alligators slumbered powerless in their lairs. The language of poetry was the magic that could liberate me from myself, transform me into another person, transport me to places far away. . . (ibid, p. 101).

For Baca, writing is a transformative act — a rising up:

When at last I wrote my first words on the page, I felt an island rising beneath my feet like the back of a whale. As more and more words emerged, I could finally rest: I had a place to stand for the first time in my life. The island grew, with each page, into a continent inhabited by people I knew and mapped with the life I lived (p. 103).

Early in my teaching career I came to see literacy as a tool that students could use to know themselves and to heal themselves as Baca writes in his essay. As I discuss in "Writing the Word and the World" (see page 58), I realized I needed to take those feelings of inadequacy that Baca writes about and get at the social roots of that alienation and despair — to help students use words as a passage into interrogating society. We need to move beyond sharing and describing our pain to examining why we're in pain and figuring out how to stop it.

I use the term "rising up" because reading and writing should be emancipatory acts. When students are taught to read "the word and the world," as Brazilian educator Paulo Freire (Freire and Macedo, 1987) wrote, then their minds become unshackled. As Freire insisted, teaching students just to read is not enough. We must teach students how to "read" not only novels and science texts, but cartoons, politicians, schools, workplaces, welfare offices, and Jenny Craig ads. We need to get students to "read" where and how public money is spent. We need to get students to "read" the inequitable distribution of funds for schools. This is "rising up" reading — reading that challenges, that organizes for a better world.

In "A Talk to Teachers," James Baldwin (1985) wrote:

The paradox of education is precisely this — that as one begins to become conscious one begins to examine the society in which he is being educated. The purpose of education, finally, is to create in a person the ability to look at the world for himself, to make his own decisions. . . . But no society is really anxious to have that kind of person around. What societies really, ideally, want is a citizenry which will simply obey the rules of society. If a society succeeds in this, that society is about to perish. The obligation of anyone who thinks of

himself as responsible is to examine society and try to change it and to fight it — at no matter what risk. This is the only hope society has. This is the only way societies change.

My first taste of Baldwin's paradox came around the issue of language. For years, I'd felt shame about my own nonstandard language and watched my words to make sure they didn't sound like "home." When I came to understand how language can be a tool of domination and that my home language wasn't wrong, it was simply the language of people without money, I became angry. Out of that anger, that rising up, I developed a unit on the politics of language (see Chapter 4) so that students in my English classes could understand the power of language to not only shape our self-concept, but to limit access to power.

In fact, each chapter in this book came out of what Baldwin described as the obligation "to examine society and try to change it and to fight it." In the fall of 1975, I entered Jefferson High School, located in the heart of a predominantly working-class African-American neighborhood in Portland, Oregon, as a temporary Title I Reading teacher. Straight from student teaching in an almost all-white lower-class middle school, straight from a white working-class community, I landed in the place that not only shaped me, but profoundly changed me by the time I was forced by reconstitution to leave the school 22 years later.

> **I use the term "rising up" because reading and writing should be emancipatory acts.**

At Jefferson I found it necessary to teach reading and writing as liberating acts. I discovered that my students were more engaged in learning when we stopped reading novels as ends in themselves and started reading and examining society — from cartoons to immigration laws to the politics of language — and taking action, as Baldwin says, to "change it and to fight it."

I'm sure some teachers, parents, and administrators might be concerned about teaching students to rise up because it becomes synonymous with out-of-control classrooms. As bell hooks (1994) wrote:

The unwillingness to approach teaching from a standpoint that includes awareness of race, sex, and class is often rooted in the fear that classrooms will be uncontrollable, that emotions and passions will not be contained. To some extent we all know that whenever we address in the classroom subjects that students are passionate about there is always a possibility of confrontation, forceful expression of ideas or even conflict.

As I confess in the opening chapter, "Creating Community Out of Chaos," conflict does happen. But so does engagement and empowerment. And besides, what's the alternative? With so many schools reproducing failure and alienation, our real choice is between confronting the hard issues directly or watching them bubble up through cracks in a thousand less constructive ways.

And rising up is a metaphor for students imagining a different kind of society. My student Deanna Wesson said her social justice education taught her that she didn't have to accept inferiority. It taught her to demand more from schools and society. Poet Martín Espada (1994) wrote, "Any progressive social change must be imagined first, and that vision must find its most eloquent possible expression to move from vision to reality. Any oppressive social condition, before it can be changed, must be named and condemned with words that persuade by stirring the emotions, awakening the senses. Thus the need for the political imagination."

This collection of work focuses on teaching for social justice. It comes out of my years at Jefferson, working with colleagues and parent activists in the Rethinking Schools, National Coalition of Education Activists, and National Writing Project communities.

I am acutely aware of the words of African revolutionary Amilcar Cabral, "Tell no lies. Claim no easy victories." It's a warning my partner and co-teacher Bill Bigelow reminds me to take to heart when I start "talking story" about my classroom. So let me open this book by using Cabral's words to proclaim there were no easy victories in any of these lessons. But there is hope. ∎

References

Baldwin, James. *The Price of the Ticket*. New York: St. Martin, 1985, p. 325.

Chevigny, Bell Gale (Ed.). *Doing Time: 25 Years of Prison Writing*. New York: Arcade, 1999.

Douglass, Frederick. *Narrative of the Life of Frederick Douglass: An American Slave*. Cambridge, MA: Belknap Press of Harvard University, 1960.

Espada, Martín. "Foreword," in Espada, Martín (Ed.), *Poetry like Bread: Poets of the Political Imagination from Curbstone Press*. Willimantic, CT: Curbstone, 1994.

Freire, Paulo, and Macedo, Donaldo. *Literacy: Reading the Word and the World*, South Hadley, MA: Bergin & Garvey, 1987.

hooks, bell. *Teaching to Transgress: Education as the Practice of Freedom*. London: Routledge, 1994, p. 39.

Acknowledgements

Teaching might appear to be a solo act: When the door closes, it's usually just one teacher and her students. But we're never alone in our classrooms. Mentors, colleagues, the writers we love, former students, even our families crowd in with us — giving guidance, challenging us, or reminding us to behave. Ultimately, teaching is a collective performance. And so, I've discovered, is writing.

There would be no book without my life companion Bill Bigelow. Our first year teaching together Bill turned my pedagogy upside down with his questions and analysis; through his role plays and emphasis on social justice he brought Paulo Freire's words, "Conflict is the midwife of consciousness," to bear on the classroom where we taught Literature and U.S. History. Over the years he has read every draft I've written and continued to comment and advise — even when I threw the drafts at his head. If they awarded Nobel Prizes for teaching, Bill would take home the first honor.

From the first day of my "education" at Jefferson to my last, nothing had a more profound effect on my teaching than the students of Jefferson High School. Their humor, their abilities to overcome adverse situations, their wisdom, their willingness to forgive me for my faults, and their criticism marked me. Daily they demonstrated how much students know about the world that is too often not a part of the official curriculum. It's difficult to single out a few students when I've taught so many. But some students have become family and colleagues over the years: Katy Barber, Pamela Clegg, Rochelle Eason, Portia Hall, Khalilah Joseph, Meg Niemi, Mira Shimabukuro, Nicole Smith-Leary, Damon Turner, Alejandro Vidales, Dyan Watson, Deanna and Stacy Wesson, Amanda and Aaron Wheeler-Kay, Cresta White, and Jenelle Yarbrough.

As I noted, teaching is not a solo act. I was fortunate to belong to an outstanding Language Arts department. We were a contentious group, but through our disagreements and discussions we found hard nuggets of truth that I savored in my classroom. And while we came at teaching from different perspectives, we were united in our commitment to our students. I was honored to work with Mary Ayala, Gail Black, Mary Burke-Hengen, Therese Cooper, Ruthann Hartley, Tim Hardin, Pam Hooten, Jim Straughan, Jeanette Swenson, and Millie Wriggle.

The Oregon Writing Project taught me both the value of examining my own practice and the importance of looking to classroom teachers for answers. I am indebted to Nat Teich and Vince Wixon for their baptism into the project, to Tim Gillespie and Kim Stafford who continue to be writing allies. Mary Bothwell, the mother of Language Arts in Portland Schools, modeled how to fight ferociously on behalf of all students. Michelann Ortloff demonstrates that heart and intellect are powerful partners in classroom teachers and administrators. Cynthia MacLeod, Portland Writing Project co-director, not only taught my daughter Anna how to write and think, she teaches me each summer the art of quiet contemplation before speaking. Molly Chun, who completes our Writing Project triad, is small in stature, but huge in her impact on my understanding of early childhood reading and writing development.

My work was also honed by a series of study/action groups that came to be known as Portland Area Rethinking Schools. Over the years, members have included Renée Bald, Bill Bigelow, Gloria Canson, Andy Clark, Jeff Edmundson, Jackie Ellenz, Ruth Hubbard, Laurie King, Sylvia McGauley, Tom McKenna, Ethan Medley, Karen Miller, Michelle Miller, Bill Resnick, Doug Sherman, Eddy Shuldman, Jessie Singer, Kent Spring, Julie Treick, Jamie Zartler, and Jan Zuckerman. This group helped me think more critically about issues both inside and outside the classroom from tracking to school funding to testing. Ruth Hubbard gave me the joy of quiet walks, where she encouraged and pushed my writing when I fell into the doldrums. Sandra Childs is my critical ally in teaching and literature.

My articles and assumptions met the scrutiny of the national Rethinking Schools editorial board and staff: Bill Bigelow, Beverly Cross, Joanna Dupuis, Brenda Harvey, Stan Karp, David Levine, Bob Lowe, Larry Miller, Barbara Miner, Bob Peterson, Kathy Swope, Rita Tenorio, and Mike Trokan. Their critiques and questions about my writing as well as our meetings and discussions serve as sessions of critical reflection and honest re-appraisal.

Beverly Cross read my manuscript and gave me invaluable critical advice when I was at a crossroads. Leon Lynn, Rethinking Schools book-publishing director, has been more generous in his praise and his patience than I deserve. Carol Ringo has done a terrific job researching photos and permissions for the book and compiling the index.

Bob Peterson has been a critical ally as well as a friend for many years. From his fiery speeches about equity in education to his poems about nature to his wacky and wonderful ideas that created Rethinking Schools, he is the Tom Paine of the social justice education movement.

My friend and colleague Stan Karp never fails to give searingly honest reviews of my writing, teaching, and life. His humor, friendship, and political analysis have seen me through many rocky situations — on hiking trails as well as in life.

The National Coalition of Education Activists (NCEA) has become a school of education for those of us engaged in the work of transforming public education and society. Working with the brilliant and passionate anti-racist educator Enid Lee gave me new frameworks to guide my teaching.

Without Deborah Menkart prodding me to produce a teaching guide for *Rites of Passage*, many of the classroom lessons in this book would not exist.

Educators Alma Flor Ada, Carole Edelsky, Herb Kohl, Sonia Nieto, Patrick Shannon, Ira Shor, Geneva Smitherman, and Beverly Tatum have provided me theoretical insights as well as support for my classroom work.

My mother, Lena Christensen, taught me the basics of teaching when she raised me: Keep your expectations high and pin their writing to the wall. My sister, Colleen Furnish, cheered me, fed me, watched my daughters, and believed in me. Because of my brother, Billy, I am perhaps the only teacher to have her articles hung on the walls of a bar ("BC's" in Eureka, California). And my sister, Tina, taught me the value of seeing beyond a person's actions to their motivations, and of opening my hands when I want to make a fist.

My daughters Anna and Gretchen Hereford have been the greatest gifts in my life. They have become women warriors whose words land on the side of justice and integrity. Each day I walk into a classroom, I am reminded that the children I teach are as precious to their parents as my daughters are to me. I am humbled.

A POEM FOR THE WOMEN IN MY DEPARTMENT

I see the hand of time on us —
corralled in our small classrooms
each morning,
like the heifers
my grandmother milked.
We graze on words
and suckle children
each year,
dawn to dusk
in our tidy, colorful stalls.

Now age spots
freckle our hands,
and the skin on our necks
and arms demonstrates
the power of gravity.
I watch the gray
weave its way
through our hair,
traveling like ivy,
holding us together,
unruly sisters,
while veins bubble up,
making roadmaps from ankle to thigh.

I want us to climb back in our stalls,
flick our tails over our spreading rumps,
chew our words,
and tell you
how beautiful we've become
this September.

— Linda Christensen

Notes to the Reader

In many ways this book is the teaching history of my years at Jefferson High School in Portland, Oregon. Most chapters developed out of "aha" moments from a class; a conversation with colleagues, students, or parents; a stirring talk; anger; or out of the pain of walking away at the end of the year wondering how I could "do it better" in the fall. For example, I wrote "Standard English: Whose Standard?" after hearing Tony Baez deliver a moving keynote speech on the English-only movement at a National Coalition of Education Activists conference. His insights about linguistic discrimination helped me make sense of the discrimination I had experienced for speaking a white working-class language growing up, and the prejudice that my predominately African-American students at Jefferson confronted in their lives. "Writing the Word and the World" came after I started teaching with Bill Bigelow and realized that I had missed huge opportunities to engage students in reflecting on the broader social contexts of their lives.

The teaching ideas evolved during my work in three classes: a lower track freshman class, an untracked junior level Literature and U.S. History course for which students received both English and U.S. history credit, and an untracked senior English class, Contemporary Literature and Society. Each chapter begins with a story-based discussion of key issues about particular areas of teaching, followed by lessons, student samples, and handouts that can be reproduced for classroom use.

I've discovered that my students learn new writing styles or reading techniques more effectively when I provide them with models from my previous students, perhaps because these pieces are more accessible than the work of professional writers. Some of the models contain errors that I did not correct because the pieces were first drafts — a dialogue journal or free write generated to capture thoughts while reading or in reaction to a movie or improvisation. These were not meant to be final drafts. Most of the student pieces were first published in *Rites of Passage*, Jefferson's literary magazine that I started in the mid-'80s.

I have used students' first and last names throughout the book except when I wanted the student to remain anonymous.

While the chapters proceed somewhat chronologically, based on when I teach each unit, there is no recipe here. For example, many lessons in the chapter "Building Community Out of Chaos" are spread out during the year. I use them to break up the doldrums, to continue to nurture connections between students, or to provide a pause between longer units.

Although the poetry chapter is in the middle of the book, I teach poetry throughout the year. While I do teach the units on the politics of language and cartoons nearly every year, my curriculum frequently changes in response to students' needs. My immigration unit, for example, emerged after I overheard students making disparaging remarks about immigrants and in response to proposed anti-immigration laws.

Although the writing in this book spans a period of more than ten years, it is still very much a work in progress. I had wanted to include lessons I didn't have time to polish and chapters that still needed rethinking. But I finally realized that writing a book is like teaching — there are victories to celebrate and inevitable gaps to mourn. And in teaching, as in life, *a luta continua*: the struggle continues. ■

Building Community Out of Chaos

Building Community Out of Chaos

One winter break I read a book on teaching that left me feeling desolate because the writer's vision of a joyful, productive classroom did not match the chaos I faced daily in my high school. My students straggled in, still munching on Popeye's chicken, wearing Walkmen, and generally acting surly because of some incident in the hall during break, a fight with their parents, a teacher, a boyfriend or girlfriend. That year, more than ever, they failed to finish the writing started in class or to read the novel or story I assigned as homework. Too often they were suffering from pains much bigger than I could deal with: homelessness, pregnancy, the death of a brother, sister, friend, or cousin due to street violence, the nightly spatter of guns in their neighborhoods, the decay of a society.

For too many days during that first quarter I felt like a prison guard trying to bring order and kindness to a classroom where students laughed over the beating of a man at a local mall, made fun of a classmate who was going blind, and mimicked the way a Vietnamese girl spoke until they pushed her into silence.

Each September I have this optimistic misconception that I'm going to create a compassionate, warm, safe place for students in the first days of class, because my recollection is based on the final quarter of the previous year. In the past that atmosphere did emerge in a shorter time span. But the students were more homogenous, and we were living in somewhat more secure and less violent times. While students shared the tragedies of divorce and loss of friendships, their class talk was less often disrupted by the pressure cooker of society — and I was more naive and rarely explored those areas. We were polite to each other as we kept uncomfortable truths at bay.

Now, I realize that classroom community isn't always synonymous with warmth and harmony.

Politeness is often a veneer mistaken for understanding, when in reality it masks uncovered territory, the unspeakable pit that we turn from because we know the anger and pain that dwell there. During my years at Jefferson High School in Portland, Oregon — where the interplay of race, class, and gender created a constant background static — it was important to remind myself that real community is forged out of struggle. Students won't always agree on issues, and the fights, arguments, tears, and anger are the crucible from which a real community grows.

Still, I hate discord. When I was growing up, I typically gave up the fight and agreed with my sister or mother so that a reconciliation could be reached. I can remember running to my "safe" spot under my father's overturned rowboat, which hung over two sawhorses in the back yard, whenever anger ran loose in our house.

Too often these days I'm in the middle of that anger, and there's no safe spot. My first impulse is to make everyone sit down, be polite, and listen to each other — a great goal that I've come to realize doesn't happen easily. Topics like racism and homophobia are avoided in most classrooms, but they seethe like festering wounds. When there is an opening for discussion, years of anger and pain surface. But students haven't been taught how to talk with each other about these painful matters.

I can't say that I've found definitive answers, but as that year ended, I knew some of the mistakes I'd made. I also found a few constants: To become a community, students must learn to live in someone else's skin, understand the parallels of hurt, struggle, and joy across class and culture lines, and work for change. For that to happen, students need more than an upbeat, supportive teacher; they need a curriculum that encourages them to empathize with others.

Cleo Photography

Sharing Power and Passion

Before I could nurture student empathy, I had to find a way to connect with them. Ironically, violence was the answer.

In the fall of 1994 none of the get-acquainted activities that I count on to build a sense of community worked in my fourth block class. Students didn't want to get up and interview each other. They didn't want to write about their names. They didn't want to be in the class, and they didn't want any let's-get-to-know-each-other games or activities. Mostly, our 90-minute blocks were painfully long as I failed daily to elicit much response other than groans, sleep, or anger. It's hard to build community when you feel like you're "hoisting elephants through mud" as my friend Carolyn says. I knew it was necessary to break through their apathy and uncover something that made these students care enough to talk, to read, to write, to share — even to get angry.

In the first days, the only activity that aroused interest was when they wrote about their history as English students — what they liked, what they hated, and what they wanted to learn. Many of these students skulked in the low-track classes and they were angry — not about tracking, because they weren't aware that another kind of education might be possible, but about the way their time had been wasted on mean-

ingless activity. "The teacher would put a word on the board and then make us see how many words we could make out of the letters. Now what does that prepare me for?" Larry asked. This complaint I could understand. But they also hated reading novels and talking about them because novels "don't have anything to do with our lives." The other constant in many of their written responses was that they felt stupid.

For the first time, they got excited. I knew what they didn't want: worksheets, sentence combining, reading novels and discussing them, writing about "stuff we don't care about."

Reverberations Across Time and Culture

My fourth block class first semester was Senior English, a tracked class where most of the students were short on credits to graduate — as DJ said, "We're not even on the five year plan" — but long on humor and potential. They came in with their fists up and their chins cocked. They had attitudes. Many of them already had histories with each other.

Our year opened with a storm of violence in the city. The brother of a Jefferson student was shot and killed. Two girls were injured when random bullets were fired on a bus. A birthday party at a local restaurant was broken up when gunfire sprayed the side of

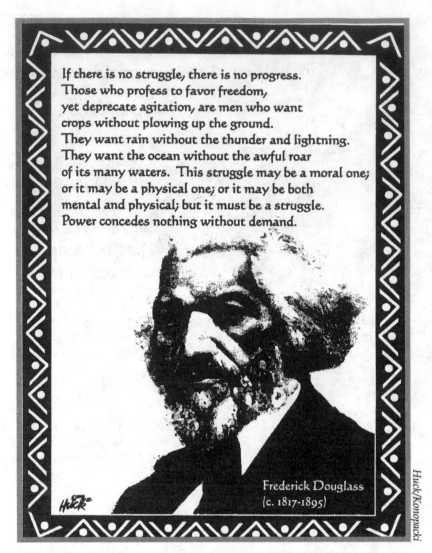

If there is no struggle, there is no progress.
Those who profess to favor freedom,
yet deprecate agitation, are men who want
crops without plowing up the ground.
They want rain without the thunder and lightning.
They want the ocean without the awful roar
of its many waters. This struggle may be a moral one;
or it may be a physical one; or it may be both
mental and physical; but it must be a struggle.
Power concedes nothing without demand.

Frederick Douglass
(c. 1817-1895)

Huck/Konopacki

In an attempt to get them involved in the novel, I read aloud an evocative passage about the unemployed peasants sweeping through the Chinese countryside pillaging, raping, and grabbing what was denied them through legal employment. Suddenly students saw their own lives reflected back at them through Chen, a minor character in the book, whose anger at losing his job and ultimately his family led him to become an outlaw. Chen created a new family with this group of bandits. Students could relate: Chen was a gang member. I had stumbled on a way to interest my class. The violence in China created a contact point between the literature and the students' lives.

This connection, this reverberation across cultures, time, and gender, challenged the students' previous notion that reading and talking about novels didn't have relevance for them. They could empathize with the Chinese but also explore those issues in their own lives.

This connection also created space to unpack the assumption that all gangs are bad. Chen wasn't born violent. He didn't start out robbing and killing. Lalu, the novel's main character, remembered him as a kind man who bought her candy. He changed after he lost his job and his family starved. Similarly, kids in gangs don't start out violent or necessarily join gangs to "pack gats" and shoot it out in drive-bys.

Because the tendency in most schools is to simultaneously deny and outlaw the existence of gangs, kids rarely talk critically about them.

A few years ago, scholar Mike Davis wrote an article analyzing the upsurge of gang activity in Los Angeles. He found it linked to the loss of union wage jobs. When I raised Davis' research, kids were skeptical. They saw other factors: the twin needs of safety and belonging. I hadn't explored Portland's history enough to know whether our situation was similar to Los Angeles, but I suspected economic parallels.

Our discussion of gangs broke the barrier. Students began writing about violence in their own lives and neighborhoods. DJ explained his brushes with violence:

> [T]he summer between my sophomore and junior years, some of my friends were getting involved in

the building. So violence was on the students' minds. I couldn't ignore the toll the outside world was exacting on my students. Rather than pretending that I could close my door in the face of their mounting fears, I needed to use that information to reach them.

But I didn't know what to teach them. I needed to engage them because they were loud, unruly, and out of control otherwise. But how? I decided to try the "raise the expectations" approach and use a curriculum I designed for my Contemporary Literature and Society class, which received college credit.

During those initial days of listening to these seniors and trying to read the novel *Thousand Pieces of Gold* (1991), a biography of a Chinese woman sold into prostitution and slavery in Northwest in the 1800s, I discovered that violence aroused my students. Students weren't thrilled with the book; in fact they weren't reading it. I'd plan a 90-minute lesson around the reading and dialogue journals they were supposed to be keeping, but only a few students were prepared. Most didn't even attempt to lie about the fact that they weren't reading and clearly weren't planning on it.

a new gang called the Irish Mob. . . . My friends were becoming somebody, someone who was known wherever they went. The somebody who I wanted to be. . . . During the next couple of weeks we were involved in six fights, two stabbings, and one drive-by shooting. We got away on all nine cases. The next Saturday night my brother was shot in a drive-by. The shooters were caught the same night.

Kari wrote that she joined a gang when she was searching for family. Her father lost his job; her mother was forced to work two jobs to pay the rent. Kari assumed more responsibility at home: cooking dinner, putting younger brothers and sisters to bed, and cleaning. While at middle school, Kari joined the Crips. She said at first it was because she liked the "family" feel. They wore matching clothes. They shared a language and nicknames. In a neighborhood that had become increasingly violent, they offered her protection. She left the gang after middle school because she was uncomfortable with the violence.

Students were surprised to learn that Phu, a recent immigrant from Vietnam, was also worried about her brother who had joined a gang. Her classmates were forced to reevaluate their initial assessments of her. While she had seemed like an outsider, a foreigner, her story made a bond between them.

At first, I worried that inviting students to write about violence might glorify it. It didn't turn out that way. Students were generally adamant that they'd made poor choices when they were involved in violent activities. As DJ states in his essay, "I wanted to be known wherever I went . . . . But I went about it all wrong and got mixed in. . . . It was nothing I had hoped for. Sure I was known and all that, but for all the wrong reasons."

More often students shared their fears. Violence was erupting around them and they felt out of control. They *needed* to share that fear.

Through the topic of violence I captured their interest, but I wanted them to critique the violence rather than just describe it.

I had hoped to build a community of inquiry where we identified a common problem and worked to understand it by examining history and our lives. That didn't happen. It was still early in the year, and students were so absorbed in telling their stories and listening to others it was difficult to pull them far enough away to analyze the situation. I didn't have enough materials that went beyond accusations or sensationalism about gangs and economics, but the topic itself also presented practical and ethical problems, especially around issues of safety and confidentiality. What happened if students admitted belonging

to gangs? What if a student discussed participating in a drive-by? My line with students had been, "What's shared in this class, stays in this class," with caveats about abuse and suicide prevention. Would I be able to keep that promise?

I want to be clear: Bringing student issues into the room does not mean giving up teaching the core ideas and skills of the class; it means using the energy of their connections to drive us through the content.

For example, students still had to write a literary essay. But they could use their lives as well as Lalu's to illustrate their points. Students scrutinized their issues through the lens of a larger vision, as Lamont did when he compared the violence in his life to the violence in Lalu's:

Lalu isn't a gang member, but some of the folks, or should I say, some of the enemies she came in contact with reminded me of my enemies. Bandits in the story represented the worst foes of my life. In some ways bandits and gangs are quite similar. One would be the reason for them turning to gang life. Neither of them had a choice. It was something forced upon them by either educational problems or financial difficulties. It could have been the fact that their families were corrupt or no love was shown. Whatever the reasons, it was a way of survival.

Finding the heartbeat of a class isn't always easy. I must know what's happening in the community and the lives of my students. If they're consumed by the violence in the neighborhood or the lack of money in their house, I'm more likely to succeed in teaching them if I intersect their concerns.

Building community means taking into account the needs of the members of that community. I can sit students in a circle, play getting-to-know-each-other games until the cows come home, but if what I am teaching in the class holds no interest for the students, I'm just holding them hostage until the bell rings.

A Curriculum of Empathy

As a critical teacher I encourage students to question everyday acts or ideas that they take for granted (see "Standard English: Whose Standard?" p. 100 and "Unlearning the Myths that Bid Us," p. 40). But I also teach them to enter the lives of characters in litera-

> **I couldn't ignore the toll the outside world was exacting on my students. Rather than pretending that I could close my door in the face of their mounting fears, I needed to use that information to reach them.**

ture, history, or real life they might otherwise dismiss or misunderstand. I don't want their first reaction to difference to be laughter or withdrawal. I try to teach them how to empathize with people whose circumstances might differ from theirs. Empathy is key in community building.

I choose literature that intentionally makes students look beyond their own world. In a class I co-taught with social studies teacher Bill Bigelow we used an excerpt from Ronald Takaki's *Strangers From a Different Shore* (1990) about Filipino writer Carlos Bulosan. Bulosan wrote, "I am an exile in America." He described the treatment he received, good and bad. He wrote of being cheated out of wages at a fish cannery in Alaska, being refused housing because he was Filipino, being tarred and feathered and driven from town.

We asked students to respond to the reading by keeping a dialogue journal. (See page 48 for more on dialogue journals.) Dirk wrote, "He's not the only one who feels like an exile in America. Some of us who were born here feel that way too." As he continued reading, he was surprised that some of the acts of violence Bulosan encountered were similar to those endured by African Americans. In his essay on immigration, Dirk chose to write about the parallels between Bulosan's life and the experiences he's encountered:

> When I was growing up I thought African Americans were the only ones who went through oppression. In the reading, 'In the Heart of Filipino America' I found that Filipinos had to go through a lot when coming to America. I can relate with the stuff they went through because my ancestors went through sort of the same thing.

Dirk went on to describe the parallels in housing discrimination, lynching, name-calling, and being cheated out of wages that both Filipinos and African Americans lived through.

Besides reading and studying about "others," Bill and I wanted students to come face to face with people they usually don't meet, as a way of breaking down their preconceived ideas about people from other cultures. During this unit we continued to hear students classify all Asians as "Chinese." In the halls, we heard students mimic the way Vietnamese students spoke. When writing about discrimination, another student confessed that she discriminated against the Mexican students at our school. We paired

---

At first, I worried that inviting students to write about violence might glorify it. It didn't turn out that way. More often students shared their fears.

---

our students with English-as-a-second-language students who had come from another country — Vietnam, Laos, Cambodia, Eritrea, Mexico, Guatemala, Ghana. They each interviewed their partner and wrote a profile of the student to share in class. Students were moved by their partners' stories. One student whose brother had been killed at the beginning of the year was paired with a girl whose sister was killed during the war in Eritrea. He connected to her loss and was amazed at her strength. Others were appalled at how these students had been mistreated at Jefferson. Many students later wrote about the lives of their partners in their essays on immigration.

Besides making immigration a contemporary rather than a historical topic, students heard the sorrow their fellow students felt at leaving "home." In our "curriculum of empathy," we wanted our class to see these students as individuals rather than ESL students, "Chinese" students, or an undifferentiated mass of Mexicans.

A curriculum of empathy puts students inside the lives of others. By writing interior monologues, acting out improvisations, taking part in role plays, by creating fiction stories about historical events, students learn to develop understanding about people whose culture, race, gender or sexual orientation differs from theirs. This is imperfect and potentially dangerous, of course, because sometimes students call forth stereotypes that need to be unpacked.

"Things changed for me this year," Wesley wrote in his end-of-the-year evaluation. "I started respecting my peers. My attitude has changed against homosexuals and whites." Similarly, Tyrelle wrote, "I learned a lot about my own culture as an African American but also about other people's cultures. I never knew Asians suffered. When we wrote from different characters in movies and stories I learned how it felt to be like them."

Sharing Personal Stories

Building community begins when students get inside the lives of others in history, literature, or down the hallway, but students also learn by exploring their own lives and coming to terms with the people they are "doing time" with in the classroom. Micere Mugo, a Kenyan poet, said, "Writing can be a lifeline, especially when your existence has been denied, especially when you have been left on the margins, especially when your life and process of growth have been subjected to attempts at strangulation." Many of our stu-

Jim Whitney

dents have been silenced in school, their stories denied or left unheard. Their histories have been marginalized to make room for "important" people, their interests and worries passed over so we can teach Oregon history or *The Scarlet Letter*.

To develop, students need to learn about each other's lives as well as reflect on their own. When they hear personal stories, classmates become real instead of cardboard stereotypes: rich white girl, basketball-addicted Black boy, brainy Asian. Once they've seen how people can hurt, once they've shared pain and laughter, they can't so easily treat people as objects to be kicked or beaten or called names. When students' lives are taken off the margins and placed in the curriculum, they don't feel the same need to put down someone else.

Any reading or history lesson offers myriad opportunities for this kind of activity. I find points of conflict, struggle, change, or joy and create an assignment to write about a parallel time in their lives. We've had students write about times they've been forced to move, been discriminated against or discriminated against someone else, changed an attitude or action, worked for change, lost a valuable possession. Obviously, losing a treasured item does not compare to the

Native Americans' loss of their land, but telling the story does give students a chance to empathize with the loss as well as share a piece of themselves with the class. All they have to empathize with is the reservoir of their own experiences — clearly limited, but all we have to build on.

Creating Passages between Students

When I was a child growing up in Eureka, California, my mother took me to the pond in Sequoia Park on Sundays to feed the ducks. They'd come in a great wash of wings and waves while I broke the bread into pieces to throw to them. I loved to watch them gobble up the soggy loaf, but I began noticing how some ducks took more than others. In fact, some ducks were pushed to the side and pecked at.

I've noticed the same thing happens in classrooms. Students find someone whom they think is weak and attack them.

In my fourth block class, the victim was Jim. He'd been in my class the year before. I'd watched him progress as a writer and thinker. In his end of the year evaluation, he drew a picture of himself as a chef; his writing was the dough. In an essay, he explained how writing was like making bread. He was proud of his achievements as a writer.

In both classes, Jim was a victim. He was going blind because of a hereditary disease. It didn't happen overnight, but he struggled with terror at his oncoming blindness. Because he was steadily losing his eyesight, he was clumsy in the classroom. He couldn't see where he was going. He knocked into people and desks. He accidentally overturned piles of books. Students responded with laughter or anger. Some days he cried silently into the fold of his arms. He told me, "I know the darkness is coming." Several male students in the class made fun of him for crying as well.

> **I came to understand that the key to reaching my students and building community was helping students excavate and reflect on their personal experiences, and connecting them to the world of language, literature, and society.**

One day, Amber was in a typically bad mood, hunched inside her too-big coat and snarling at anyone who came near. When Jim bumped her desk on the way to the pencil sharpener and her books and papers tumbled on the floor, she blew up at him for bumbling around the room. Jim apologized profusely and retreated into his shell after her attack.

A few days later I gave an assignment for students to write about their ancestors, their people. First, they read Margaret Walker's poems, "For My People" and "Lineage" and others. I told them they could imagine their people as their immediate ancestors, their race, their nationality or gender. Jim wrote:

To My People With Retinitis Pigmentosa

Sometimes I hate you
like the disease
I have been plagued with.
I despise the "sight" of you
seeing myself in your eyes.
I see you as if it were you
who intentionally
damned me to darkness.
I sometimes wish
I was not your brother;
that I could stop

the setting of the sun
and wash my hands of you forever
and never look back
except with pity,
but I cannot.
So I embrace you,
the sun continues to set
as I walk into darkness
holding your hand.

Students were silenced. Tears rolled. Kevin said, "Damn, man. That's hard."

Amber apologized to Jim in front of the class. At the end of the year she told me that her encounter with Jim was one of the events that changed her. She learned to stop and think about why someone else might be doing what they're doing, instead of immediately jumping to the conclusion that they were trying to annoy her.

My experience is that given a chance, students will share amazing stories. Students have told me that my willingness to share stories about my life with them opened the way for them to tell their stories. Students have written about rape, sexual abuse, and divorce, as well as drug and alcohol abuse. And through their sharing, they make openings to each other. Sometimes it's just a small break. A crack. A passage from one world to the other. And these openings allow the class to become a community.

Students as Activists

Community is also created when students struggle together to achieve a common goal. Sometimes the opportunity spontaneously arises out of the conditions or content of the class, school, or community. During the first year Bill Bigelow and I taught together, we exchanged the large student desks in our room with another teacher's smaller desks without consulting our students. We had 40 students in the class, and not all of the big desks fit in the circle. They staged a "stand in" until we returned the original desks. We had emphasized Frederick Douglass' admonition that power concedes nothing without a demand — and they took it to heart.

One year our students responded to a negative newspaper article, about how parents feared to send their children to our school, by organizing a march and rally to "tell the truth about Jefferson to the press." During the Columbus quincentenary, my students organized a teach-in about Columbus for classes at Jefferson. Of course, these "spontaneous uprisings" only work if teachers are willing to give

8

over class time for the students to organize, and if they've highlighted times when people in history resisted injustice, making it clear that solidarity and courage are values to be prized in daily life, not just praised in the abstract and put on the shelf.

But most often I have to create situations for students to work outside the classroom. I want them to connect ideas and action in tangible ways. Sometimes I do this by asking students to take what they have learned and create a project to teach at nearby elementary or middle schools. After students critique the media (see "Unlearning The Myths That Bind Us," p. 40), they are usually upset by the negative messages children receive, so I have them write and illustrate books for elementary students. Students in Literature and U.S. History write children's books about Abolitionists, the Nez Perce, Chief Joseph, and others. They brainstorm positive values they want children to receive, read traditional and contemporary children's books, critique the stories, and write their own. They develop lesson plans to go with their books. For example, before Bev read her book about John Brown she asked, "Has anyone here ever tried to change something they thought was wrong?" After students shared their experiences, she read her book. Students also created writing assignments to go with their books so they could model the writing process.

Students were nervous prior to their first teaching engagements. As they practiced lesson plans and received feedback from their peers, there was much laughter and anticipation. They mimicked "bad" students and asked improper questions that had nothing to do with the children's book: Is she your girlfriend? Why are your pants so baggy? Why does your hair look like that?

When they returned from the other schools, there were stories to share: children who hugged their knees and begged them to come back; kids who wouldn't settle down and listen; kids who said they couldn't write. My students proudly read the writings that came out of "their" class. They responded thoughtfully to each student's paper.

Lamont, a member of my English 12 class, was concerned by the number of young children who join gangs. He and several other young men wrote stories about gang violence and took them to our neighborhood elementary school. He strode into the class, wrote "GANGS" in big letters on the board and sat down. The fifth-grade class was riveted. He and his teaching mates read their stories and then talked with students about gangs. He wrote after his visit:

For a grown person to teach a kid is one thing. But for a teenager like myself to teach young ones is another. Kids are highly influenced by peers close to their age or a little older. I'm closer to their age, so they listen to me. . . . Some of these kids that I chatted with had stories that they had been wanting to get off their chest for a long time. . . . When I came to class with my adventures of being a gangster, that gave them an opportunity to open up. Spill guts. [No one] should object to me teaching these shorties about gang life, telling them that it's not all fun and games. It's straight do or die. Kill or be killed.

The seriousness the students showed was in sharp contrast to the seeming apathy they had displayed at the year's beginning.

Through the year, I came to understand that the key to reaching my students and building community was helping students excavate and reflect on their personal experiences, and connecting them to the world of language, literature, and society. We moved from ideas to action, perhaps the most elusive objective in any classroom.

Community and activism: These are the goals in every course I teach. The steps we take to reach them are not often in a straight path. We stagger, sidestep, stumble, and then rise to stride ahead again. ∎

References

McCunn, Ruthann. *Thousand Pieces of Gold*. Boston: Beacon, 1991.

Takaki, Ronald. *Strangers from a Different Shore: A History of Asian Americans*. New York: Penguin, 1990.

To Say the Name Is to Begin the Story

"To say the name is to begin the story," according to the Swampy Cree Indians. In my English courses we begin our "story" together by saying our names — and by telling the history of how we came to have them. Because the first day of class lays a foundation for the nine months that follow, I want our year to begin with respect for the diverse cultural heritages and people represented not only at Jefferson High School, but in the world.

Initially, I started the year with writing about our names because I was appalled that several weeks into the new school year, students still would not know each other's names. Telling about our names was my way of saying up front that the members of the class are part of the curriculum — their names, their stories, their histories, their lives count. But I realized a few years ago that I was missing an opportunity to frame the question of naming more broadly. So this naming ritual has also become a way to say from the jump that naming is personal, cultural, and political. In this case, to say the name is also to begin questioning whose story is told.

I start class by asking students the name of the river connecting Oregon and Washington. When they say, "Columbia," I tell them that the first people here called it "Che Wana" — Big River. I ask them to name the volcano that blew ash on Washington and Oregon in 1980; when they respond, "Mount St. Helens," I tell them that the Cowlitz who lived here first named it "Loo-Wit." Then we talk about how people who have the power to name also have

> **Telling about our names was my way of saying up front that the members of the class are part of the curriculum — their names, their stories, their histories, their lives count.**

the power to tell the story. I explain that in this class we will listen for whose voices get heard and whose have been silenced.

Students and I talk about how naming traditions differ depending on family, cultural group, nationality, or religious affiliation. We look at some of the naming traditions in Vietnam, Laos, Cambodia, and Mexico. I give examples from my family, where the first son was named using the first initial and the middle name of the father. My grandfather was William Meyer, my father was Walter Meyer, and my brother was William Meyer. My brother broke the tradition by naming his first son Steven Troy. I broke tradition by not taking my husband's name — and my mother and sister still addressed their letters to Linda Hereford, not Linda Christensen, ten years after my divorce.

We also speak — using student knowledge as well as mine — of how historically some groups of people were denied their names. Many people from Eastern Europe had their names shortened at Ellis Island because their last names were too long and too difficult for the officials to pronounce. When Africans were stolen from their homeland, their names and their history were stripped as well. I share the following story that my friend, Bakari Chavanu, wrote about changing his name:

> *I changed my name to Bakari Chavanu six years ago and my mom still won't pronounce it. The mail she sends me is still addressed to Johnnie McCowan. I was named after my father. When I*

Bill Bigelow

brought up the subject with her of changing my name, she said my father would turn over in his grave, and "besides," she said, "how could you be my son if you changed your name?"

I knew she was responding emotionally to what I decided to do. I knew and respected also that she was, of course, the giver of my life and my first identity, but how do I make her understand the larger picture? That the lives of people are more than their families and their birth names, that my identity was taken from me, from her, from my father, from my sister, from countless generations of my people enslaved for the benefit of others? How do I make her understand what it means for a kidnapped people to reclaim their identity? How do I help her understand the need for people of African descent to reclaim themselves?

In addition to Bakari's moving piece, I use an assortment of prompts to get students started writing. I've stumbled across name poems or stories over the years that I read to students as a way of priming the writing pump. One of my favorites is Marge Piercy's "If I had been called Sabrina or Ann, she said" (1985). Piercy fools around with her name —

makes fun of it in a playful way. Because my name is Linda Mae, I could identify with Piercy's dismal view of her name. I wanted a name like Cassandra, something fancy and long. My name sounded like a farm girl's and I wanted to be sleek and citified. I also love Sandra Cisneros' "My Name" from her book *The House on Mango Street* (1991). Cisneros' character, Esperanza, uses delicious details to describe her name, "In English my name means hope. In Spanish it means too many letters. It means sadness, it means waiting. It is like the number nine. A muddy color. It is the Mexican records my father plays on Sunday mornings when he is shaving, songs like sobbing."

Teaching Strategy:

I like to begin this activity with a combination of story and poem, humor and seriousness, so students can choose their own route to the assignment.

1. Students read Chavanu's story, Piercy's poem and Cisneros' piece about names. We discuss how differently each writer views his or her name. We pause to look at lines and point out specific details. For example, Piercy doesn't say she hates her name, she plays with it. "Name/

like an oilcan, like a bedroom/ slipper, like a box of baking soda,/ useful, plain . . . ."

2. We read student samples from previous years. I find it helpful to save these from year to year as students often look up to their older school-mates and find it amusing and powerful to see examples of their writing. The following poem written by my student Mary Blalock is a great example of how students can mix personal history, songs, even religion into their poems:

Jean-Claude Lejeune

Mary

Mary was a hand-me-down
from Grandma.
I was
the "Little Mary"
on holiday packages.
Merry Christmas.

Mary, mother of God,
who is a strong woman
in a male dominated religion.
Me,
a lone girl,
in a world of testosterone.
Because of her,
it means sorrow and grief —
I am very sad about this.

"How does your garden grow?" they often ask.
With colorful fruit like the pictures
I attempt to paint,
and beautiful flowers like the poems
I try to write.

They had
three little kids in a row,
and the middle one's me.

Mary, Mary, not always contrary.

Another student, Sekou Crawford, wrote his "name poem" as a story about how his mother came to name him Sekou. Because it has dialogue and setting, it is a good model of how the assignment can be written as prose:

I have a very unusual name. Not as unusual as I used to think because just last year I came face to face with another Sekou. He didn't look much like me, and we probably had very little in common, but when I stood in front of him and shook his hand, I felt we had some kind of secret bond. I could tell he felt the same way.

One day I asked my mom about my name, "How did you come to name me Sekou?"

"Well," she said, "I used to work with convicts, tutoring them, and one day as I walked across the prison courtyard, I heard someone yell, 'Hey, Sekou!' I thought to myself, 'Wow. What great name.' And I remembered it."

I didn't know how I felt being named after some inmate, but I've always been thankful for having it. I couldn't imagine hearing my name and wondering if they were talking to me or the other guy with the same name. I wouldn't like walking into a little gift shop and seeing my name carved onto a key chain. I've heard that somewhere in Northern Africa my name is quite common.

My name has a special meaning. Sekou Shaka, my first and middle name, together mean learned warrior. That's the way I'd like to see myself: Fighting the battle of life with the weapon of knowledge.

Sam Austin wrote his piece after soaking in the flavor of Sandra Cisneros' description:

My name is an all encompassing, fully endowed, drenched and soaked, burnt and charred entity, glazed over with a dark molasses finish. And then given a strong strawberry smoke. It's a sweet song that every time you hear it sounds better than the last.

If spoken correctly, it can get you the sweetest of love or the harshest of hate. Sam to Sammy to Samuel. I've heard those plus some. A man from the streets once told me it's not what you do, but how good you look doing it. And he's halfway right. If you flip my name just right, it gives the feel of an old 1930s gangster Dillinger, or a modern day Casanova. It's the way the girl down the street tosses in that extra long am into my name. "Hey Saaaaam." Or the way that pretty girl with her sensual accent throws that low and long aaah into my name.

I'll go out of my way just to walk by and get that low and steamy, "Hi Saam," from her window. My name really doesn't get any better than that.

3. After saturating students in name poems and prose, I ask students to write about their name. They can write their piece as a story or as a poem. They can tell the history of their name, the meaning of their name, memories or anecdotes connected to their names. They can choose to write about their feelings about their names or their nicknames. The only boundary on the assignment is that they write something about their name.

4. We start writing in class before the period ends, but I encourage students to talk with their parents — if they live with them — to find out the history behind their names. Their homework is to finish the writing and bring their piece to class the following day. We share our work using the read-around method (see the detailed description of read-arounds which begins on page 14).

Susan Lina Ruggles

While no assignment creates instant classroom camaraderie, this exercise does provide a forum for students to share their names and their histories with their classmates. From such a humble beginning, respect can grow. ■

References

Cisneros, Sandra. *The House on Mango Street*. New York: Vintage, 1991, pp. 10-11.

Piercy, Marge. "If I Had Been Called Sabrina or Ann, She Said," in *From My Mother's Body*. New York: Knopf, 1985, p. 122.

The Read-Around: Raising Writers

The read-around is the classroom equivalent to quilt making or barn raising. It is the public space — the *zocolo* or town square — of my room. During our read-arounds, we socialize together and create community, but we also teach and learn from each other. If I had to choose one strategy as the centerpiece of my teaching, it would be the read-around. It provides both the writing text for my classroom and the social text, where our lives intersect and we deepen our connections and understandings across lines of race, class, gender, sexual orientation, and age.

The Read-Around as Writing Text

During the read-around, students provide each other accessible models of writing. I encourage them to listen for what "works" in their peers' pieces, to take notes on what they like, and then to use those techniques in their own writing. During the read-around I point out particular writing strategies. I might note how Aaron used a list in his poem or how Brandon opened his essay with an anecdotal introduction. I might ask Alisha to re-read a section of her essay so that we can notice her transitions. I do this consistently in each read-around to bring students' attention to the writers' tools. In her portfolio evaluation Heather wrote about what she learned from her classmates:

> When I listen to other people's writing, I hear things I love or wish I'd written myself. Most of the time that's where I get my inspiration. Sometimes I catch myself saying, "I wish I could write like so-and-so."

Then I think, "What was it about his/her piece that I liked?" When I figure that out, I'm that much closer to being a better writer. I use their papers as examples. I steal their kernels of ideas and try to incorporate them into my own writing. For example, I love how Ki uses her personal history in her writing, so I try that out for myself. I like Lisa's use of unusual metaphors, so I try as hard as I can to steer clear of the generic type I've been known to use in the past.

Because students learn to listen closely to each other's papers for both ideas and literary tools, they can identify those strategies and use them in their own writing.

Students in every class I've taught have made it clear that the read-around was the best part of my teaching. Adam wrote:

> There is so much to learn about good writing. I know that a lot of what shaped my writing was not the diagramming of sentences or finding the subject and verb that we learned in grade school, but the desire to learn more about what I'm hearing around me. Just hearing the work of good writers makes an incredible difference. When I find something I really like, I ask myself, "What was it about that piece that made me get all goosebumpy?" That's why I think it is really important to have those read-arounds in class. Not only does the author get to hear comments about his/her work, but the rest of the class gets a chance to hear some pretty amazing stuff. Like when we heard Nicole's home language paper, I don't think there was anyone who wasn't touched by it. Everyone

Jim Whitney

A read-around at Jefferson High School.

had felt, at some point, like that and her paper was able to capture those feelings and describe them perfectly. At the same time, everyone thought, "How can I write like that?" We all learned from the paper. Now, this is only one example, but almost every day we share, something like this happens.

Starting with What Works

At the beginning of the year, I ask students to write a compliment to each student in the class about their piece. I make it clear that no one is allowed to make critical comments about a paper. We focus on the positive — on what works. As each person reads, classmates take notes and give positive feedback to the writer. We also applaud each writer for having the courage to read in front of the class.

I require that all students read some assignments like the "Where I'm From " poem (see page 18). I also offer to read pieces anonymously for shy or reluctant students. Some students are eager; their hands are always in the air. Other students are too cool; this is why I give them points for sharing. They can maintain their smooth facade, and act like they are just reading for the extra credit.

Sometimes students want to share, but they need to be coaxed. I use National Writing Project teacher

Keith Caldwell's technique of teasing students into reading: "Who's dying to share, but doesn't want to raise their hand?"

For most personal assignments, I allow students to pass, but I encourage them to share at least a paragraph. We also share informally along the way to a finished piece — openings and evidence in essays; figurative language in poetry; dialogue, blocking, or characterization in narratives. My willingness to share my life opens the doors for students to share theirs. I write stories about my father's alcoholism, my poor test scores, my sister's wayward ways, and my first marriage to an abusive man.

Students respond to the content of the piece — what they like about the arguments, the ideas. They respond to its style. I ask them to be specific. What line, what phrase did they like? Did they like the imagery, the repetition? Instead of working on a deficit model — what's wrong with this piece — we work on a positive model: What's right? What can we learn from it? As Pete noted in his class evaluation:

The way you have us make comments (what did you like about the piece of writing) has helped me deal with people. My skin is thick enough to take a lot of abuse just because I've always had a fairly high opinion of some of the things I can do. I didn't realize a lot of other people don't have that

advantage. After a while I found out positive criticism helped me more than negative too.

Pulling in Reluctant Writers

Not all students in an untracked class arrive on the due date with a paper in hand. To be sure, some students haven't taken the time to do the work, but others can't find a way to enter the work; they either don't know where to start or they feel incapable of beginning. Even my pep talks about "bending the assignment to find your passion" or "just write for 30 minutes; I'll accept whatever you come up with as a first draft" don't entice these students. That's why I'm not a stickler about deadlines.

> **I make it clear that no one is allowed to make critical comments about a paper. We focus on the positive — on what works.**

During read-arounds the students who wrote papers will spawn ideas for those who either couldn't write or who haven't learned homework patterns yet. Listening to how Amanda, Alyss, or Deanna approached the assignment helps teach reluctant writers a way to enter the writing. Sometimes students write a weak "just get it done" paper, then hear a student piece that sends them back home to write with more passion.

There are advantages for both the strong and the weak writer in this process. While the struggling writer gets an opportunity to hear drafts and figure out a writing strategy, the strong writer gets feedback: What worked? Was there a spot where listeners got confused? In reading their papers aloud, writers often notice the places where the language limps and needs tightening. They notice repetitions that need to be deleted. Also, during the second part of the year, the class begins to offer critique: Where isn't the piece working?

The Town Square

The read-around is also the place we share our lives. As students listen to each other's stories they try to feel what it's like to be in someone else's skin. Jessica Rawlins wrote:

> *Never before have I sat in a circle and expressed my opinion about rape, internment, and injustice with my peers and listened while they agreed or disagreed. Never has the teacher said, "I didn't know that. . . . Tell me how you feel." Talking about our lives was a rare treat in most classes and it only happened on holidays and special free days. In here it was part of the lesson. We educated each other through our writing. We brought the*

beauty out of our skin and onto plain paper.

While the read-around provides the writing text and it helps us share crucial stories from our lives, it can also miss some important teachable moments. For this reason, my colleague Bill Bigelow and I developed what we called the "collective text," so we could step back from the writing and figure out what our individual stories said about ourselves and our society (see "Writing the Word and the World," page 58). For example, when students in my sophomore class read pieces about times when they were either the victims or the perpetrators of acts of unkindness, we stepped back and examined the stories for common threads. Students discovered that they didn't "act for justice" when they felt they might be the victim of the next attack. This reading of the "collective text" allowed us to talk about how we might become allies for people in the future.

Creating a Safe Space for Sharing

Some students love to share their writing. Reading aloud in class is a conversation, gossip session, a chance to socialize in a teacher-approved way. Unfortunately, too many students arrive with bruises from the red pen, so when we begin the year, it's necessary to build their confidence.

Teaching Strategy

1. Seat the students in a circle — or the nearest approximation. Students should not have their backs to each other. This way they can see each other and be seen as they read. The attention will be focused on the reader.

2. Distribute as many blank strips of papers as there are students in the class. Students write a compliment to each classmate as he/she reads.

3. Students write each reader's name on the paper. So if Vonda volunteers to read her paper first, everyone in the class writes Vonda's name on their strip. (This is also a way for students to learn their classmates' names.)

4. Tell students they must respond with a positive comment to each writer. Emphasize that by listening and "stealing" what works in their classmates' writing, they will improve their own. Write a list of ways to respond on the board:

   Respond to the writer's style of writing. What do you like about how the piece was written? Do you like the rhyme? The repeating lines? The humor? (Later, these points can change, particularly if you are focusing on a specific skill — like introductions, transitions, evidence, and imagery.)

Respond to the writer's content. What did the writer say that you liked? Did you like the way Ayanna used a story about her mother to point out how gender roles have changed?

Respond by sharing a memory that surfaced for you. Did you have a similar experience? Did this remind you of something from your life?

As the writer reads, write down lines, ideas, words or phrases that you like. Remember: you must compliment the writer.

5. As students write each compliment, tell them to sign their slip so the writer knows who praised them.

6. Ask for a few volunteers to share their praise with the writer. This is slow at first, so try modeling it. This is an opportunity to teach writing: Point out dialogue, description, attention to detail.

7. Tell students to look at the writer and give that person the compliment. Usually, students will look at the teacher and say what they liked about the student's piece. I tell the writer to call on students who have raised their hands. Establish early on that all dialogue in the class does not funnel through the teacher.

8. If the class does not immediately respond, offering extra credit can elicit positive oral comments. In my classes where defiance is a badge of honor, I give points. This allows some people a "cover" for giving positive feedback: "I just do it for the points." Whether they actually do it for the extra credit or not, their compliments contribute to a positive classroom climate.

9. After everyone has read, ask students to hand

> *Sometimes students write a weak "just get it done" paper, then hear a student piece that sends them back home to write with more passion.*

out their compliment strips to each other. (This is usually chaotic, but it's another way for students to identify who's who is the class and to connect with each other.)

10. After the first few read-arounds, I drop the strips of paper and rely on oral feedback. But I find that in some classes I need to have them take notes for the collective text as a way of keeping them on task — so they don't write love letters or complete a math assignment during the read-around.

When It Doesn't Work

Some classes move into read-arounds like my black Lab takes to water. Others are more reluctant. There are awkward silences after I say, "What do you like about that piece?" Sometimes students come in carrying past histories with each other that make them fearful about sharing. One year Bill and I taught a class we nicknamed "the class from hell." They not only had a history; they had a present. A few students made fun of classmates and held us all hostages to their anger. We read more pieces anonymously that year. We bribed students with points. We brought in graduates from previous years to model appropriate behavior. Bill and I sat next to the troublemakers and attempted to "control" their negative comments by placing our bodies in their path. Some days we resorted to sending the offenders to the library or the dean's office during our read-around.

Classes usually warm up during the first quarter. The strategy takes time, persistence, and energy, but it's worth it. As Jenni Brock wrote in her class evaluation, "The read-arounds are totally awesome stud vicious. They really helped the class to become closer. They teach us so much about each other." And I would add — about writing. ∎

Where I'm From: Inviting Students' Lives Into the Classroom

WHERE I'M FROM

I am from clothespins,
from Clorox and carbon-tetrachloride.
I am from the dirt under the back porch.
(Black, glistening
it tasted like beets.)
I am from the forsythia bush,
the Dutch elm
whose long gone limbs I remember
as if they were my own.

I am from fudge and eyeglasses,
from Imogene and Alafair.
I'm from the know-it-alls
and the pass-it-ons,
from perk up and pipe down.
I'm from He restoreth my soul
with a cottonball lamb
and ten verses I can say myself.

I'm from Artemus and Billie's Branch,
fried corn and strong coffee.
From the finger my grandfather lost
to the auger
the eye my father shut to keep his sight.
Under my bed was a dress box
spilling old pictures,
a sift of lost faces
to drift beneath my dreams.
I am from those moments —
snapped before I budded —
leaf-fall from the family tree.

— George Ella Lyon

I remember holding my father's hand as he read my story hanging on the display wall outside Mrs. Martin's third-grade classroom on the night of Open House. I remember the sound of change jingling in Dad's pocket, his laughter as he called my mom over and read out loud the part where I'd named the cow "Lena" after my mother and the chicken "Walt" after my father. It was a moment of sweet joy for me when my two worlds of home and school bumped together in a harmony of reading, writing, and laughter.

In my junior year of high school, I skipped most of my classes, but each afternoon I crawled back through the courtyard window of my English class. There were no mass assignments in Ms. Carr's class: She selected novels and volumes of poetry for each student to read. Instead of responding by correcting my errors, she wrote notes in the margins of my papers asking me questions about my home, my mother, my sister who'd run away, my father who'd died three years before.

These two events from my schooling capture part of what the editors of *Rethinking Our Classrooms: Teaching for Equity and Justice* (1994) meant when we encouraged teachers to make students feel "significant" in our classrooms:

> *The ways we organize classroom life should seek to make children feel significant and cared about — by the teacher and by each other. Unless students feel emotionally and physically safe, they won't share real thoughts and feelings. Discussions will be tinny and dishonest. We need to design activities where students learn to trust and care for each other. Classroom life should, to the greatest extent possible, pre-figure the kind of democratic and just society we envision, and thus contribute to building that society. Together students and teachers can create a "community of conscience," as educators Asa Hilliard and George Pine call it.*

A PUBLICATION OF RETHINKING SCHOOLS

Image Productions

Mrs. Martin and Ms. Carr made me feel significant and cared about because they invited my home into the classroom. When I wrote and included details about my family, they listened. They made space for me and my people in the curriculum.

In my classrooms at Jefferson High School, I've attempted to find ways to make students feel significant and cared about as well, to find space for their lives to become part of the curriculum. I do this by inviting them to write about their lives, about the worlds from which they come. Our sharing is one of the many ways we begin to build community together. It "prefigures" a world where students can hear the home language from Diovana's Pacific Islander heritage, Lurdes' Mexican family, Oretha's African-American home, and my Norwegian roots, and celebrate without mockery the similarities as well as the differences.

Sometimes grounding lessons in students' lives can take a more critical role, by asking them to examine how they have been shaped or manipulated by the media, for example. But as critical teachers, we shouldn't overlook the necessity of connecting students around moments of joy as well.

I found a poem by George Ella Lyon in *The United States of Poetry*[1] that I use to invite my students' families, homes, and neighborhoods into the classroom (see page 18).

> **As critical teachers, we shouldn't overlook the necessity of connecting students around moments of joy.**

Lyon's poem follows a repeating pattern, "I am from . . . ." that recalls details, evokes memories — and can prompt some excellent poetry. Her poem allows me to teach about the use of specifics in poetry, and writing in general. But the lesson also brought the class together through the sharing of details from our lives and lots of laughter and talk about the "old ones" whose languages and traditions continue to

---

[1] *The United States of Poetry* (see reference) is a book and a video. *The United States of Poetry* introduces students to political poetry as well as to some old and new poets from diverse racial and social backgrounds. The video uses a music video format and demonstrates performance poetry. I use both the book and video with my high school students. Most of the pieces are more appropriate for older students, but some pieces, like "Where I'm From," could be used with elementary students as well.

permeate the ways we do things today.

Teaching Strategy:

1. After students read the poem out loud together, I note that Lyon begins many of her lines with the phrase, "I am from." I remind the class of William Stafford's[2] advice to find a hook to "link the poem forward" through some kind of device like a repeating line, so the poem can develop a momentum. I suggest they might want to use the line "I am from" or create another phrase that will move the poem.

2. We go line by line through the poem. I ask students to notice the details Lyon remembers about her past. After we read, I ask students to write lists that match the ones in Lyon's poem and to share them out loud. This verbal sharing sparks memories and also gives us memories to share as we make our way through the lesson:

   • Items found around their home: bobby pins or stacks of newspapers, grandma's teeth, discount coupons for a Mercedes. (They don't have to tell the truth.)

   • Items found in their yard: broken rakes, dog bones, hoses coiled like green snakes. (I encourage them to think of metaphors as they create their lists.)

   • Items found in their neighborhood: the corner grocery, Mr. Tate's beat up Ford Fairlane, the "home base" plum tree.

   • Names of relatives, especially ones that link them to the past: Uncle Einar and Aunt Eva, Claude, the Christensen branch.

   • Sayings: "If I've told you once. . . ." (The students have a great time with this one. They usually have a ready supply that either brings me back to childhood or makes me want to steal their families' lines.)

   • Names of foods and dishes that recall family gatherings: lutefisk, tamales, black-eyed peas.

   • Names of places they keep their childhood memories: Diaries, boxes, underwear drawers, inside the family Bible.

3. We share their lists out loud as we brainstorm. I encourage them to make their piece "sound like home," using the names and language of their home, their family, their neighborhood. The students who write vague nouns like "shoes" or "magazines" get more specific when they hear their classmates shout out, "*Jet,*" "*Latina,*" "pink tights crusted with rosin." Out of the chaos, the sounds, smells, and languages of my students' homes emerge in poetry.

4. Once they have their lists of specific words, phrases, and names, I ask them to write. I encourage them to find some kind of link or phrase like "I am from" to weave the poem together, and to end the poem with a line or two that ties their present to their past, their family history. For example, in Lyon's poem, she ends with "Under my bed was a dress box/spilling old pictures. . . . I am from those moments . . . ."

5. After students have written a draft, we "read around." (See page 14 for a detailed description of this activity.) This is an opportunity for students to feel "significant and cared about," in

---

I AM FROM
SOUL FOOD AND HARRIET TUBMAN
By Lealonni Blake

I am from get-togethers
and Bar-B-Ques
K-Mart special with matching shoes.
Baseball bats and BB guns,
a violent family is where I'm from.

I am from "get it girl"
and "shake it to the ground."
From a strict dad named Lumb
sayin' "sit yo' fass self down."

I am from the smell of soul food
cooking in Lelinna's kitchen.
From my Pampa's war stories
to my granny's cotton pickin'.

I am from Kunta Kinte's strength,
Harriet Tubman's escapes.
Phyllis Wheatley's poems,
and Sojourner Truth's faith.

If you did family research,
and dug deep into my genes.
You'll find Sylvester and Ora, Geneva and Doc,
My African Kings and Queens.
That's where I'm from.

---

[2]William Stafford, Oregon's poet laureate for many years, published many outstanding books of poetry as well a two wonderful books on writing: *Writing the Australian Crawl and You Must Revise Your Life.* See references.

I AM FROM PINK TIGHTS AND SPEAK YOUR MIND
By Djamila Moore

I am from sweaty pink tights encrusted in rosin
bobby pins
Winnie-the-Pooh
and crystals.

I am from awapuhi ginger
sweet fields of sugar cane
green bananas.

I am from warm rain cascading over
taro leaf umbrellas.
Crouching beneath the shield of kalo.

I am from poke, brie cheese, mango,
and raspberries,
from Marguritte
and Aunty Nani.

I am from speak your mind
it's o.k. to cry
and would you like it if someone did that to you?

I am from swimming with
the full moon,
Saturday at the laundromat,
and Easter crepes.

I am from Moore and Cackley
from sardines and haupia.
From Mirana's lip Djavan split,
to the shrunken belly
my grandmother could not cure.

Seven diaries stashed among
Anne of Green Gables.
Dreams of promises
ending in tears.
Solidifying to salted pages.

I am from those moments of
magic
when life remains a
fairy tale.

the words of *Rethinking Our Classrooms*, as they share their poems.

6. Seated in our circle, students read their poems. After each student reads, classmates raise their hands to comment on what they like about the piece. The writer calls on his/her classmates and receives feedback about what is good in the poem. I do stop from time to time to point out that the use of a list is a technique they might "borrow" from their peer's poem and include in their next poem or in a revision. I might note that the use of Spanish or home language adds authenticity to a piece and ask them to see if they could add some to their poem. After a few read-around sessions I can spot writing techniques that students have "borrowed" from each other and included in their revisions or in their next piece: dialogue, church sayings, lists, exaggeration.

"Where I'm From" is an opening lesson in a year of critical teaching. As we create schools and classrooms that are "laboratories for a more just society than the one we now live in," we need to remember to make our students feel significant and cared about. These kinds of lessons keep me going, too. When the gray days of budget cuts, standardized tests, school restructuring plans gone awry, and kid-bashing talk in the teacher room pile up one after another like layers of old newspapers on your back porch, pull out George Ella Lyon's poem and invite the stories and voices of your students into the classroom. ∎

References

Bigelow, Bill, et al. *Rethinking Our Classrooms*: *Teaching for Equity and Justice*. Milwaukee, WI: Rethinking Schools, 1994, pp. 4-5.

Blum, Joshua, Holman, Bob, and Pellington, Mark (Eds.). *The United States of Poetry*. New York: Harry N. Adams, 1996.

Stafford, William. *Writing the Australian Crawl*. Ann Arbor, MI: University of Michigan Press, 1978.

Stafford, William. *You Must Revise Your Life*. Ann Arbor, MI: University of Michigan Press, 1986.

I AM FROM . . .
By Oretha Storey

I am from bobby pins, doo-rags
and wide toothed combs.
I am from tall grass, basketballs and
slimy slugs in front of my home.
I am from prayer plants that lift
their stems and rejoice every night.

I am from chocolate cakes and deviled
eggs that made afternoon snacks just right.
I am from older cousins and hand me downs
to "shut ups" and "sit downs."

I am from Genesis to Exodus
Leviticus too.
Church to church, pew to pew.

I am from a huge family tree,
that begins with dust and ends with me.

In the back of my mind there lies a dream
of good "soul food" and money trees.
In this dream I see me on top makin'
ham hocks, fried chicken
and smothered porkchops.
I am from family roots and blood,
Oh, I forgot to mention love.

I AM FROM
SWINGSETS AND JUNGLE GYMS
By Debby Gordon

I am from jars for change collections,
cards from Grandma,
and chocolate milk.

I am from swingsets and jungle gyms
rusted metal mounted in dirt
used by many kids,
well broken in.

I am from the cherry tree,
and the pudgy faces climbing out on the branches
for a piece of juicy red fruit.

I am from tattle-tales,
keep-it-froms,
and "shut-up and listen to me."

I am from Rice Crispy Treats,
and pretty rings,
from Melvin and Earline.

I'm from Will and Sharon's long branch,
chunky Peanut-Butter and Jelly,
from the house we lost to fire,
and surgeries we all have had.

I am from the old scrapbooks,
where pictures,
remind me of days that live only in the minds
of those of us who were there.

I am from the people who paved a way for me,
I am from the best that could be,
and I am the best I could be.

Image Productions

Sweet Learning

According to my friend Eddy Shuldman, when children first learned to read Hebrew the rabbi placed a drop of honey on each letter of the alphabet. When children mastered the letter, they licked the honey to make the learning sweet.

I like the image of "sweet learning" because too often in school we speak of "rigor" and "getting tough" without talking about the joy of education, the thrill of discovering something new.

Some of my "sweetest" learning took place on Humboldt Bay in northern California. On Saturday mornings my father and I piled into our old Ford and headed to Eureka's waterfront. We'd stop at the California Fruit Market on 2nd Street, where Pop bought a newspaper, a pack of chocolate pinwheel cookies for me, and a few groceries for his friend Big Ernie. Then we'd climb into the rowboat and my Saturday lessons would begin. On Humboldt Bay my father taught me how to cast off from the dock and how to row. Once we moored our skiff at Big Ernie's dock, my father showed me how to secure the boat to the dock, find tube worms on the pilings at low tide, thread them on a hook, throw my line and reel in fish.

I no longer live on Humboldt Bay, but the memory of my father's teaching stays with me. When I visited a Roma village outside of Letanovce, Slovakia, I was struck by how much education took place in the village. (The Roma are more commonly known by the derogatory term "Gypsy." Most prefer to be called Roma.) Children learned to gather wood, build fires, dip water from the well and carry it home. They learned how to cook, clean, and sew from their family members — just as my father taught me.

This lesson on sweet learning brings our students' lives, their families and cultures — whether they are Roma, African-American, Laotian, Irish, or Norwegian — into our classrooms while we nurture students' reading and writing skills. I use it at the beginning of the year so I can learn something about the cultural background of my students, and so they can share their identity in positive ways with the rest of the class.

Image Productions

Teaching Strategy:

1. As students read out loud two stories written by my former students — "In My Father's Kitchen" by Laura Tourtillott (see next page) and "Abuelita" by Alejandro Vidales (see page 26) — I ask them to think about what Laura learned in her father's kitchen and what Alejandro learned from his grandmother.

2. After we've discussed what Laura and Alejandro learned, we go through each story and look for the "elements of fiction" that help the writers tell their story (see handout on page 29). I ask students to circle the dialogue and underline the descriptions of characters and setting.

3. I start the writing by making a list on the board of people who've taught me over the years:

   • My father taught me to row a boat and fish.

   • My father also taught me how to be a friend.

   • My mother taught me how to make clam chowder.

   • Darrell, my brother-in-law, taught me how to drive a car.

   • Billy, my brother, taught me how to find egrets' nests in trees.

   • Tina, my sister, taught me how to make a platter of food look elegant.

   • My friend, Katherine Weit, taught me how to stand up for what I believe.

   As I create my list and talk about each person and what they taught me, I ask students to make their own lists of sweet learning experiences.

4. When it looks like most students have five or six people on their lists, I ask them to share a few. Sometimes when students get stuck and can't think of one person to write about, hearing their classmates' lists helps get them started.

5. Before students begin their drafts, we discuss the elements of fiction again — particularly dialogue, character description, and setting description — and I ask them to include these elements as they tell their story about a sweet learning experience. Their homework is to finish the writing and bring the draft to class.

The Read-around:

6. After the first read-around (see page 14 for a complete desciption of this activity), I require students to take notes as they listen to their classmates read, but we don't exchange slips of papers. In this writing, I also ask students to keep track — take notes — on what "sweet learning" took place. What did their classmate learn? Where did the learning take place? What were the conditions for the learning? In other

In My Father's Kitchen
By Laura Tourtillott

I enter the kitchen to a spiced earthy smell and steamy windows. At the stove a tall, red-haired man is stirring a large pot.

"What're you making, Daddy?" I ask.

"Applesauce. Wanna stir while I knead the bread?"

"Sure. But can I knead, too?" I try not to sound whiny, but kneading is my favorite part. After Dad goes through a few turns of the dough, we switch places. My hands are smaller, and since I'm nearly two feet shorter than he is, I have a hard time.

As I go back to stirring, I know the muscles in my arms will complain tomorrow, and I may not be able to use the monkey bars, but I am happy anyway. After he puts the dough back on the fridge to rise some more, he gives me instructions for the applesauce.

"Laura, you hold the jar while I spoon the sauce in, okay?"

"All right," I say, careful not to let the hot apples burn my fingers.

When we have filled three jars I ask, "Why is there still some at the bottom of the pot?"

"Because I'm going to cook it down and make apple butter," he says with a smile, "but you don't have to eat any."

I feel my eyes bulge. My tongue does a quick pass over my lips. Daddy knows apple butter is my favorite. "No!" I say. "I want some."

And he wraps me in his arms where I can feel his warm, deep laugh coming up from his belly button.

We still commune in the kitchen, Daddy and I, absorbed in the sweetest smells and brightest colors in our small house. Spices, vinegars, oils, and expensive fish all come out from their cupboards to be arranged by my father's fingers into something more beautiful to see and taste than they could ever dream of being on their own.

In my father's kitchen, I learned to read, multiply, dance, hug, stand up straight, create, feel . . . and I'm just now learning to cook. In my father's kitchen he makes magic.

words, did they learn by doing? Watching? Practicing? Did someone give them a manual? Did they get praised?

Instead of controlling the dialogue myself, I ask the writer to call on classmates who want to share their positive comments with the writer. I admit — with apologies to Alfie Kohn — that I shamelessly shower students with points at the beginning of the year. By January, they are conditioned to listening closely and praising each other.

The Discussion

After students have read and shared, we talk about the "collective text" of our stories. What were the conditions that made for sweet learning? Who did students learn from? Typically students discover that they have learned a lot from the people in their homes. No one handed them a manual on "how to build a fire," instead they learned by watching and practicing under the guidance of a significant adult. We talk about what schools could learn about teaching from these "experts" in our lives.

As a teacher, I want to acknowledge the wisdom that resides in my students' homes. Because I live in a society that honors the wealthy and tends to hold in greatest esteem "high status" formal knowledge, I must find ways to honor the intelligence, common sense, and love that beats in the hearts of my students' families. In my classroom, I want every student to feel pride in where they come from, in their heritage, and the people who clothe, shelter, and teach them. ∎

Abuelita

By Alejandro Vidales

At the age of 6, I came to live in the United States. My grandmother was so excited. She painted the most beautiful images of how it would be. "Mijo, we are going to go to a better place. We are going to a place where the streets are made of gold, where dollars grow on trees, and most importantly, where you can become somebody."

When I got here, we lived in San Diego, California, right next to the ocean. I remember going to the beach, listening to the seagulls, feeling the breeze on my face, looking at the waves drifting to the shore, feeling the last sun rays hitting my skin. It was magic. Every Saturday, my grandmother and I walked along the shore, picking up sand dollars and sea shells. She helped me build sand castles. "No, aoi, no. Primero tienes que hacer tu figura." I would laugh and hug her. She wasn't only my grandmother; she was my friend.

I didn't like school because I didn't understand anybody. At the time, I didn't speak English. When I got home, my abuelita became my school. She taught me how to read and write in Spanish. And while learning Spanish, I was able to pick up English.

I liked studying with my abuelita because after we finished, she would cook dinner. Man, could she cook! I remember her wrinkled hands grinding the corn, then chopping fresh tomatoes, tomatillos, onions, and chiles. Every cut exact, just how she wanted. She made the best salsa. Sometimes my friends would come to my house for dinner. But most of the time, it would only be the two of us having dinner together because my uncles were never home and my mom was too busy working.

I never met my grandfather or father, so my abuelita took the responsibility of guiding me. She taught me how to clean, sweep, mop, cook, and even wash and iron my own clothes. She also taught me how to be independent, respectful, responsible, and how to treat women.

As I write this piece, I clearly remember her words: "Mijo, I brought you here so you can do something with your life. I want you to get your education and become a great lawyer or doctor or whatever you want. Show everybody that a Mexicano can make a difference and that you don't need to shoot anybody or steal to get attention. I believe in you, and I know you will accomplish anything you put your mind to."

Now that I am a senior in high school, I am going to graduate and go to college because I don't plan on letting my abuelita or myself down. I want to thank my abuelita for raising me to become a real man.

A PUBLICATION OF RETHINKING SCHOOLS

Jean-Claude Lejeune

Childhood Narratives

My students were a delightful blend of colors, sexual orientations, and grade levels. They differed in the activities they enjoyed: Some loved football and basketball; some loved ballet; others were into soap operas and the telephone. The two things they shared were the school building and my classroom. Because I wanted them to get comfortable sharing across their lines of difference, I decided to take them back to their childhood where they could find some early memories to bring them together while we also worked on their writing skills.

I brought cookies and milk and set up my high school classroom to resemble a preschool play room. In one corner I had Matchbox cars and a plastic roadway. The opposite corner held a table full of Legos. One side

> **I try to get students to see, hear, smell, taste the memory — to create a movie in their heads of the childhood memory so their writing will be more detailed.**

was cleared for jump rope. Jacks were ready on the floor. I even dared to bring modeling clay and finger paints. There was a "station" with children's books, blankets, and pillows.

At first, students were scornful of the "childish toys," but they quickly moved into action. They spent that class period munching on cookies and moving from station to station in animated play. (The teacher in the room below came up after a particularly long bout of double-dutch jump rope.) Kids connected across culture, gender, and race lines because they remembered and could laugh about common games.

The next day we talked about our favorite games, books, and toys. Out of our discussion and play, students wrote pieces evoking their favorite childhood games and memories.

TEACHING STRATEGY:

PREWRITING

1. I bring toys to class. Even if I don't spend the entire day engaged in "frivolous activity," students can recall the toys or games they used as children. Often they will find connections because of their age. They remember Cabbage Patch dolls, Big Wheel bikes. They can talk about My Little Pony, G.I. Joes, and Barbie dolls. I allow them some time to revel in these details. The more they talk, the more specific memories return.

2. Prior to reading the student models, we read and discuss the elements of fiction (see next page).

3. We read "Neighborhood Hassle" by Stephenie Lincoln (see page 31), "My Name is Not Kunta Kinte" by DeShawn Holden (page 32), and "Super Soaker War" by Bobby Bowden (see page 34). Some of the pieces reactivate the sharing or trigger memories in a quiet class.

4. Using the "Childhood Narrative Reading Analysis Sheet" (see page 35), I ask students to examine the student pieces for narrative criteria as they read. Does the writer tell a story? Use dialogue and description? I find that students are more likely to use these elements in their own writing if I pre-teach them using student models.

5. I ask students to list toys, games, and activities they cherished as children. Sharing items from the list out loud sometimes deepens the memories. While this might seem like a lot of "wasted" class time, the more time students spend talking, the more memories and details surface. They need to steep in the details in order to write the pieces.

6. I go over the Narrative Criteria Sheet (see page 36) with students, so they know what they are aiming for in their writing.

7. Prior to narrative writing, I frequently take students on a guided visualization. Students read over their list and circle one childhood memory they want to write about. I close the blinds, turn out the lights, ask them to get comfortable, and close their eyes. (I joke around as I do this. "I promise no one will look at you. Put your head on the desk if you think they might." I exaggerate taking big breaths, rolling my shoulders. . . .)

I pause about 20 to 30 seconds between each question so they can raise the memory. I say, "Remember the event. Imagine the room or playground or park where the memory took place. What does it look like? What does it smell like? What sounds do you remember? Who else was there? What did they say?" There are no set questions for these visualizations, but I try to get students to see, hear, smell, taste the memory — to create a movie in their heads of the childhood memory so their writing will be more detailed. If they can't recall exactly what someone said, I tell them to make up something that fits their memory of the event.

DRAFTING

8. To transition from the guided visualization to the writing, I tell students that when I turn on the lights I want them to write as fast as they can because sometimes they will capture forgotten memories when they write fast. This is a first draft. I also say, "Write this as if you were talking to a friend. Tell the story." Students start writing in class and finish the draft at home.

SELF REFLECTION

9. After students have finished the draft, I ask them to reflect on it using the Childhood Narrative Criteria Sheet.

PEER FEEDBACK: THE READ-AROUND

10. Before we begin the read-around (see page 14 for a complete description of this activity), I tell students that they must take notes on their classmates' stories. I want them to think about the narrative criteria — story line, dialogue, character description — but to also think about what they like in the piece, including use of language and evocative details that help them "see" the story. As each student reads his/her paper, the rest of the class takes notes. After the "writer" finishes, we applaud, then give specific feedback about what "worked" in the piece.

REVISION

11. Using the feedback from their Childhood Narrative Criteria Sheet, the feedback from paired-share — where students pair off and read their stories to each other — and the read-around, students work on a revision. I find that hearing other students read their pieces out loud often stimulates students to go back to their own pieces with renewed energy and ideas because they've heard examples that work.

Elements of Fiction

1. Dialogue

Dialogue helps the reader understand the characters. Use real language and make each character sound distinct. Each person's "voice" is like a fingerprint — unique. Find places in your story where you tell, instead of using dialogue, to make your characters come alive:

Tell: Her mother told her to go to her room.

Dialogue: "Tina, you had better get in here and clean up this nasty bedroom. If you're not in that room cleaning by the time my foot hits the stairs, you're in big trouble," my mom said as she stood at the bottom of the stairs.

Helpful Hints: When creating dialogue, avoid words like exclaimed, bellowed, and proclaimed. The more sensational the speaking verb is, the more likely it will call attention to itself. You want your reader to focus on the dialogue.

2. Blocking

Think of blocking as "stage directions." It tells where the characters are and what they are doing while they are talking. The blocking sets the scene, creates a place for the dialogue to happen. Ask yourself: Are your characters disembodied voices? What are they doing while they are talking? Walking? Looking out the window? Tapping a pencil? Make us see them.

Where is the character? In the kitchen? Sitting on the sofa? In the third desk in a science classroom? Be specific.

Example: In this example from the book *Coffee Will Make You Black*, note how April Sinclair uses blocking to show the reader what the character is doing while she's speaking. This gives the reader a visual image of the scene. The italicized section is blocking.

Mama sat down on my unmade bed. She rubbed her hands nervously against her housedress.
"What are you talking about? What did they say?"

In the following excerpt from a piece by student writer Michelle Lee, notice how the blocking helps the reader visualize the speaker and his actions:

"You betta' listen to yo' little sista," ordered Justin. *The rest of the kids stood with their backs to the sun looking at me and Justin standing face to face.*

3. Interior monologue

What is the character thinking and feeling while the dialogue and action are happening? This literary device helps the reader discover more information about the character or the story.

Example: Interior monologue from "The Bracelet" by student Chetan Patel:

"Hi," I whispered to a girl staring at me. She answered with a roll of her blue eyes. *Back then I wished I had those eyes. Life would have been so much easier. No more standing on the bus, not dirty bathrooms! Would it make a difference to wash in a clean sink? Or use an unclogged toilet? I liked having a bathroom that smelled clean, without bugs crawling at my feet.* The bell rang, and I came back to reality.

4. Setting Description

Describe the setting. Where is this story taking place? In Escape from New York Pizza? Make us smell the salami and tomato sauce. Let us hear the cooks talking in the background. Tell us the color of the restaurant walls.

Example: Setting description from "My Nerves Wasn't All She Got On" by student Pamela Clegg:

I knew she had opened up the hall closet, and I'll be the first to say this closet was a mess. This was the reserve closet for me and my sister. Whenever we heard our mother coming up the stairs, we would throw anything and everything that was on the floor in this closet: shoes, underwear, clean socks, dirty socks, towels, dolls, paper, pop cans, books, anything.

5. Character Description

Describe the characters. What do they look like? What are they wearing? What are their habits? Their background?

Example: from *What Looks Like Crazy on An Ordinary Day*, by Pearl Cleage:

> The Good Reverend himself was a revelation. Tall, white-haired, and sixtyish, the Rev looked like an aging Cab Calloway and preached like Jesse Jackson. He had a long, black robe with full sleeves that billowed out like wings when he raised his arms in praise or flung them wide in surrender. His voice was rich and more powerful than his slender frame would lead you to believe.

In the following example, student writer Stephenie Lincoln draws word pictures for her readers:

> Little Ronnie was the fat one. He never did anything but instigate and eat. He had on one of those polyester T-shirts that was brown and orange, with some brown pants. They looked like they both had been painted on.

6. Figurative Language — metaphors & similes

Figurative language makes the reader see everyday things and people in a new way — metaphors and similes make comparisons, sometimes between the known and the unexplored. For example in the sentence, "His teeth were like a weasel's, sharp and pointed, but twisted and bunched at the roots," A person's teeth are compared to a weasel's teeth. Although we think of using figurative language in poetry, it helps strengthen narrative and essay writing.

7. Personification

This literary device gives human qualities to non-humans. For example, if I wrote, "The moon wept at the end of each month," I would be giving the moon the human quality of emotion.

Example: from *Billy* by Albert French:

> "The shades had been drawn in the room where Lori lies, the late-afternoon sunlight coming through the window *is weakened and lets the darkness cuddle up in the corner.*"

8. Flashback

You create a flashback when the character remembers something from his/her past that helps build the story. A flashback is not essential, but it is a good tool to give background on a character. Usually something triggers the memory:

> As she drove down the highway, she saw a lone light in the distance. *It reminded her of the time her father. . . .*

Sometimes you can just begin: "He remembered. . . ."

9. Scene and Summary

A summary gives the reader a quick sketch of what is happening or what has happened. Often these are places that you need to go back and fill out with more details. Scenes, on the other hand, create a mental movie for your readers — they can see, hear, sometimes even smell what you're writing about.

Example of summary: from a piece by student Erika Mashia:

> I was excited about the game against Benson. It was an important game, and I was nervous about the outcome. Sarah Green was an obstacle our team would have to overcome. Benson had a clear height advantage, but that's never stopped me. I beat both Imé and Kenny at the hoop. Steph and I have our outside shots down, and. . . .

Example of scene:

> A wave of must and heat hit me when I ran through the doors to Benson's gym. The crowd rose to their feet shouting, "Tiger power!" as we made our entrance. "It's on," Steph said as we took off our huge, yellow warm-up shirts. "We can do it."
>
> Steph's the talker. I get clear and focused. When I'm playing, the band, the cheerleaders, even the yelling between the "boys'" teams melts into the walls. It's just me, the ball, my team — and in this game, Sarah Cooper.

Neighborhood Hassle
By Stephenie Lincoln

"I wish you guys would hurry up," I yelled, looking up towards the hoop. I was standing by the wire fence that was off to the right. The boys on the block were playing basketball. They never let me play because I was a girl and they didn't want girls with them.

It was a sunny day. Birds were flying by and all the neighborhood kids were out all over-playing kickball, stickball, catch, tag, anything. I had just come out from eating one of my favorite lunches, peanut butter and jelly, so I was ready to ball.

"You ain't playin' so you might as well leave," Timmy said. Timmy was about an inch taller than me. He wasn't skinny, but he wasn't fat either. He had a nappy mini afro and he always wore too little shorts and shirts with Coasters from Volumes.

"Oh yes I am, and just for that, you gone be the first person I beat," I said. All the other boys was like, "OOH." So when they got finished playin, Timmy called me out. The winner of one-on-one stays on the court until he/she loses.

"Now, these is the rules: game is 5, ain't no outs, and winner gets ball."

"O.K.," I said, and we started.

"You got first ball since you a girl," he said. That was his first mistake.

I took the ball out top. We were on the corner of Michigan and Webster at the Frazier's hoop that had been nailed up to the top of the garage. On the right side was a fence and on the left were bushes.

The bushes were very tall and had big green leaves that were also glossy. On the other side of the bush lived a lady that we all called crazy. She looked like a monster cluck.

I had Timmy all to myself. I faked left, crossed over to the right, went through my legs, and layed it up with my left hand. Timmy was embarrassed. Now all the rest of the boys were going crazy. They never knew I could ball.

I was always a tomboy, but I never let them know I could ball because they were so mean. But I was fed up. So I had decided it was time to school 'em.

It was my ball again. I dribbled to my left, crossed to my right, and busted a"J."

"In yo face Timmy," I said like I was all that. "My ball." I went right, tried to go through my legs, and Timmy stripped me. He laid it up and the score was 2-1, me. His ball. All the fellas was jumpin'up and down now yellin', "Go Timmy, don't let no girl beat you."

Little Ronnie was the fat one. He never did anything but instigate and eat. He had on one of those polyester T-shirts that was brown and orange, with some brown pants. They looked like they both had been painted on. He had curly hair and the prettiest white teeth.

Jimmy was Timmy's lil brother. He was the little tagalong with Timmy's old pants and shirt on. But Jimmy wore those little brown Dexters, and his hair was always combed. He had a cute little dimple in his left cheek and some of the most chocolate colored skin.

Timmy was grinnin'now. He had the ball and pulled up for a two pointer. I blocked it, turned and layed it up. Score was 3-1, my ball. I drove in strong to the right and pulled up for another "J."

"Cheating," I said. "Yes. Money."

The boys were laughing now. Timmy got so mad that on my next out he knocked me down so hard I could have cried.

He had a little grin on his face like, ``Yeah, now what Steph?"

I was wearing my favorite jean shorts and my Aries T-shirt with my blue and white old school Nikes. I was lookin' too cute. And he had pushed me onto the dirty ground. My shorts were all dusty. I think I might have even had a few pebbles in my pants. Anyways, I was pissed off and hurt. But I got up and socked him in the face.

"Oh my goodness," yelled Jimmy, his little bro.

"She socked him," yelled Ronnie.

By then other neighborhood kids were watching. They had never seen me play either. Plus I was playing Timmy, the best boy baller on the block.

"Get up Timmy, get up," they all started yelling.

I just walked down the little so-called court and turned left leading home. As I walked, I kicked the cherry tree that was on the right of me. By the time I turned the corner, I saw Mr. Johnson.

"Steph, wus the matter?" he asked.

"Nothing," I said sounding as if it was his fault I had been pushed on the ground in my favorite jean shorts.

The next day I went outside. I was sitting under the tree in front of our house. I had on my pink overalls and white T-shirt and sandals. I was making some mud pies and was interrupted by Timmy.

"I'm sorry, Steph, for treating you like that." He continued, "Do you wanna play again?"

Feeling kind of fresh cause I had got the best of him, I said, "Yeah, but don't let me have to kick yo butt again."

So I washed my hands on the side of the house and went in to put on my old school Nikes. When I came out Timmy, Jimmy, and Ronnie were standing at the end of my steps. When I walked down the stairs, they moved out of my way.

We walked to the Frazier's hoop and we got our ball on. From then on, they never told me I couldn't play with them.

My Name is Not Kunta Kinte

By DeShawn Holden

I am not Kunta Kinte; I recited to myself after being woke up by my mother. If she called my name one more time, I might as well have breathed my last breath. I didn't care that lions roar. That didn't scare me one bit, but my mom did. Hey, I figured I could take my time since she was waking me up the butt-crack of dawn.

The obnoxious sunrays beamed into my eyes. I really didn't want to go to the berry field, but I had to go in order to make some pocket change. This didn't motivate me too much. What do you expect? A nine year old to take money over sleep? I don't think so.

Rushed by parents and siblings, I walked right out of the house with eye boogers still in the corners of my eyes and slobber stretching from my mouth to my ear. I didn't care until my grandmother, Mrs. Rise and Shine herself, who goes to bed at 8 p.m. and starts her day at 3 a.m. said, "Boy, why haven't you washed your face? You look like you been sleeping in a barn. And you didn't even bother to comb yo' ole nappy head. Looks like chickens been having their way with it."

She meant well, even though it sounded pretty harsh. I love my grandmother. She was light in spirit, but heavy every where else. She was a strong woman, a warrior, and a survivor. My grandmother loved me in spite of all my mischievous, devilish, sneaky ways. She always managed to speak life when I was bad and everyone else wanted to speak death. She said that I was going to be the one to grow up to be a preacher.

We finally made it to the land flowing with rows of raspberry bushes and big ole dirt clods that me and my brother Bunky and my nephew Mario used to throw at one another when no one was looking. Bunky was the oldest, then me, then Mario. I was the strongest. Bunky was the smartest, and Mario was the skinniest. Boy, was he skinny. He was so skinny he could be on the "Feed the hungry" commercials and make millions. When we stepped out of the car, I could smell the sweet perfume of berries.

"Come on. Y'all let's get started. The quicker we get started, the quicker we can get out of here," my impatient sister insisted. I was with her on this one. The thirteen adults and three children crowded the untouched ripe rows of berry bushes. Everyone tied the berry-stained bucket to their waist and scarves to their heads, ready to sing the old slave field songs, "I don't feel no ways tired." Each adult took the mile long rows for themselves and Bunky, Mario, and me took a row together. These rows were too big to handle by ourselves.

After working the hot 90-degree weather for hours the three of us grew tired. Ka plunk. "Ouch, Shawn. That hurt. I'm tellin' on you."

"Tell tell, go to jail. Hang yo drawls on a rusty nail," I teased Mario.

"Y'all betta stop that before Mama sees you," Bunky said, sounding afraid.

"Oh hush, yo ole scaredy cat before I make you eat this dirt clod," I tried to sound tough, even though I wasn't.

"Do it and see if I don't hurt you."

I looked at Bunky and started building up my inner strength because I knew if I made him eat dirt, I'd need to run for my life. Bunky could beat me up even though I didn't want to admit it. Pow! I did it and I wasn't afraid. Bunky bent over spitting chunks of dirt out of his mouth.

"What does it taste like?" Mario asked while he rolled on the ground cracking up laughing at Bunky.

"You stupid bald headed monkey, I'm gonna get you," Bunky had steam comin' out of his ears.

I saw that and took off running. He chased me and I ran through the berry vines, sliding in the dirt, in the outhouse, out of the outhouse, hiding behind a bush. I had outsmarted him.

My grandmother was walking on her way to our row to check up on us. We had started up our war again. Every man for himself. But Bunky was especially trying to go after me. He was throwing dirt clods with all his might at me. He threw his last dirt clod so hard; it went past me, past Mario, down three rows of berry vines at the speed of light. Smack! It hit my grandmother right square in her back.

Now, my grandmother always stickin' up for me and takin' my side and never blaming me, but this time, she cried out from the pit of her belly, "SHAWN, COME HERE NOW!" On my way comin' she found a switch and went to whoopin' on my head. "Now didn't I tell you about chuckin' that dirt?"

"But. . . ."

"Don't but me boy. I'm gonna beat that devil outta you. Now get over there and pick that row by yourself. And I better not see one berry left behind."

Walking to my new row, mad and hurt, "Shoot, that wasn't even me," I thought to myself. "Grandma's not fair." My heart was shattered and my ears grew irritated by the teasing laughter of smart aleck Bunky and "Feed the hungry" Mario.

Super Soaker War

By Bobby Bowden

It was a hot day on Mississippi Street. The sun was blaring down like a heat lamp, and the sky offered no protection with clouds or smog. My older brother and Roxie our dog were on the porch. The dog's tongue hanging out of his mouth like a pink slug.

The four of us: Damon the biggest and strongest of us, Maquinji, a big, plump, asphalt Black kid, only a little taller than me, me the dirty white kid with skinned knees and dirty pro-wings, and Nathan the fastest and the littlest. All of us had decided to play war. Now every one wanted to be on Damon's team. It just happened that I was his best friend that week. So he picked me to be on his team. Man, on Damon's team I felt that we could be like twin brothers.

Now, this game was played with super soakers. The object was to tag one of the other team's members with water from the water gun. One team had a base, and the other tried to take it over.

"Garage is our base," I shrieked.

"Nuh-hu," replied Maquinji, idly picking at one of the numerous scabs on his elbow.

"Rock, paper, scissors for it," said Damon.

One, two, three. They both threw scissors. The game continued, one two three. Damon threw rock and Maquinji threw scissors. "Yeeaaa, we got it!" I shouted like a lotto winner.

Maquinji glared at me, "So what man? You gotta' be so loud?"

Damon and I hurried to Damon's garage. The garage was about six trillion years old and had seen more that a million of our wars. It had been the home and base of numerous amounts of clubs and had been my pouting place for four years. If it could talk, it would probably be in an asylum. Damon took the secret way up to the roof, and I guarded the front door.

After three minutes of waiting, Damon and I became impatient and decided to hunt down Maquinji and Nathan. We saw Maquinji hiding in some bushes, crouched like a cat. We got him in a crossfire and started shooting. Damon's stream of water went over the bush and hit me.

"Got you, got you, we win!" exclaimed Maquinji streaking out of the bushes.

"What are you talking about it was Damon that got me not you, so I am still alive." I retorted, shaking my gun at him.

"Man you are lying!" shouted Maquinji getting in my face.

Then just on time to save me from getting my ass kicked, Damon had a light bulb. "Hey guys, my dad just finished painting my room, we could use the left over paint."

"Yea, each team could have a different color," said Nathan as though it had been his idea.

What a good idea. Our team was white paint and theirs was brown. Now it was easy to tell who killed who. We played with our paint-filled super soakers for a full three hours. Then we went home. My dad saw me and my clothes and quietly asked me if I preferred paper or leather.

"Whatcha mean, Kit?" I inquired innocently, not knowing he was offering me a choice between a book or a belt.

I got a beating for punishment. All four of us also had to give that garage a well-deserved cleaning, and then we had to paint it entirely by hand.

Childhood Narrative Reading Analysis Sheet

Assignment:
Read the model childhood narratives. As you read, fill out the following criteria sheet.

Narrative Criteria:

1. Does the story tell a personal experience based on something that really happened? What is the narrative about?

2. Is there a clear story line: beginning, middle, and end? Did the story feel complete?

3. What was the writer's controlling idea? Was there a sense of change or did the writer learn or gain something during the story? What?

Literary Elements:
Mark each of these elements in the story. (See the Elements of Fiction, page 29.)
If you have a highlighter or colored pencils, color each of the elements with a different color. If not, put the number of the element in the margin of your paper. For example, every time you find dialogue put #1 in the margin next to it.

___1. Dialogue

___2. Blocking

___3. Character Description

___4. Setting Description

___5. Figurative Language

___6. Interior monologue*

___7. Flashback*

* These two are nice but not necessary.

Narrative Criteria Sheet

Literary Elements:

Mark each of these elements on your draft. If you have a highlighter or colored pencils, color each of the elements with a different color. If not, put the number of the element in the margin of your paper. For example, every time you use dialogue put #1 in the margin next to it. (The elements marked * are not essential, but give your writing more depth.)

___1. Dialogue
- What are the characters saying?
- Do they each have a "voice print?"

___2. Blocking
- What are the characters doing while they are talking? Leaning against a wall? Tossing a ball in the air?
- Where are they located?

___3. Character Description
- What does the character look like?
- Smell like?
- What is the character wearing?
- Can we tell the character's age?
- Is the character bossy? Shy? Rowdy?

___4. Setting Description
- Where does the story take place?
- What does it look like?
- Smell like?
- What's on the walls?

___5. Figurative Language*
- Did you use metaphors and similes — comparisons?
- Did you use personification — giving human qualities to non-humans?

___6. Interior monologue*
- What is going on inside the character's head?
- What is the character thinking while the action is happening?

___7. Flashback*
- This is fancy stuff. Does the character remember a time when…?

Discipline: No Quick Fix

Image Productions

Creating a climate of respect is easy to talk about and hard to practice.

Ideally, we want a space where students listen respectfully and learn to care about each other. A sign in our hallway reads: "No Racist or Sexist Remarks." I've often said, "I just don't tolerate that kind of behavior."

But sometimes it's like saying, "I don't tolerate ants." I occasionally have ants in my kitchen. I can spray chemicals on them and saturate the air with poison and "not tolerate" them, or I can find another solution that doesn't harm my family or pets in the process. If I just kick kids out of class, I "don't tolerate" their actions, but neither do I educate them. And it works about as well as stamping out a few ants — more show up to replace the ones I eliminated. I prepare them for repressive solutions where misbehavior is temporarily contained by an outside authority, not really addressed. Sometimes I am forced to that position, but I try not to use "outside force" as a solution to my classroom disruptions.

Dealing with Discipline

Students in one Literature and U.S. History class Bill Bigelow and I co-taught during the early 1990s were often rude to each other. Their favorite put down was "faggot." (This in a class where a young woman came out as a lesbian.) During the first weeks, several young women complained that they had been called names by boys in class. They felt the hostility and wanted to transfer out. They didn't feel comfortable sharing their work or even sitting in the class because they were pinched, hit, or called names when Bill's and my backs were turned. As one of the main, but certainly not the only, instigators, Wesley wrote in his end of the year evaluation, "I started the year off as I finished the last year: bad, wicked and obnoxious. I was getting kicked out of class and having meetings with the deans about my behavior every other day."

For critical teachers trying to build community, this creates a serious problem. Do we eliminate this student? When, after trying time-outs, calling his home, talking with his coach, and keeping him after class, we finally kicked Wesley out, his friends said, "They're picking on him." Not true. But it set us up as the bad guys and divided us from the students we wanted to win over.

Increased police presence in the school neighborhood created situations where students gained honor by taunting the cops in front of their peers. This carried over to class, where we represented the same white authority as the police until students got to know us. While Wesley was not skilled academically, in other respects he was brilliant. He was an artist at toeing the line between acceptable and unacceptable behavior while creating total chaos in the process. He'd raise his hand and make perfectly nice comments about someone's paper in such a way that the entire class knew he was mocking the whole procedure. Even with Bill and me both in the classroom, he defeated us at every turn. Clearly, we were playing on his terrain, and he knew the game better than we did even if we'd taught longer than he'd been alive.

Here we were teaching about justice, tolerance, equality, and respect, and yet when we had a problem with a talented student who didn't want to go along, we turned him over to the deans. Ultimately, what lesson did that teach our students? That we talked a good game, but when pushed we responded like other traditional teachers? That we might profess to believe in everyone's potential, but in practice could not act on this belief? It's a complex issue. I don't want to keep the class from progressing because of one or two students, but I don't want to "give up" on students either. On bad days, I threw Wesley out. On good days, I tried to look behind his behavior and figure out what motivated it.

In teaching students to read for race, class, and gender biases in books, I tell students to look behind the words to discover what the text is really saying. Likewise, in working with "problem" students in class, I need to look behind students' actions. What motivates this behavior? How can I get to the root of the problem? In my experience, the more negatively students feel about themselves and their intellectual ability, the more cruel or withdrawn they are in the classroom.

Tyrelle, Wesley's classmate, wrote early in the year that he felt stupid. "My problem is I don't like to read because I don't think the class would like it. Every time I try to write or do something my teachers told me, 'That's stupid, you did it wrong, or you can't spell.' My friends [who were classmates] say it too. I don't say anything. I just act like I don't hear it, but I really do."

One day I overheard his friends teasing him about his spelling. After class I talked with him about it. I arranged for him to come in so we could work privately on his skills. Because so many of his friends were in the class, he was afraid to ask for help. His way of dealing with the problem was to close down — put his head on his desk and sleep — or make fun of people who were trying to do their work. This did not totally stop, but once he found a way into his writing he would usually settle down and work.

> **In my experience, the more negatively students feel about themselves and their intellectual ability, the more cruel or withdrawn they are in the classroom.**

During the second semester Tyrelle wrote, "You guys have helped me become a better person because you were always after me, 'Tyrelle, be quiet. Tyrelle, pay attention.' After a while I learned how to control myself when it was time to." He'd also learned to separate himself from his friends so he could work.

Wesley, who admitted to being "bad, wicked and obnoxious," was also a victim of poor skills and low academic self-esteem. He'd sneak in after school for help with his writing, or I'd go over the homework readings and teach him how to "talk back" to the author. Sometimes he'd call me at home when he was stuck. At the end of the year his mother said, "He told me that he didn't think he could write. Now he says he knows how."

With both of these students, recognizing the cause of the behavior — embarrassment over poor skills — and helping them achieve success helped to change their behavior. And once the withdrawn or antisocial actions stopped, they contributed to the community rather than sabotaged it. This was not a miraculous, overnight change. On some days, the behavior backslid to day one, but most times there was steady improvement.

Why did Wesley and Tyrelle come in after school to work one-on-one? Ultimately, they knew we cared about them. Everything, from the curriculum — an anti-racist curriculum that tackled issues they confronted in their lives — to the home phone calls in the evening to see if they understood the work, to attending their sports games, demonstrated that we were on their side.

Insider Tricks:
Parents and Coaches as Allies

I have yet to discover a quick fix for out of control behavior. I try calling my students' homes in September to establish contact and expectations. I usually ask parents or grandparents, "Is there anything you can tell me that will help me teach your child more effectively?" Parents know their child's history in school and can give important insights. One parent, for example, told me that her son needed to have instructions in writing as well as orally because he didn't process oral information.

When my daughter didn't turn in a project, her teacher called me. I discovered that her class had long-term work that students needed to complete at home. I appreciated the call because Anna had insisted that she didn't have homework. Her teacher made me realize how much parents need to hear from teachers — not only for keeping track of homework, but so we can work in tandem.

Often working with a coach or activities advisor helps because they've established strong one-on-one relationships. They also have access to an area where the student feels successful. One coach, for example, told me that "Jeremy" had just realized that he would play high school basketball, maybe college ball, but he'd never be a pro. He'd turned from gangs to sports in the seventh grade, and the vision that had fueled him was the NBA. Suddenly, that dream crashed against reality. He practiced hours every day, but he knew he wouldn't make it. His attitude had been sour and nasty for weeks. He needed a new vision. This information helped me to understand Jeremy and allowed me to get out the college guide and talk about choices. His final essay was "Life After Sports."

The Night Life of a Teacher

Mostly, I call students at night and talk with them after the day is over, their friends are no longer around, and both of us have had a chance to cool down. Students joke about how they can't get away with anything because Bill and I call their homes. I overheard one student say, "Man, I got to go to class today otherwise they'll call my uncle tonight." Perhaps it's just letting them know we care enough to take our time outside of school that turns them around. ∎

Unlearning The Myths That Bind Us

Unlearning the Myths That Bind Us:
Critiquing Cartoons and Society

I was nourished on the milk of American culture: I cleaned the dwarves' house and waited for Prince Charming to bring me life; I played Minnie Mouse to Mickey's flower-bearing adoration, and, later, I swooned in Rhett Butler's arms — my waist as narrow and my bosom every bit as heaving as Scarlett's. But my daddy didn't own a plantation; he owned a rough and tumble bar frequented by loggers and fishermen. My waist didn't dip into an hourglass; in fact, according to the novels I read my thick ankles doomed me to be cast as the peasant woman reaping hay while the heroine swept by with her handsome man in hot pursuit.

Our students suckle the same pap. Our society's culture industry colonizes their minds and teaches them how to act, live, and dream. This indoctrination hits young children especially hard. The "secret education," as Chilean writer Ariel Dorfman (1983) dubs it, delivered by children's books and movies, instructs young people to accept the world as it is portrayed in these social blueprints. And often that world depicts the domination of one sex, one race, one class, or one country over a weaker counterpart. After studying cartoons and children's literature, my student Omar wrote, "When we read children's books, we aren't just reading cute little stories, we are discovering the tools with which a young society is manipulated."

Beverly Tatum, who wrote the book *Why Are All the Black Kids Sitting Together in the Cafeteria?* (1997) helps explain how children develop distorted views of people outside of their racial/cultural group:

> *The impact of racism begins early. Even in our preschool years, we are exposed to misinformation about people different from ourselves. Many of us grow up in neighborhoods where we had limited opportunities to interact with people different from our own families. . . . Consequently, most of the early information we receive about "others" — people racially, religiously, or socioeconomically different from ourselves — does not come as a result of firsthand experience. The secondhand information we receive has often been distorted, shaped by cultural stereotypes, and left incomplete. . . .*

Cartoon images, in particular the Disney movie **Peter Pan**, *were cited by the children [in a research study] as their number one source of information. At the age of three, these children had a set of stereotypes in place.*

Children's cartoons, movies, and literature are perhaps the most influential genre "read." Young people, unprotected by any intellectual armor, hear or watch these stories again and again, often from the warmth of their mother's or father's lap. The messages, or "secret education," linked with the security of their homes, underscore the power these texts deliver. As Tatum's research suggests, the stereotypes and world view embedded in the stories become accepted knowledge.

I want my students to question this accepted knowledge and the secret education delivered by cartoons as well as by the canon. Because children's movies and literature are short and visual we can critique them together. We can view many in a brief period of time, so students can begin to see patterns in media portrayals of particular groups and learn to decode the underlying assumptions these movies make. Brazilian educator Paulo Freire (in Shor and Freire, 1987) wrote that instead of wrestling with words and ideas, too often students "walk on the words." If I

Jean-Claude Lejeune

want my students to wrestle with the social text of novels, news, or history books, they need the tools to critique media that encourage or legitimate social inequality.

To help students uncover those old values planted by Disney, Mattel, and Nike, and construct more just ones, I begin this "unlearning the myths" unit with two objectives. First I want students to critique portrayals of hierarchy and inequality in children's movies and cartoons. Then I want to enlist them to imagine a better world, characterized by relationships of respect and equality.

Exposing the Myths:
How to Read Cartoons

Prior to watching any cartoons, I ask students to read the preface and first chapter of Ariel Dorfman's book *The Empire's Old Clothes: What the Lone Ranger, Babar, and Other Innocent Heroes Do to Our Minds* (1983).

Students keep track of their responses in a dialogue journal. (See page 48 for a complete discussion of dialogue journals). I pose the question: Do you agree with Dorfman's position that children receive a "secret education" in the media? Do you remember any incidents from your own childhood that support his allegations?"

This is difficult for some students. The dialogue journal spurs them to argue, to talk back, and create a conversation with the writer. Dorfman is controversial. He gets under their skin. He wrote:

> *Industrially produced fiction has become one of the primary shapers of our emotions and our intellect in the twentieth century. Although these stories are supposed to merely entertain us, they constantly give us a secret education. We are not only taught certain styles of violence, the latest fashions, and sex roles by TV, movies, magazines, and comic strips; we are also taught how to succeed, how to love, how to buy, how to conquer, how to forget the past and suppress the future. We are taught more than anything else, how not to rebel.*

Many students don't want to believe that they have been manipulated by children's media or advertising. No one wants to admit that they've been "handled" by the media. They assure me that they make their own choices and the media has no power over them

— as they sit with Fubu, Nike, Timberlands or whatever the latest fashion rage might be. And Dorfman analyzes that pose:

> There has also been a tendency to avoid scrutinizing these mass media products too closely, to avoid asking the sort of hard questions that can yield disquieting answers. It is not strange that this should be so. The industry itself has declared time and again with great forcefulness that it is innocent, that no hidden motives or implications are lurking behind the cheerful faces it generates.

Justine, a senior in my Contemporary Literature and Society class, was bothered by Dorfman's quest "to dissect those dreams, the ones that had nourished my childhood and adolescence, that continued to infect so many of my adult habits." In her dialogue journal she responded:

> Personally, handling the dissection of dreams has been a major cause of depression for me. Not so much dissecting — but how I react to what is found as a result of the operation. It can be overwhelming and discouraging to find out my whole self image has been formed mostly by others or underneath my worries about what I look like are years (17 of them) of being exposed to TV images of girls and their set roles given to them by TV and the media. It's painful to deal with. The idea of not being completely responsible for how I feel about things today is scary. So why dissect the dreams? Why not stay ignorant about them and happy? The reason for me is that those dreams are not unrelated to my everyday life. They influence how I behave, think, react to things. . . . My dreams keep me from dealing with an unpleasant reality.

In looking back through this passage and others in her dialogue with Dorfman, Justine displayed discomfort with prying apart her identity and discovering where she received her ideas; yet, she also grudgingly admitted how necessary this process was if she wanted to move beyond where she was at the time. Her discomfort might also have arisen from feeling incapable of changing herself or changing the standards by which she was judged in the larger society. But she knew such questioning was important.

In a later section of her journal, she wrote, "True death equals a generation living by rules and attitudes they never questioned and producing more children who do the same." Justine's reaction may be more articulate than some, but her sentiments were typical of many students. She was beginning to peel back the veneer covering some of the injustice in our society, and she was dismayed by what she discovered.

Charting Stereotypes

I start by showing students old cartoons because the stereotypes are so blatant. We look at the roles women, men, people of color, and poor people play in the cartoons. I ask students to watch for who plays the lead. Who plays the buffoon? Who plays the servant? I encourage them to look at the race, station in life, body type of each character. What are the characters' motivation? What do they want out of life? What's their mission? If there are people of color in the film, what do they look like? How are they portrayed? What would children learn about this particular group from this film?

How does the film portray overweight people? What about women other than the main character? What jobs do you see them doing? What do they talk about? What are their main concerns? What would young children learn about women's roles in society if they watched this film and believed it? What roles do money, possessions, and power play in the film? Who has it? Who wants it? How important is it to the story? What would children learn about what's important in this society?

As they view each episode, they fill in a chart answering these questions. (See page 51.) Students immediately start yelling out the stereotypes because they are so obvious. Early in the unit, I show a Popeye cartoon, "Ali Baba and the 40 Thieves" that depicts all Arabs with the same face, same turban, same body — and they are all thieves swinging enormous swords. At one point in the cartoon, Popeye clips a dog collar on helpless Olive Oyl and drags her through the desert. Later, the 40 thieves come riding through town stealing everything — food, an old man's teeth, numbers off a clock — even the stripe off a barber pole. The newer cartoons — like *Mulan, Aladdin,* and *Pocahontas* — are subtler and take more sophistication to see through, but if students warm up on the old ones, they can pierce the surface of the new ones as well.

On first viewing, students sometimes resist critical analysis. After watching a Daffy Duck cartoon, for example, Kamaui said, "This is just a dumb little cartoon with some ducks running around in clothes." Then students start to notice patterns — like the absence of female characters in many of the older cartoons. When women do appear, they look like Jessica Rabbit or Playboy centerfolds — even in many of the

> If I want my students to wrestle with the social text of novels, news, or history books, they need the tools to critique media that encourage or legitimate social inequality.

new and improved children's movies.

After filling in a few charts, collectively and on their own, students write about the generalizations children might take away from these tales. From experience, I've discovered that I need to keep my mouth shut for a while. If I'm the one pointing out the stereotypes, it's the kiss of death to the exercise. Besides, students are quick to find the usual stereotypes on their own: "Look, Ursula the sea witch is ugly and smart. Hey, she's kind of dark looking. The young, pretty ones only want to hook their man; the old, pretty ones are mean because they are losing their looks." Kenneth noticed that people of color and poor people are either absent or servants to the rich, white, pretty people. Tyler pointed out that the roles of men are limited as well. Men must be virile and wield power or be old and the object of "good-natured" humor. Students began seeing beyond the charts I'd rigged up for them. They looked at how overweight people were portrayed as buffoons in episode after episode. They noted the absence of mothers, the wickedness of step-parents.

Later in the unit, Mira, a senior, attacked the racism in these Saturday morning rituals. She brought her familiarity with Native American cultures into her analysis:

> Indians in Looney Tunes are also depicted as inferior human beings. These characters are stereotypical to the greatest degree, carrying tomahawks, painting their faces, and sending smoke signals as their only means of communication.

Help Me Syndrome
By Hasina Deary

It's a typical cartoon scene: Popeye off sailing or toting a sledge hammer doing whatever Popeye does to make a living, while Olive Oyl who does not have a job lounges around. Olive is skinny to the point of hospitalization. Popeye obviously does not share his spinach. Olive Oyl, in her frail condition has a tendency to be vulnerable to Bluto's frequent abductions. Bluto is the big, brawny bully who Popeye grapples with from cartoon to cartoon. Poor Olive is whisked away by the hair or thrown kicking and screaming over Bluto's shoulder. Her only salvation is knowing that Popeye will be coming to save her. "Help me, help me, Popeye!" Magically, he hears Olive's call for help. Popeye, her hero. He struggles with his can of spinach, but in the end the tattooed avenger saves Olive Oyl. It is so silly. Olive Oyl's only redeeming quality as a woman is the fact she is never stuck in the kitchen. Popeye, the strong and courageous, also prepares his own meals.

Why wasn't Olive ever smart enough to lock the doors so Bluto couldn't get in or clever enough to save herself? It is a disgusting example of the "Help Me Syndrome" so often portrayed in cartoons.

In **Sleeping Beauty,** the silly little princess pricked her finger, causing an entire kingdom to slumber. Peace was restored after the prince rode into town, fought with a witch in dragon's form, then kissed the Sleeping Beauty. All is well, another princess saved.

Why are women constantly in need of male rescue? Does the industry feed on some women's twisted fantasy to be saved by a make-believe Prince Charming? It might be said that these are old cartoons and women today have evolved. But Disney's three latest productions have at least one scene where the female character's life was in jeopardy, only to be spared by her male counterpart.

In **The Little Mermaid,** Eric steers a ship's mast through the evil Ursula's torso, freeing Ariel from the curse. After Belle from Beauty and the Beast tries to leave the castle she is attacked by slanty-eyed wolves. Lucky for her, the Beast came and fought off the angry hounds. A sigh of relief is breathed, another pretty face saved. Even in **Aladdin,** Disney's most progressive cartoon, Aladdin, the street-smart hero, first comes to Princess Jasmine's aid when she nearly has her hand cut off after being accused of thievery. In the end of the movie, we see Jasmine trapped in a huge hourglass. Her cries for help are drowned out by the sand that fills the glass. Finally, Aladdin breaks the glass to save Jasmine. Ahh.

While the women in Disney's three recent cartoons are a step up from the non-stop pathetic whining of Olive Oyl, they still lack independence and basic survival skills. They may be called a heroine, but by no means are they the woman hero. Indeed, they are merely girls in need of rescue. The misconception that females must be male-dependent is reiterated, even if they basically have things going for them. Belle wanted more than her "provincial life." So they want more, but never can they attain it by themselves.

Rarely do we see brave women saving others. Wonder Woman is the only woman cartoon character I know who has ever been the rescuer. She saves men, women, and children (but mostly women and children). Of course, she has to have Super Heroine powers to do it. She could not just be Mindy MacGyver, the normal girl, who uses her mind to solve probems. Instead cartoons are made about beautiful girls who sing and read, and bright-eyed, headstrong princesses who are all capable of thinking, but ultimately succeed because of the love of a man. I think it is time to change the outdated formulas of love and near-death rescue scenes. I challenge the cartoon makers to find a new happy ending.

They live in tipis and their language reminds the viewer of Neanderthals. We begin to imagine Indians as savages with bows and arrows and long black braids. There's no room in our minds for knowledge of the differences between tribes, like the Cherokee alphabet or Celilo salmon fishing.

A Black Cinderella?

After viewing a number of cartoons, Kenya scolded parents in an essay, "A Black Cinderella? Give Me A Break." She wrote: "Have you ever seen a Black person, an Asian, a Hispanic in a cartoon? Did they have a leading role or were they a servant? What do you think this is doing to your child's mind?" She ended her piece, "Women who aren't white begin to feel left out and ugly because they never get to play the princess." Kenya's piece bristled with anger at a society that rarely acknowledges the wit or beauty of women of her race. And she wasn't alone in her feelings. Sabrina wrote, "I'm not taking my kids to see any Walt Disney movies until they have a Black woman playing the leading role."

> **The newer cartoons — like "Mulan," "Aladdin," and "Pocahontas" — are subtler and take more sophistication to see through, but if students warm up on the old ones, they can pierce the surface of the new ones as well.**

Both young women wanted the race of the actors changed, but they didn't challenge the class or underlying gender inequities that also characterize the lives of Cinderella, Ariel, and Snow White.

Kenya's and Sabrina's anger is justified. There should be more women of color who play the leads in these white-on-white wedding cake tales. Of course, there should also be more women of color on the Supreme Court, in Congress, as well as scrubbing up for surgeries. But I want students to understand that if the race of the character is the only thing changing, injustices may still remain.

So I have students read Mary Carter Smith's delightful retelling of Cinderella, "Cindy Ellie, A Modern Fairy Tale" (1989), which reads like laughter — bubbly, warm, spilling over with infectious good humor and playful language. In Smith's version, Cindy Ellie, who lived in East Baltimore, was "one purty young Black sister, her skin like black velvet." Her father, "like so many good men, was weak for a pretty face and big legs and big hips." Her stepmother "had a heart as hard as a rock. The milk of human kindness had curdled in her breast. But she did have a pretty face, big legs, and great big hips. . . . Well, that fool man fell right into that woman's trap."

Cindy Ellie's stepsisters were "two big-footed, ugly gals" who made Cindy Ellie wait on them hand and foot. When the "good white folks, the good Asian folks, and the good Black folks all turned out and voted for a good Black brother, running for mayor" there was cause for celebration, and a chance for Cindy Ellie to meet her Prince Charming, the mayor's son. With the help of her Godma's High John the Conqueror Root, Cindy Ellie looked like an "African Princess." "Her rags turned into a dazzling dress of pink African laces! Her hair was braided into a hundred shining braids, and on the end of each braid were beads of pure gold! . . . Golden bracelets covered her arms clean up to her elbows! On each ear hung five small diamond earrings. On her tiny feet were dainty golden sandals encrusted with dazzling jewels! Cindy Ellie was laid back!"

The students and I love the story. It is well told and incorporates rich details that do exactly what Sabrina, Kenya, and their classmates wanted: It celebrates the beauty, culture, and language of African Americans. It also puts forth the possibility of cross-race alliances for social change.

But, like the original tale, Cindy Ellie's main goal in life is not working to end the plight of the homeless or teaching kids to read. Her goal, like Cinderella's, is to get her man. Both young women are transformed and made beautiful through new clothes, new jewels, new hairstyles. Both have chauffeurs who deliver them to their men. Cindy Ellie and Cinderella are nicer and kinder than their stepsisters, but the Prince and Toussant, the mayor's son, don't know that. Both of the Cinderellas compete for their men against their sisters and the rest of the single women in their cities. They "win" because of their beauty and their fashionable attire. Both of these tales leave young women with two myths: happiness means getting a man, and transformation from wretched conditions can be achieved through consumption — in their case, through new clothes and a new hairstyle.

I am uncomfortable with those messages. I don't want students to believe that change can be bought at the mall, nor do I want them thinking that the pinnacle of a woman's life is an "I do" that supposedly leads them to a "happily ever after." I don't want my female students to see their "sisters" as competition for that scarce and wonderful commodity — men. As Justine wrote earlier in her dialogue journal, it can be overwhelming and discouraging to find that our self-images have been formed by others, but if we don't dissect them, we will continue to be influenced by them.

Writing as a Vehicle for Change

Toward the end of the unit, students write essays

Looking Pretty, Waiting for the Prince

By Lila Johnson

[As a senior, Lila Johnson uncovered the "secret education" that cartoons, advertising, and the media slipped into her life. She wrote this article to educate others about the inaccurate visions Disney & Co. sell children.]

My two brothers and I lived for our daily cartoon fix. We hungered for the vibrant reds, blues, and yellows that raced around our screen for an insane hour or two.

When we were away from the tube, we assumed the roles of our favorite characters: Bugs Bunny, that wise-cracking, carrot-munching rabbit; Yosemite Sam, rough and tough shoot-'em-down cowboy; and Popeye, the all-American spinach-guzzling sailor. We took our adopted identities outside and to school where our neighbors and friends did the same.

Now, as a senior in high school, I see that cartoons are not just lighthearted, wacky fun. Animated material touches on such sensitive issues as roles of men and women in society, and people of color.

Cartoons are often the birthplace of the cultural stereotypes we learn and remember, as I do today: the idea that Indians are savages — tomahawks and moccasins, teepees and war paint — the bad guys who pursued my favorite cowboys, or the belief that Arabs have nothing better to do than to tear across deserts in robes while swinging fierce swords and yelping like alien creatures.

These notions didn't just occur to my brothers and me magically. We saw Indians in our afternoon cartoons and on some of our favorite Disney movies like **Peter Pan**. We witnessed villainous Arabs thieve their way through violent episodes of **Popeye**.

What is not seen in relation to people of different cultures can be as harmful as some of the things that are seen. People of color are rarely seen as the heroes of animated presentations. I can think of only one Disney classic where a person of color is the principal and heroic character — **The Jungle Book**. Not an impressive list.

Children search for personal identity. In first grade I adored Bonnie Bondell, a girl in my class. She wasn't a cartoon character, but she could have been. She had glossy blonde hair and blue eyes. She had a sparkly smile and a sweet voice. She could have been Cinderella's younger sister or Sleeping Beauty's long lost cousin. For those reasons, I longed to be just like her.

I look at old photos of myself now, and have decided that I was pretty cute. I wasn't a traditional cutie, and that's exactly what bothered me then. My father is African-American and my mother is German and Irish. Put the two together and I'm the result. Olive complex-ion, dark curly hair, brown and green eyes. All wrong. At least according to the "Fairy Tale Book of Standards."

The pride that I had in myself as a person with a colorful heritage did not blossom before it was crushed. The pride that I had in myself as a female was following the same path.

Women's roles in cartoons lack the cleverness and depth of their male counterparts. Instead, they are laced with helplessness and ignorance. The women are often in need of rescue — they seem incapable of defending or helping themselves. When they aren't busy being rescued, they spend their time looking pretty, waiting for a prince.

In first grade, these illustrations moved me to action. They influenced me to push aside my slacks and rustic bike and turn to dresses and dolls. I had to start practicing perfection if I was going to be happy. Weak, helpless, boring, I struggled to be all of those, then I could call myself a princess, an awkward one, but a princess nonetheless.

At the same time, my brothers swung guns and swords like they were attached to their hands. They tossed aside their piles of books and tubs of clay — heroes didn't read or create — they fought! So they flexed their wiry muscles and wrestled invisible villains. They dressed, ate, talked, became miniature models of their violent heroes.

Sometimes it was fun, like a game, playing our parts. But we began to feel unhappy when we saw that some things weren't quite right. As I said — I wasn't Bonnie Bondell or Cinderella. My brothers, never destined to be hulks, went to great lengths to grow big, but gallons of milk and daily measurements didn't help. It wasn't a game anymore.

I have some fond memories of those afternoons with my brothers, yet I know that I will also remember them for the messages I swallowed as easily as gum drops. My newfound awareness has enabled me to better understand those messages I absorbed and the ones I observe daily, whether on billboards, in movies, or in magazines. I see them in a new light. A critical one. I don't have to be a princess to be happy or pretty. I don't need to rely on characters to learn about real people.

I proudly perceive myself as an exuberant, creative, responsible, open-minded individual who will never be reduced to a carbon copy of a fictional being.

critiquing cartoons. I hope that these will encourage students to look deeper into the issues — to challenge the servant/master relationships or the materialism that makes women appealing to their men. For some students the cartoon unit exposes the wizardry that enters our dreams and desires, but others shrug their shoulders at this. It's okay for some people to be rich and others poor; they just want to see more rich people of color or more rich women. Or better yet, be rich themselves. They accept the inequalities in power and exploitative economic relationships. Their acceptance teaches me how deep the roots of these myths are planted and how much some students, in the absence of visions for a different and better world, need to believe in the fairy tale magic that will transform their lives — whether it's a rich man or winning the lottery.

Many students write strong critiques following the viewing. But venting their frustrations with cartoons — and even sharing it with the class — can seem an important but limited task. Yes, they can write articulate pieces. Yes, they hone their arguments and seek the just-right examples from their viewing. Through critiques and the discussions that follow, they are helping to transform each other — each comment or observation helps expose the engine of our society, and they're both excited and dismayed by their discoveries.

But what am I teaching them if the lesson ends there? That it's enough to be critical without taking action? That we can quietly rebel in the privacy of the classroom while we practice our writing skills, but we don't really have to do anything about the problems we uncover, nor do we need to create anything to take the place of what we've expelled? Those are not the lessons I intend to teach. I want to develop their critical consciousness, but I also hope to move them to action.

For some the lesson doesn't end in the classroom. Many who watched cartoons before we start our study say they can no longer enjoy them. Now instead of seeing a bunch of ducks in clothes, they see the racism, sexism, and violence that swim under the surface of the stories.

Pam and Nicole swore they would not let their children watch cartoons. David told the class of coming home one day and finding his nephews absorbed in Looney Tunes. "I turned that TV off and took them down to the park to play. They aren't going to watch that mess while I'm around." Radiance described how she went to buy Christmas presents for her niece and nephew. "Before, I would have just walked into the toy store and bought them what I knew they wanted — Nintendo or Barbie. But this time, I went up the clerk and said, 'I want a toy that isn't sexist or racist.'"

Students have also said that what they now see in cartoons, they also see in advertising, on prime time TV, on the news, in school. Turning off the cartoons doesn't stop the sexism and racism. They can't escape, and now that they've started analyzing cartoons, they can't stop analyzing the rest of the world. And sometimes they want to stop. Once a student asked me, "Don't you ever get tired of analyzing everything?"

During a class discussion Sabrina said, "I realized these problems weren't just in cartoons. They were in everything — every magazine I picked up, every television show I watched, every billboard I passed by on the street." My goal of honing their ability to read literature and the world through the lens of justice had been accomplished at least in part. But as Justine wrote earlier, at times my students would like to remain "ignorant and happy." Without giving students an outlet for their despair, I was indeed creating "factories of cynicism" (Bigelow, et al., 1994) in my classroom — and it wasn't pretty.

Taking Action

I look for opportunities for students to act on their knowledge. In Literature and U.S. History class, these occasions have presented themselves in the form of unfair tests and outrageous newspaper articles about Jefferson that provoked spontaneous student activism (Bigelow, et al., 1994). But in my Contemporary Literature and Society class, I discovered that I had to create the possibility for action.

Instead of writing the same classroom essays students had written in years before, I asked students to create projects that would move beyond the classroom walls. Who could they teach about what they learned? I wanted their projects to be real. Who could their analysis touch enough to bring about real change? Students filled the board with potential readers of their work: Parents, peers, teachers, children's book authors, librarians, Disney, video store owners, advertisers.

My only rule was that they had to write a piece using evidence from cartoons or other media. Don't just rant in general, I told them. Use evidence to support your thesis. The examples might come from cartoons, advertisements, novels, your mother or father's advice. You might use lines from TV or movies. You don't have to stick to cartoons — use the world.

We discussed possible options:

- Focus on one cartoon — critique it, talk about it in depth. Write about Mulan or Peter Pan. Using the chart, analyze the representation of men, women, people of color, and poor people in that movie.

- Focus on the portrayal of one group. Write about how women, men, African Americans,

Latinos, Arabs, overweight people or the poor are depicted and give examples from several cartoons or across time. (See "Help Me Syndrome," page 43)

- Take an issue — like the representation of women — and relate it to your life and/or society at large. (See "Looking Pretty, Waiting for the Prince," page 45)

One group of playful students wanted to create a pamphlet that could be distributed at PTA meetings throughout the city. That night they went home with assignments they'd given each other — Sarah would watch Saturday morning cartoons; Sandy, Brooke, and Carmel would watch after-school cartoons; and Kristin and Toby were assigned before-school cartoons. They ended up writing a report card for the various programs. They graded each show A through F and wrote a brief summary of their findings:

"DUCK TALES: At first glance the precocious ducks are cute, but look closer and see that the whole show is based on money. All their adventures revolve around finding money. Uncle Scrooge and the gang teach children that money is the only important thing in life. Grade: C-

"TEENAGE MUTANT NINJA TURTLES: Pizza-eating Ninja Turtles. What's the point? There isn't any. The show is based on fighting the 'bad guy,' Shredder. Demonstrating no concern for the townspeople, they battle and fight, but never get hurt. This cartoon teaches a false sense of violence to kids: fight and you don't get hurt, or solve problems through fists and swords instead of words. Grade: D

"POPEYE: This show oozes with horrible messages from passive Olive Oyl to the hero 'man' Popeye. This cartoon portrays ethnic groups as stupid. It is political also - teaching children that Americans are the best and conquer all others. Grade: F

On the back of the pamphlet, they listed some tips for parents to guide them in wise cartoon selection.

Catkin wrote about the sexual stereotyping and adoration of beauty in children's movies. Her article described how she and other teenage women carry these messages with them still:

Women's roles in fairy tales distort reality — from Jessica Rabbit's six-mile strut in Who Framed Roger Rabbit? *to Tinker Bell's obsessive vanity in* Peter Pan. *These seemingly innocent stories teach us to look for our faults. As Tinker Bell inspects her tiny body in a mirror only to find that her minute hips are simply too huge, she shows us how to turn the mirror into an enemy. . . . And this scenario is repeated in girls' locker rooms all over the world.*

Because we can never look like Cinderella, we begin to hate ourselves. The Barbie syndrome starts as we begin a life-long search for the perfect body. Crash diets, fat phobias, and an obsession with the materialistic become commonplace. The belief that a product will make us rise above our competition, our friends, turns us into addicts. Our fix is that Calvin Klein push-up bra, Guess jeans, Chanel lipstick, and the latest in suede flats. We don't call it deception; we call it good taste. And soon it feels awkward going to the mailbox without makeup.

Catkin wanted to publish her piece in a magazine for young women so they would begin to question the origin of the standards by which they judge themselves.

Most students wrote articles for local and national newspapers or magazines. Some published in neighborhood papers, some in church newsletters. Lila Johnson's article "Looking Pretty, Waiting for the Prince" (see page 45) and Hasina Deary's "Help Me Syndrome" (see page 43) have both been published nationally.

The writing in these articles was tighter and cleaner than for-the-teacher essays because it had the potential for a real audience beyond the classroom walls. The possibility of publishing their pieces changed the level of students' intensity for the project. Anne, who turned in hastily written drafts last year, said, "Five drafts and I'm not finished yet!"

But more importantly, students saw themselves as actors in the world; they were fueled by the opportunity to convince some parents of the long-lasting effects cartoons impose on their children, or to enlighten their peers about the roots of some of their insecurities. Instead of leaving students full of bile, standing around with their hands on their hips, shaking their heads about how bad the world is, I provided them the opportunity to make a difference. ■

References

Bigelow, Bill, et al. *Rethinking Our Classrooms: Teaching for Equity and Justice.* Milwaukee, WI: Rethinking Schools, 1994, p. 4.

Dorfman, Ariel. *The Empire's Old Clothes: What the Lone Ranger, Babar, and Other Innocent Heroes Do to Our Minds.* New York: Pantheon, 1983, p. ix.

Smith, Mary Carter. "Cindy Ellie, A Modern Fairy Tale," in Goss, Linda (Ed.). *Talk That Talk: An Anthology Of African-American Storytelling.* New York: Touchstone, 1989, pp. 396-402.

Shor, Ira and Freire, Paulo. *A Pedagogy for Liberation.* South Hadley, MA: Bergin & Garvey, 1987, p. 10.

Tatum, Beverly. *'Why Are All the Black Kids Sitting Together in the Cafeteria?' And Other Conversations About Race.* New York: Basic Books, 1997, pp. 4-5.

Dialogue Journal Strategy:
Their Eyes Were Watching God

As you read the novel *Their Eyes Were Watching God*, keep track of passages and page numbers you want the class to come back to for discussion. Write your reaction to these passages.

1. SOCIAL QUESTIONS — Look for race, class, gender inequalities. For example, in *Their Eyes Were Watching God* Grandma says, "Ah can't die easy thinkin' maybe de menfolks white or Black is makin' a spit cup outa you." You might want to comment about this quote. It might remind you of something your grandmother said. It might be a quote you want the class to talk about.

2. GREAT WRITING —Look for a line, a phrase, a paragraph that you think is great writing. You might want to "steal" some ideas or words from this passage for a poem or to use in an essay or story. Ultimately, learning to recognize good writing helps you write better.

3. QUESTIONS — It could be that you don't understand something that is going on in the novel or in a passage. These questions usually lead to rich classroom discussion. For example: Why did the men both respect and hate Joe Sparks? Why wouldn't Joe let Janie tell stories on the porch with the men?

4. TALK BACK — Get mad at the character or the storyteller. Talk back. Disagree. Shout. These are also great discussion starters. "Nanny shouldn't have pushed Janie to get married. . . ."

5. MEMORIES — Every text changes somewhat depending on the reader and his/her experiences. You might hear yourself saying, "That reminds me of. . . ." What memories click on when you read? Did you have a grandmother who told you stories? Do you and your friends sit on the porch and tell stories? Do you know someone like Tea Cake? Don't lose those memories: they are the key to your writings.

6. AHA'S — As you read, you might start to notice a thread that you want to follow — Janie's interaction with men; how men treat women; how Hurston uses the porch stories. Keep track of those threads. When it comes time to write an essay, you will have all the evidence you need.

7. OTHER READINGS — Sometimes as we read, other books or movies come to mind. It's good to write those down. Sometimes we learn by making comparisons. For example: Joe Starks reminds me of Mr._____ in *The Color Purple*.

8. LITERARY TECHNIQUES — In number two, I asked you to keep track of great writing — lines, phrases — but I'd also like you to watch for literary techniques: use of imagery, flashback, blocking, dialogue. Notice how Hurston gets folks off and on the stage. Again, noticing these contributes to your own ability to write.

Student Sample of a Dialogue Journal:
Their Eyes Were Watching God

Observations/Quotes	Reactions & Reflections
"Thank yuh fuh yo' compliments, but mah wife don't know nothin' 'bout no speech-makin'. Ah never married her for nothing like dat…She's uh woman and her place is in de home." (p. 40)	It's interesting to me that men who think they have a little bit of power, abuse it. They have to be in control of everything, their work and their women. If they only knew that they don't have much power at all.
"That's the way it went, too. The women get together the sweets and the men look after the meats." (p.42)	When did this begin? With hunting and gathering? The men hunted and the women gathered? In modern times this translates to the man cooking the meat and the women dealing with the sweets.
"Ah told you in de very first beginnin' dat Ah aimed tuh be uh big voice. You oughta be glad, 'cause dat makes uh big woman outa you." (p. 43)	Do men think that they substantiate a woman? Make her? Do some women like this? I don't like it.
"What Ah don't lak 'bout de man is, he talks tuh unlettered folks wit books in his jaws." "Showin' off his learning." (p. 46)	I know people like this. They try to make themselves look important by showing off how much they know. They put others down, want them to feel one down, inferior if they haven't read as much or completed college.
"He tagged on and swallowed to kill time." (p. 46)	Interesting way to describe swallowing.
"A pretty doll-baby lak you is made to sit on de front porch and rock and fan yourself." (p. 49)	What's up with that? So pretty women are supposed to sit and fan themselves? What about ugly women? Fat women? I don't like this man.

Charting Stereotypes

Young children often learn some of their first lessons in front of the TV set. From cartoons, children learn how boys and girls act, what our society values, and how to react to people who may differ from the mainstream. As you watch the cartoons today, begin to think about the education that children soak up while they view. Of course, I can hear you already: "Cartoons are innocent fairy tales." Keep that assumption, but also imagine for a moment that children might learn some lessons. Using the chart, take notes on the following questions as you view:

• Who plays the lead?

• Who plays the buffoon?

• Who plays the servant?

• Look at the race, station in life, body type of each character.

• What are the characters' motivations? What do they want out of life? What's their mission?

• If there are people of color in the film, what do they look like? How are they portrayed? What would children learn about this particular group from this film?

• What about women other than the main character? What jobs do you see them doing? What do they talk about? What are their main concerns? What would young children learn about women's roles in society if they watched this film and believed it?

• What roles do money, possessions, and power play in the film? Who has it? Who wants it? How important is it to the story? What would children learn about what's important in this society?

• How does the film portray overweight people?

Charting Stereotypes

	Character's Name	Character's Name	Character's Name
Women			
Men			
People of Color			
Poor People			

Praise Poems

As I try to equip students to "unlearn the myths that bind them" in history, literature, and popular culture, I find it necessary to balance the critical stance we strive for in class with times of laughter and playfulness. I want to create more opportunities for joy.

But even in those moments of joy, of community building, I want students to think critically about the world. In class, we read poems by Lucille Clifton, Langston Hughes, Maya Angelou, Mari Evans, Countee Cullen, and others who celebrate African-American culture and beauty. We also read poems by Martín

Skjold Photographs

I encourage students to praise themselves, their "people," their culture, their language, their school, their neighborhood.

Espada, Gary Soto, Naomi Shihab Nye, Pablo Neruda, Carolyn Forché, and Lawson Inada who celebrate the language, music, history of other cultures.

"Praise poems" I call them. Many of these poets found it necessary to praise themselves because the standards of beauty and acceptance in the dominant culture were European-American. For example, Clifton and Angelou praise big women — rejecting the norm of beauty that holds thinness as the standard. Mari Evans' poem "Who Can Be Born Black" and Dudley Randall's "Blackberry Sweet" both sing the beauty of Blackness.

Writing praise poems gives us a positive way to look at ourselves, but these poems also speak against the negative portrayals students too often see associated with their neighborhood, their school — in the case of Jefferson High School — race, language, gender, sexual orientation, size — the list is endless. This is a poetry assignment I return to again and again as my students and I explore thematic units throughout the year. I encourage students to praise themselves, their "people," their culture, their language, their school, their neighborhood.

Of course, this is awkward. Most students have been taught that bragging is not acceptable. That's why I frame the idea socially and historically. When Lucille Clifton writes in her poem "homage to my hips": "these hips are big hips/ they don't like to be held back./ these hips have never been enslaved . . . these hips are mighty hips/ these hips are magic hips," she critiques the way women have been judged as well as the treatment of African Americans.

As we talk about standards of beauty and materialism in the "Unlearning the Myths" unit, students gain permission to criticize commercially produced images. In writing about themselves, students learn to praise their own attributes that often have been overlooked or held in contempt by society. Some students love the opportunity to point out what's good about them. Curtina Barr wrote:

What the Mirror Said —
In admiration of Lucille Clifton's poetry

The mirror told me,
"Yo' skin the color of coffee
after the cream's been poured in.
Yo' body's just the right size —
not too plump,
not too thin.
Yo' lips like cotton candy
sweet and soft.
Yo' sho' done good.
Yo' like a city,
strong and tall,
though deep in yo' eyes
I can still see yo' pain,
yo' smile and laugh.
Keep doin' yo' thang.

Damon wrote a praise poem about his backside. Marcus wrote about his luscious lips. Aaron Wheeler-Kay wrote about his eyes in a poem called, "I Got the Blues":

Blue eyes
Yes, Ma'am.
Blue.
Like the ocean —
No, blue like new jeans.
Stiff and comfy —
No, blue like hard times.
Yeah.
Blue like cold steel and oil.
Blue like the caress of jazz at a funeral.
The azure ice cubes in my head
Melt hearts.
Yes, blue like lightning in a desert storm.
Blue like twin sapphires blazing in a jeweler's palm.
Blue like my baby.
Like my baby blues.
Blue like cold lips in winter,
Indigo stains
In an optical vein.
I got the blues
And they got a tale
To tell.

Jean-Claude Lejeune

As students read aloud, the poems bring kinship and often a great deal of laughter to our classroom community. When Marcus returned two years after he graduated, we still laughed about his "luscious lips."

Teaching Strategy:

1. When we read the poems by Angelou, Clifton, and others, I ask the students to talk about what the poets are praising and why they might feel it necessary to praise themselves.

2. I ask students to think of something about themselves, their bodies, homes, community, school, culture, or language that deserves praise, but that may not often receive praise. I ask a few students to share their ideas so they can help shake loose some ideas for classmates who are stuck.

3. As I select the poems — whether they are models to help us praise ourselves in the "Unlearning the Myths" unit, praise our homes and cultures in the immigration unit (see Chapter 6, page 143), praise our language in the "Politics of Language" unit (see Chapter 4, page 99), or praise our school or neighborhood after negative media coverage — I look for poems that provide a pattern or hook. Clifton's "what the mirror said," for example, is a great opening for students. They can look in the mirror and pay homage to themselves as Curtina Barr did, or they can praise their heritage as Chetan Patel did in his poem "Tiger Eyes" (see page 54). It helps if students have several ideas of how to begin their poems. I try to use models from both professional and student writers.

4. Sometimes students get stuck in this — and other — assignments. Some have difficulty praising themselves. I understand this problem because I haven't been able to write a decent

TIGER EYES
By Chetan Patel

I look into a mirror
and watch the history inside of me
flood out.
I see the Kshatriya warrior,
sword in hand,
the Sudra laborer,
working hard at his feet.
I see the stories passed
under the Banyan tree
and the cleansing Ganges,
slicing down the Himalayas.
I see the village Panchayat,
the Lok Sabha,
the House of People.
I see the deep fried Samosas,
full of carrots and peas,
wrapped in flour,
ready to eat.
I see the river flooding
in the monsoons,
the locus lying
in the fields of Jammu.
I see the tiger eyes
waiting in the high grass,
for me to come back
and relive the past.

praise poem about myself either, so I allow students to find their own passion in the assignment, but to remember the intent of the poem: praise something that may not traditionally be valued in our society. With classes of younger students, I sometimes begin by asking them to write a paragraph describing an object, and then a paragraph about how they came to have the object. They can use these details in their poems.

Students have written odes to the Spanish language, their skin, their weight, a mother's hands, animal cookies, ham, a grandfather's hat, tap dance, coffee, Jefferson High School, chocolate chip cookies, the color red, writing, and more. The ode becomes a form they return to frequently in their writing.

Sarah Scofield, whose beautiful reading of Neruda's poetry in Spanish allowed her to share her linguistic talent with classmates, wrote this poem:

Ode to Spanish

A language
As beautiful as music:
Melodious verbs
Harmonious adjectives
Rhythmic nouns
Intertwine as I speak
An orchestra of words
Conducted by my tongue
I compose
A new song
As those around me listen
Musical sentences
Rich with the notes
Of culture
A romance language
Stirring the hearts
Of its listeners
The music plays on
As I watch with wonder how
My untrained yet experienced tongue
conducts the orchestra
and the music pleases me

5. I usually turn the lights off and ask students to find a space where they can write quietly. Some like to sit on the floor, others on the windowsill, some turn their desks to the wall. This allows them time to get prepared. Then I tell students that when I turn the lights back on they must begin writing in silence.

If I want students to imagine a more just society, I must spend time teaching them how to find what's good as well as to find what's bad. My classroom provides a small space to undermine a social system that daily damages my students with belittling messages. In this space, I hope to help students not only construct a critique, but also to build a community that can laugh and share joy. ■

Bibliography of Praise Poems

Angelou, Maya. "Ain't That Bad" and "Phenomenal Woman," in *And Still I Rise*. New York: Random House, 1978.

Clifton, Lucille. "homage to my hips" and "what the mirror said," in *Good Woman: Poems and a Memoir 1969-1980*. (American Poets Continuum Series, Vol. 14.) Rochester, NY: BOA Editions, 1989.

Evans, Mari. "Who Can Be Born Black?" in Miller, E. Ethelbert (Ed.), *In Search of Color Everywhere: A Collection of African-American Poetry*. New York: Stewart, Tabori, & Chang, 1994.

Forché, Carolyn. "The Morning Baking," in *Gathering the Tribes*. New Haven and London: Yale University Press, 1976.

Hongo, Garrett. "Who Among You Knows the Essence of Garlic?" in *Yellow Light*. Middletown, CT: Wesleyan, 1982.

Inada, Lawson. "On Being Asian American," in Chin, Frank (Ed.), *Aiiieeeee!: An Anthology of Asian-American Writers*. New York: Mentor, 1991.

Jeffers, Lance. "My Blackness Is The Beauty of This Land," in Miller, E. Ethelbert (Ed.), *In Search of Color Everywhere: A Collection of African-American Poetry*. New York: Stewart, Tabori, & Chang, 1994.

Kono, Juliet. "The Cane Cutters" in *Hilo Rains*. Honolulu, HI: Bamboo Ridge Press, 1988.

Neruda, Pablo. "Ode to My Socks," in *Selected Odes of Pablo Neruda* (with translation by Margaret Sayers Peden). Berkeley, CA: University of California Press, 1990.

Nye, Naomi Shihab. "Blood," in Blum, Joshua, Holman, Bob, and Pellington, Mark (Eds.), *The United States of Poetry*. New York: Harry N. Abrams, Inc., 1996.

Randall, Dudley. "Blackberry Sweet," in Miller, E. Ethelbert (Ed.), *In Search of Color Everywhere: A Collection of African-American Poetry*. New York: Stewart, Tabori, & Chang, 1994.

Rose, Wendy. "Heredity," in *The Halfbreed Chronicles and Other Poems*. Los Angeles: West End Press, 1985.

Soto, Gary. "Ode to a Tortilla," in *Neighborhood Odes*. New York: Scholastic, 1994.

Troupe, Quincy. "A Poem for 'Magic.'" in Miller, E. Ethelbert (Ed.), *In Search of Color Everywhere: A Collection of African-American Poetry*. New York: Stewart, Tabori, & Chang, 1994.

Woody, Elizabeth. "Hand Into Stone," in *Hand Into Stone*. New York: Contact II Publications, 1988.

GURL
By *Mary Blalock*

From Adam's rib
it's prophesied
I came,
but that's his story.

I'm walking on my own
down these streets
with a stop sign on every corner,
taking my time.
I've got no place to go 'cept forward.

Down these highways without a road map,
down these sidewalks,
where the cracks want to break my mother's back,
where the city is crowded.

I'm walking on my own.

I'm not on a stairmaster,
and I won't wait for an elevator,
I'm taking the fire escape
to the top floor.

If I want to,
I'll walk all around the world,
taking the long way
or the shortcuts,
'cross the countries and through the oceans.
I won't be swimming.
I'll walk
on my own.

KOOL-AID
By Jenelle Yarbrough

You soothed me on hot summer days
and relaxed me on humid summer nights.
I remember blue skies and green grass
when we used to rest in Grammy's yard.

I always knew we were her favorites.
Don't worry.
I believe you.
I know you're really made with 1/3 less sugar,
but Grammy still thinks you're sweet.
I think Grammy admires your nationality.
You know, Grammy doesn't know too many
foreigners.
She adores your red native color,
the fact you come from somewhere Tropical
and have an ethnic name like Punch.
And that scent you wear,
Grammy loves it.
She says it smells fruity, but yet subtle.
And she'll swear when she kisses you,
you taste like Sweet Tarts.
I agree with Grammy.
'Cause in our eyes, Kool-Aid is the one.

ODE TO ROCKY ROAD
By Erin Brock

Dipping and curving,
sweet white treasures
hidden underground.
I hold the carton
in my hands
and chisel away,
the plump and light clouds
hidden in creamy,
cold chocolate.
Using my spoon as a shovel,
I break up a rock
of chocolate nuts
and let it melt in my mouth,
A river of ice cream
runs down my chin.
I shave off the first layer,
an archeologist
savoring her work,
seeking the mysteries of ice cream
in a barrel of calories.

DRAGON DANCE
By Loi Nguyen

Tung . . . tung . . . tung
Dragon dance, dragon dance
head and tail
legs and feet
moving
Tung . . . tung . . . tung
Dragon dance, dragon dance
drums play loud
head jump up
tail run down
open the mouth
cut down bargain
bite sweet treat
Tung . . . tung . . . tung
Dragon luck
Dragon strong
like a young man's
big shoulders
Tung . . . tung . . . tung
Dragon dance, dragon dance

Writing the Word and the World

Writing the Word And the World*

I heard that Alice Walker said if we write long enough and hard enough we'll heal ourselves. Maybe that's true. But I've come to see that it's not enough.

I've watched kids write through rapes, parental abuse, the humiliation of the SATs and tracking, the daily bombardment of messages from commercials ("you are not pretty enough, strong enough, smart enough"), budget cuts that mean they won't get any loans or scholarships for college — but these kids passed out of my room every day and went back into the world that wounded them. I patched them up and sent them out without tools to understand — or stop — the brawl they lived with.

For the past 20 years I've worked toward empowering students to use their own voices, to plumb their lives for stories, poems, essays, to engage in a dialogue with their peers about their writing, about literature. And in many respects, I've succeeded.

Students learn to sing their lives through writing. They use writing to take the power out of their pain. Listen as Arne begins to understand his parents' divorce:

> *Mom carried his name around*
> *like a phantom pain until she had him*
> *amputated*
> *to cut off what doesn't exist*
> *takes paperwork*
>
> *Now I see things after the break*
> *were burrs*

> *clinging to her flesh*
> *Maybe she smelled his carpenter sweat*
> *in the sheets and winced*
> *Maybe the little memories*
> *were sand in her shoes*
>
> *I see now*
> *Every chance to dismantle a memory*
> *was taken —*
> *a painting off the wall*
> *love poems slipped under things*
> *maybe one side of a record*
> *she doesn't listen to anymore*
>
> *There is a time*
> *to cut off fingers when*
> *holding hands is wind*
> *on chapped lips*
>
> *I tried to stay with Father*
> *and never saw why she didn't too*
> *Now I see my mother as a lover*
> *and the name she dropped*
> *a phantom pain*

Whitney, a "remedial" freshman, bopped in and out of class, in and out of school, chose cigarette breaks over English for the first semester, but discovered a community where she could talk/write about her life

* The author expresses her thanks to Paulo Freire and Donaldo Macedo (*Literacy: Reading the Word and the World*, South Hadley, MA: Bergin & Garvey, 1987) whose work inspires hers.

and people would listen. This is what Whitney wrote after reading a short story about a mother who verbally abused her daughter:

> My mother's not an alcoholic. Well, she likes to drink when she gets home from work at night because she's tired and the wine helps her relax. . . . I don't like it when she drinks too much and comes into my room late at night and shakes me out of bed with her anger.

DeShawn Holden, a senior in my Contemporary Literature and Society class, wrote and shared stories from his neighborhood. We grew to love his childhood memories filled with wisdom from his grandmother:

> [M]y grandmother, Mrs. Rise and Shine herself, who goes to bed at 8 pm and starts her day at 3 am said, "Boy, why haven't you washed your face? You look like you been sleeping in a barn. And you didn't even bother to comb yo' ole nappy head. Looks like chickens been having their way with it."
>
> She meant well, even though she sounded harsh. I love my grandmother. She was light in spirit, but heavy everywhere else. She was a strong woman, a warrior, and a survivor. My grandmother loved me in spite of all my mischievous, devilish, sneaky ways. She always managed to speak life when I was bad and everyone else wanted to speak death.

The Power of Writing

These kids can write. They are honest. They are truth-tellers. They've discovered the power of writing down their stories. Admittedly, Gayleen didn't join in and neither did Marcus, but most students learned to love writing and sharing their lives.

Before I began my journey as a social justice teacher, when students read their pieces to the class we gave them warm and sympathetic responses. We discussed where the writing "worked," we selected lines we particularly liked, we noted how Justine used active verbs, the strong voice in Margo's piece, we asked questions in places where the writer needed to do more work, more thinking. And this was successful: Students felt they were part of a community that cared about them. They learned something about style by hearing other student models and discussing the techniques in those pieces, and they began to understand how the published writers we read in class wrote their novels, short stories, poems.

Now that I'm working on developing a classroom that focuses on justice as well as skills, we continue to look at our lives and we still respond on both the technical and the human level to each other's writing. But we also study those essays, stories, and poems as a text to get at the social roots of our feelings of alienation and inadequacy, as well as our possibility for joy and resistance (see Shor, 1987; Shor and Freire, 1987).

What emerges from students' writing over the years is that often their problems are experienced individually. Any failure or shortcoming appears the result of a personal deficiency. Sometimes it is — but often it's not. Once, for example, in Literature and U.S. History class, students came back devastated after taking the PSAT. As far as they were concerned there was no need to go to college because this test confirmed their stupidity. During an in-class discussion, Rochelle said, "The words on that test had letters arranged in ways I'd never seen before. There were math problems that Mr. Chappelle hadn't taught us, formulas my pencil had never scratched out. I just wanted someone to give me a cool drink of water and let me go on my way."

> **Students learn to sing their lives through writing. They use writing to take the power out of their pain.**

Students blamed themselves for their poor performance or blamed their teachers: "Well, if you'd taught us subject-verb agreement instead of writing, I'd have a better score on the verbal section."

Because so much feeling was generated around the test, my co-teacher Bill Bigelow and I said, "Let's look at what these tests are all about. Write about some test you've taken. It might have been the PSAT or a math or English test or the yearly Portland Achievement Levels Test. Choose either a good or bad testing experience. Think back to the experience and try to re-create it. What was the test on? How were you prepared for it? What did you feel like before you took the test? During the test? After the test? Tell it as a story or use the anecdote as your entrance into an essay on testing. Be sure to pay attention to the kinds of feelings you experienced around the testing situation." We wrote in silence for the rest of the period.

Student Read-Arounds

The next day the students, Bill, and I sat in a circle and read our papers. (See page 14 for a more complete description of this activity.) As we read our stories, we took notes on the common themes that emerged from our pieces. We asked students to listen for how the tests made people feel about themselves, their peers, and those in authority — the test-givers. It quickly became obvious that Joseph's problem was Claire's problem was Mindy's problem. Students who stung privately with humiliation discovered that they weren't alone, although where or with whom they placed the blame differed sharply. After all papers were shared, we read over our notes and wrote summaries on the similarities and differences in our pieces.

In previous years, students would have shared their stories and learned that they weren't the only ones who felt stupid after taking the tests, but since we left our sharing at that point, they might have gone home saying, "Boy, I'm sure in a class with a bunch of dummies" or "Well, I didn't do so hot on my PSAT, but then neither did Bea and she's supposed to be so smart."

In the read-around kids understand they aren't alone, but they also learn to ask why they had these similar experiences. After the testing paper, we began to question why they all came away from their test experience feeling threatened and stupid. Trisa opened the discussion by reading her summary:

> [Tests] caused us to feel nervous, made us feel stupid, conditioned us to testing and to being told what to do without questioning, made us compete against each other, fostered an "I'm better than you," appeared fair, but made us internalize the fault.

Students wrestled with their feelings and their stories. Matthew picked examples from his classmates' papers to show how tests and schools foster competition, how grades are used as rewards or punishments instead of measuring how much was learned. Elan referred back to Christen and Amy's papers to show how some of us had internalized the blame — if only we'd worked harder we'd have done a better job or received a higher score. Students continued to call on each other and to raise questions for the rest of the period.

Analyzing the Experts

As productive as this discussion was, it left students without a broader context in which to locate their feelings and new understandings. They needed to explore where these so-called aptitude and achievement tests originated and whose interests they serve. These youngsters, still smarting from their private battle with Education Testing Service's brainchild, were introduced to Carl Campbell Brigham and other testing gurus in David Owen's chapter, "The Cult of Mental Measurement" from his book *None of the Above* (1985). In dialogue journals (see page 48 for a complete description of dialogue journals), students read and fought with Brigham, whom the College Board hired in 1925 to develop an intelligence test for college admissions.

Students were shocked by what they discovered about Brigham: According to Owen, he published in the same journal as Adolph Hitler and was convinced that there should be stronger immigration laws to protect the "contamination of the American intellect" by "Catholics, Greeks, Hungarians, Italians, Jews, Poles, Russians, Turks, and — especially — Negroes" (p. 178).

The selections printed below are from student dialogue journals. They first quote from Owen's book on the left and argue, agree, paraphrase or question it in the comments that follow.

Christen, a thoughtful young Black woman, began to see connections between past and present:

Observations/Quotes	Reactions and Reflections
In his book he [Brigham] argued passionately for stricter immigration laws, and within American borders for an end to the "infiltration of white blood into the Negro."(p. 178)	This struck me because even though slavery has been over, they enslave us differently so that we will still be seen as dumb.
Brigham reserved most of his considerable scorn for Blacks, whose arrival in America he described as the "most sinister development in the history of this continent." (p. 183)	They could have kept us where we were in the first place. As far as I'm concerned we were better off.

Omar took offense at Brigham's assuming he had the right or knowledge to control someone else's life:

Observations/Quotes	Reactions and Reflections
[T]he problem of eliminating "defective strains in the present population" remained. One solution, Brigham believed, was intelligence testing. By carefully sampling the mental power of the nation's young people, it would be possible to identify and reward those citizens whose racial inheritance had granted them a superior intellectual endowment. (p. 179)	How does he know who's defective? Who appointed him population watchdog? Sounds like Hitler!

Omar also questioned the items appearing on Brigham's early Army Mental Tests which were used to assign recruits jobs during World War I:

Observations/Quotes	Reactions and Reflections
Look at the Alpha Test 8! (p. 181) The Pierce Arrow car is made in: Buffalo/Detroit.Toledo/Flint (p. 181)	This sounds like Trivial Pursuit! It's also very racist, no real thinking required, just trivia.

In another excerpt, Margo bit back:

Observations/Quotes	Reactions and Reflections
Brigham did not advocate the reestablishment of human bondage. He did believe that Blacks should be barred from mixing freely in White society. (p. 183)	What does this mean? What's the difference? Is he trying to be a nice bigot?
In recent years the College Board and ETS have described Brigham's virulent racism as a sort of irrelevant eccentricity. (p. 186)	His racism is by no means irrelevant. He has a strong grasp on who goes to college and therefore a grasp on the future of the country. I would say that is fairly relevant.

The dialogue journal allowed students to critique and question Brigham and ETS. In some cases they related it to their own experiences. A number of their questions echoed Omar's: "Who appointed him watchdog?"

Who indeed? It would be misleading for students to lay all blame for the inequities of testing at Brigham's doorstep. Through role plays, film, and source readings we explored the changes in mass education in the early 20th century and looked critically at those groups needing Brigham's tests as a sorting mechanism to preserve the status quo (see Bowles and Gintis, 1976; Nasaw, 1979).

We followed up this historical study by analyzing the correlation between today's income levels and SAT scores: On average, the higher the parents' income, the higher the score a student "earned" on the SAT. Then we looked at some of the sample vocabulary used in typical analogy questions:

HEIRLOOM:INHERITANCE::

(A) payment:currency

(B) belongings:receipt

(C) land:construction

(D) legacy:bill

(E) booty:plunder

After we pulled a few analogies apart and made some of our own from each other's background and neighborhood experiences, it became clear to students that the SAT questions measured access to upper class experience, not ability to make appropriate analogies. The test vocabulary did not reflect the everyday experience of these inner-city kids, and they said so. Through class discussion, it became evident that the test was biased towards the privileged and functioned to segregate students on the basis of social class.

After scrutinizing the test, the students concluded that Brigham's test didn't measure their intelligence, nor would it predict their success in college. When the test became demystified, when it was no longer a bogeyman; when kids saw it as an obstacle, ETS no longer held the same kind of power over them.

Trisa and her classmates became skeptical of tests, of any measure or device used to include some and exclude others. Beyond that, they sharpened their analysis of who would want devices that promoted and protected inequality.

When students see either their lives or history as inevitable, they are not encouraged to work for change. By studying problems in their lives and by rooting those problems historically, students are able to analyze this society, uncover inequality, and explore the reasons why it exists.

Critiquing Ourselves

At our end-of-the-year class evaluation, Elan said,

> Before I took this class, I hated school. I never tried. I'd never written a poem or story. I accepted what teachers told me, what I read. Now I question everything. And I write stories and poems for the fun of it.

And Justine, who argued all year with us, said, "I thought god dammit I don't want to be conscious. I just want to eat candy and ride the swings. But I learned how to think."

Claire said, "I learned from everyone in the class.... I learned how to think differently by listening to other people's stories, by seeing their growth."

Now all of this sounds great, but a problem remains. While kids learned to question, while they broke down their senses of isolation and alienation, while they pushed toward a greater knowledge of how this society functions, they were moved less often to hope and action and more often to awareness and despair than I felt comfortable with.

During the class evaluation, Amy, who planned on becoming a teacher so she could "help change the world," sat quietly and didn't volunteer her feelings about the class. After everyone else shared, I asked her what she'd thought of this course. She offered one of the strongest critiques. "You need to include some more positive aspects. We can't live in a world where it's all negative. I became overwhelmed and angry. I felt like I couldn't take it."

When Bill and I talked with her after class, she said she could see our optimism and hope, but she didn't see where it came from. She wanted to know who else was working to make it a better world. She wanted to hear those people speak, to find out what vision they had for a different society. As she spoke, I began drafting changes for next year's classes — ones that put kids in touch with real people who haven't lost their hope, who still fight the brawl and who plan to win.

Sometimes I remind myself that I'm an English teacher and I question whether I'm straying too far afield. I know my pasture is broader than nouns and verbs, stories, poems, and essays. Where does the world begin that is within my terrain? How can I

> **It became clear to students that the SAT questions measured access to upper class experience, not ability to make appropriate analogies.**

teach *The House of the Spirits* (Allende, 1985) without teaching about Chile's Socialist president Salvador Allende and General Pinochet's coup that ended Chile's democracy? My students now reach beyond the beauty, power, and seduction of their descriptive writing; they probe for the whys and ask, "Is this the way it has to be?" I no longer tranquilize their pain through writing; I'm helping them develop the tools to understand the causes of those wounds. ■

References

Allende, Isabel. *The House of the Spirits*. New York: Knopf, 1985.

Bowles, Samuel, and Gintis, Herbert. *Schooling in Capitalist America: Educational Reform and the Contradictions of Economic Life*. New York: Basic Books, 1976.

Freire, Paulo, and Macedo, Donaldo. *Literacy: Reading the Word and the World*. South Hadley, MA: Bergin & Garvey, 1987.

Nasaw, David. *Schooled to Order: A Social History of Public Schooling in the United States*. New York: Oxford UP, 1979.

Owen, David. *None of the Above: Behind the Myth of Scholastic Aptitude*. Boston: Houghton Mifflin, 1985.

Shor, Ira. *Freire for the Classroom*. Portsmouth. NH: Heinemann, 1987.

Shor, Ira, and Freire Paulo. *A Pedagogy for Liberation*. South Hadley, MA: Bergin & Garvey, 1987.

Coming Out
By Kronda Adair

Sweet 16 was the worst year of my life. But in many ways it was also the best year because of what came out of it.

After I started Teens Incorporated, my life got very interesting. Suddenly I was busy, busy, busy all the time. I had to buy a planning calendar to keep track of all the places I was supposed to be and it was almost always full. More importantly, TI sparked a period of personal growth for me that I'm sure will continue until I die. Every new subject we learned about was a new topic for debate. I was forced to decide how I felt about a lot of things I never thought about before. The main purpose of TI is to inform teens about sexuality. In the midst of educating others, I began to examine my own sexuality and question the reasons behind some of my behavior.

One day after TI rehearsal we were talking about the ever popular subject of our families. I mentioned half jokingly that before my brothers were born I was the "boy" in the family. Out of four girls I was the one who wore pants all the time, hated Barbie, loved remote control cars, sports, fishing and the outdoors in general, I was also the only one who would clean the fish. In short, I was a genuine tomboy.

After I mentioned this, my director Susan got very serious and offered to take me out to lunch if I wanted to talk about how I felt. She said that all her roommates were lesbians and it was okay.

This thought had never even entered my head and I had no clue how or why she would associate tomboyishness with homosexuality. I mean, just because you were a tomboy didn't mean you were gay. Did it? Susan's perception of my comment raised questions and answers that I didn't want to begin to contemplate. But deep down I knew I had to at least face the possibility. So that Sunday I met Susan downtown and we talked. She got me to admit that I was and had always been more comfortable with and emotionally attracted to women. Then she said that it might be just a phase, but if it wasn't I was going to have to deal with it. That was exactly what I wanted to hear. I latched onto the first part of that sentence. If it was a phase then I could ignore it until it went away. So I proceeded to do just that. Susan and I went back to work and except for once when it couldn't be helped, I never brought up our conversation again or gave any implication that I was affected by it in any way. But despite my efforts I couldn't quite go back to "life as usual." The big question was always in the back of my mind, but I didn't want to know the answer.

I found out the hard way that there was a high price for shutting off a part of yourself that way. I began to get depressed a lot without knowing why. I went through extreme mood swings from really happy to angry and eventually back to depression which usually lasted for days on end. My problems began to seem larger than they were. Inside it felt like my life was falling apart and I was under constant pressure from all directions to get even better grades. The worst part was that I closed my real feelings off from everyone. I got into a vicious downward spiral like when you eat when you're depressed and get depressed when you eat. I knew I needed help, but I was afraid to ask, and I didn't know who I could talk to that would understand when I didn't understand myself. Whenever I got close to asking for help, my low self-esteem kicked in. It was easy to think of people who were worse off than I was and feel selfish for even being depressed. I told myself no one was interested in my problems, and I should be able to handle it on my own. Except that I didn't know what "it" was.

The one thing I had going for me was that I didn't really want to die. There were a lot of times when I thought I did but once you're dead that's it. You don't get a second chance. Some people see suicide as a way to end pain but all it really does is cause more. I reached a kind of stalemate. I knew I couldn't kill myself, I couldn't feel better by myself, and I really couldn't tell anyone what was wrong.

The result of holding my emotions in for so long was that they built up until I was forced to do something to relieve the pressure. One morning in English during a quiz that I was not prepared for, I started to cry. At first it was only tears running down my cheeks and no one noticed. Then Jenny asked me if I was okay. Even as I nodded yes I started crying harder. I wanted desperately to stop, but it was totally beyond my control. I was taken to the teen clinic where I cried for 40 minutes non stop. Everyone wanted to help me, but there was nothing anyone could do. I felt completely hopeless, as if I would never have a happy moment ever again. And yet, there was still a voice in my head— call it conscience, spirit or whatever — that said it wasn't true. I could and would be happy again if I could just learn to like myself. That was the real problem. I had little or no self-esteem and I didn't like myself.

Once I came to this realization, I felt a lot better. At least now I knew what the problem was even if I didn't have a clue what to do about it. From then on I was at least able to function without losing control of my emotions. If I felt like things were building up, I found someone to talk to. I found out I didn't always have to talk about what was bothering me to feel better. Sometimes just having someone to listen was enough. Talking led to the first step of my self-esteem recovery.

I started making lists. Every day I spent five minutes writing a list of things I liked about myself. The trick was not to stop writing the entire time. It was really hard at first, but gradually my lists got longer.

Then I realized that I was my own worst enemy. I started watching and listening for the little putdowns I gave myself every day. When I caught myself saying negative things, I reversed them. Once I began to notice my own negative behavior, I noticed it in others as well. It's so easy to find yourself playing down compliments and blaming yourself for anything that goes wrong.

Then came the hardest step of all. I realized if I was going to learn to like me, I would have to discover just who I was. So I set out to answer the question I had been avoiding for so many months. Since I didn't have anyone I felt safe talking to, I turned to books. I read everything on homosexuality that I could get my hands on and when I ran out of sources close to home or school, I turned to bookstores and discovered the Catbird Seat.

The first thing I noticed when I went in was all the gay newspapers and magazines available. I started reading **Just Out**, **The Lavender Network** and **Guide** but, because they were newspapers, they were very political. I wanted to read about people, not issues. The second thing I noticed was how easy it is to find everything because the sections are clearly marked with large signs. For some reason the sign that said GAY BOOKS seemed larger than the rest. But I nerved myself and headed towards it, stopping by science fiction, psychology, fiction and children's books on the way. Finally I made it. When no one jumped out with handcuffs to drag me off to the deprogrammer, I relaxed a little.

Once I felt comfortable I started spending more and more time at the bookstore. I soaked up everything I read like a dry sponge. I was amazed at how much I identified with almost everything I read. I didn't feel so alone anymore because everything I read brought home to me the fact that there were lots of people out in the world going through the same confusion I was. Most of the books I read in the store because they were too expensive to buy, and I didn't want to take them home and risk my mom finding them.

After a while, books weren't enough anymore. Now that I knew how many people shared my feelings I wanted to know, where were they? That's when I began checking the newspaper for listings of groups and I discovered Windfire, "a social/support group for people under 21 who are gay, lesbian, bisexual or unsure."

That first meeting was like being the new kid at school. But I didn't spend two years learning to be an extrovert for nothing. Not only did I go in, but after a while I felt comfortable enough to participate in the discussion. I'd finally found a place where I could be totally me, and I didn't have to watch over my words for fear of saying the wrong thing.

It was at this point that my school and home life became a real problem. Now that I had a place to be "out" I began to resent having to be straight during the rest of the week. Having such a big secret made my writing classes harder because so many times I couldn't write the first thing that came to my head. I'm positive my work could have been better had I not felt that restriction. Besides that, the feeling of isolation I hadn't felt since middle school was back again. Knowing the cause of my isolation didn't help me feel any better. Acting like two different people took a toll on me and I knew I had to do something about it. I began to have doubts about my still-fragile self-esteem. I wondered how I could continue to feel good about myself when society kept portraying gay people as child molesters who caused the entire AIDS epidemic and even my own mother told fag jokes and voted yes on Measure 8.

Windfire was a big help. Going to it helped me keep my equilibrium and reminded me of the good things about being gay. To help me survive during the week I started buying books and reading them at home and school which helped me keep from feeling totally cut off. But I still didn't have anyone in school to talk to.

Then on Wellness Day I went to a seminar called "How to Handle Your Sexuality." After being in TI, I didn't really expect to learn anything new. I went mainly because I was curious. When I got there it was just about what I expected. I didn't learn anything new, but did like Billie a lot. I liked the way she took all the questions seriously even though the seniors had suddenly turned into giggling freshman. Then there was the fact that Billie is one of those rare people who just sends out GOOD VIBES all the time. I considered sitting through the lecture again just so I could watch her work. But last year everyone said the music seminar was sooo good so I moved on.

The music session was incredibly boring. The whole time I kept thinking that I should have stayed upstairs. Afterwards I went back to help carry pamphlets back to the clinic but mostly I went to see if there was any way I could see her again. I made an appointment for the next week. When I went in I was really nervous, but she made me feel very at ease and I never hesitated about telling her that I'm gay.

It was such a joy and a relief to tell someone. It was like half of the weight was lifted off my shoulders and school was suddenly a better place to be. Pretty soon I found someone else "safe" to tell and the weight got even lighter.

Coming out never gets any easier, but I find the more I do it, the more I want to. So far I've been lucky enough to have only supportive reactions from people I know are my real friends. Because of that I can now say to myself and to others that I like being gay. Because now I like myself and gay is just part of who I am.

Forgiveness Poems

forgiving my father

it is friday. we have come
to the paying of the bills.
all week you have stood in my dreams
like a ghost, asking for more time
but today is payday, payday old man;
my mother's hand opens in her early grave
and i hold it out like a good daughter.

there is no more time for you. there will
never be time enough daddy daddy old lecher
old liar. i wish you were rich so i could take it all
and give the lady what she was due
but you were the son of a needy father,
the father of a needy son;
you gave her all you had
which was nothing. you have already given her
all you had.

you are the pocket that was going to open
and come up empty any friday.
you were each other's bad bargain, not mine.
daddy old pauper   old prisoner,
old dead man
what am i doing here collecting?
you lie side by side in debtors' boxes
and no accounting will open them up.

— Lucille Clifton

Teenagers often harbor resentment as well as love for their parents. Theirs is an age of rebellion and separation. When I first read "forgiving my father" by Lucille Clifton (1989), I knew this was a poem I wanted to teach. During the last 20 years, I've listened as my students stormed in anger at their parents, but I've also witnessed their loyalty. As a daughter who has forgiven her mother, and as the mother of two daughters who I hope will forgive me all of my mistakes, I see this poem as essential.

As students grow into adulthood, they need to see their parents as people as well as family members. Sometimes understanding the cultural and social influences that shaped their parents helps them begin to resolve some of the issues that divide them from their mothers and fathers. For some students the pain is still too close and too fresh to forgive. Both responses are legitimate.

Teaching Strategy:

1. I begin by reading Clifton's poem. The lesson can be completed without it, but she's a tremendous poet. Her collection, *Good Woman: Poems and a Memoir 1969-1980,* provides poetry prompts for a year.

2. I read "Forgiving My Mother" by Tanya Park. (see page 67) After reading the poem, I note how she uses a stanza for each thing she forgives her mother for. I also point out the repetition of the phrase "For all the . . ." Also, I discuss how the next word signals the change for the stanza. "For all the times, for all the nights, for the friends . . ." This is an effective pattern for students.

3. Then I read "Forgiving My Father" by Justin Morris (see page 67). Clearly, Justin is not ready to let go of his anger. I ask students to list the reasons why Justin is angry. I point out the repetition in his poem: "I'd like to forgive you, Father, but . . ." We also look at the use of questions in this piece.

4. I ask students to think about who they want to forgive or not forgive. They begin my making a list of things they forgive — or don't.

5. I encourage students to create a pattern or borrow one from Tanya's or Justin's poems. Patterns sometimes help move the poem forward.

Reference

Clifton, Lucille. *Good Woman: Poems and a Memoir 1969-1980.* (American Poets Continuum Series, Vol. 14.) Rochester, NY: BOA Editions, 1989.

FORGIVING MY MOTHER
By Tanya Park

For all the times you yelled
and all the times you screamed
I forgive you.

For all the nights we had breakfast
for dinner and dinner for breakfast
I forgive you.

For all the times I felt you pushed
my daddy away
I forgive you.

For all the times we ran away
and came back,
For all the times we packed
and unpacked,

for all the friends I've lost
and all the schools I've seen,

for all the times
I was the new kid on the scene,
I forgive you.

FORGIVING MY FATHER
By Justin Morris

I'd like to forgive you Father,
but I don't know your heart.
Your face,
is it a mirror image of mine?

I'd like to forgive you Father,
but I find your absence a fire
that your face might be able to extinguish.

I'd like to forgive you Father,
but my last name isn't the same as yours
like it's supposed to be.
You rejected me, Dad,
but can I sympathize with your ignorance?
For all the birthdays
you didn't send me a card,
for the Christmases
when I'd wake up,
and you weren't sitting by the tree waiting for me
I can't forgive you.
What about the summer nights
where prospects of you began to fade?
Fade like you did seventeen years ago.
Out of my life.

I'd like to forgive you, Father,
but I don't know you.
And for that,
I hate you.

Essay With an Attitude

Say the word "essay" and students curl up like an Oregon slug encountering salt. They shrivel before this word because too often it conjures up the memory of boredom and failure. But essays don't have to be boring, and students don't have to fail. Essays can be playful; they can be as personal and provocative as poetry and stories; they can shake their fists and shout, "Injustice!" or shake us with laughter. As I tell my students, "As long as you've got an opinion, you can write an essay." And hearing them talk, I know they've got opinions.

Before we start, I tape one of my published articles to the board. The one I use has 10 drafts. I also tape the notes written on Starbuck's napkins and the backs of envelopes; the crossed-out sections, the writing on the back where I redrafted the opening, notes to myself about research I need to find for my next revision. I include the drafts where Bill Bigelow, my partner, fellow writer and teacher, scribbled notes in the margins. Following the drafts, I tape the letter I sent to Ben Nelms, an English Journal editor, the response and the final publication. I want students to see that writing is messy and sometimes hard. And like anything worth pursuing, it takes time, commitment, and practice.

> I've never found a five-step Betty Crocker boxed essay recipe. Because students don't all learn the same way or enter my class with the same background knowledge or confidence, I need to teach essay writing rather than assign it.

In her portfolio evaluation, my student Claire wrote that seeing how many times I reworked my piece before getting it "right" gave her courage to let go; she knew she could come back and revise, so she didn't have to worry over every word she wrote. On the other hand, my student Naaman said, "Maybe I better transfer to another class if it took you that many times to get it right."

Lists and Models

Writing an essay with an attitude is really about taking a position and backing it up. It's a sustained, rehearsed argument with a parent, friend or teacher, newscaster, magazine writer, advertiser, or the broader society. I begin by asking students: What makes you angry? What gets on your nerves, under your skin? What makes you want to scream when you see a movie, a commercial, or the news? Are there times when you want to shake someone in the middle of a conversation? Are there things about school that you just can't stand? (This one is always good for a full blackboard and a whole stick of chalk.)

Students make lists of what raises their hackles. Then we "share the wealth" and write their ideas on the board: curfews, suspensions, time-out rooms, dead dances, violence in the neighborhood, boring books in English classes, lack of uniforms for the soccer team, weak support for women's sports compared to men's, the way African Americans and Latinos are portrayed on the news, how overweight women or dark-skinned women never get to be the sexy lead. The lists go on and on. Everybody's got something on their mind. If they don't, the rest of the class can certainly fill up their heads.

I discovered through many failures that the way I frame the opening of this lesson and the examples I give determine the kind of responses I get. If I start with pet peeves like dandruff and dirty fingernails, I get more of a Seinfeld whining list. Because I want students to focus on larger social issues, I open the discussion with examples that steer their responses in that direction. I talk about how I hate advertisements that use women to sell products, like Black Velvet ads that feature a beautiful woman in a black velvet dress, as if she came with the purchase. Sometimes I talk about cigarette ads, like Virginia Slims, that show a hip woman with a long cigarette dangling from her fingers. "She's come a long way, baby." Yeah, right. Even more disgusting are Nike's "Just Do It" ads that celebrate the athletic achievements of women, children, and men and ignore the sweatshop exploitation of Nike workers.

Susan Lina Ruggles

Finding Evidence

Once upon a time I began teaching students to write introductions at this point. I don't anymore. Too often, students became enamored with their introduction and when they tried to write the rest of the paper, they realized they didn't have enough evidence to support their dramatic opening. Instead of forging ahead on the thesis statement, I demonstrate the importance of gathering evidence. After reading some sample essays and identifying the kinds of supporting evidence they used, we take one item from the student-generated list and brainstorm supporting evidence for that topic. One student wanted to write about increased violence in the neighborhood. "Give me some examples," I said. Students talked about recent events — the daytime shooting on a city bus that two students in the class witnessed, the street corner slaying of a former Jefferson student.

If I stop at this point, "support" becomes little more than a listing and a description. Stopping means I don't move students to a more intense scrutiny of the issues; I don't get them to ask why. Yes, there is more violence in the neighborhood and these two events prove that. But why is there more violence? How do

you account for that? What has happened recently that might contribute to the rise in violence? These are the hard questions, and if I don't push them to think more deeply about the why questions, their papers end up a recitation rather than an in-depth examination. The easy answers also lead to conclusions that more often than not, blame the victim rather than look at the economic or social conditions that have changed the neighborhood in recent years.

After I've modeled the process of gathering support for a subject, I ask students to choose one topic from the board or from their paper and list the evidence. As I work with students who ask for help or appear lost, I ask them, Why? Why are women targets of advertising? Why do more women diet than men? Why do women color or perm their hair more often than men?

Once individual work is completed, students get in groups of four or five and share their topics and help each other brainstorm evidence. With luck, the group helps them expand their lists, and, of course, I hover and push them to probe beneath the surface. For homework, they must find more evidence by talking with other people, looking up newspaper or maga-

Tar Baby

By Khalilah Joseph

During the Atlantic slave trade, Africans on plantations across the South were treated like animals. They were thought to be less than human, but even within this undignified category, they were further classified by color. It started that far back: When all Blacks were nothing, still color was an issue. The lighter you were, the closer to the house you toiled, and the less work you did. In those days, there was no beauty in color, and if you had some, you were destined to be working way out in the field. Even today, I see the remnants of the Field nigga, House nigga syndrome.

It happens in a continuous motion through music videos, movies, magazines and daily life. I can watch a video by a given artist and before the end of it, the object of desire will prance across the screen, and, of course, she'll be a honey dipped, barely-brown bombshell.

In the movie **Waiting to Exhale**, a film targeted at African-American women, the lightest woman in the movie was the male magnet. And the dark skin sister? It took her the whole movie just to get a date. Women of color are greatly downsized in the movie. Angela Bassett could be a battered wife, but could she be a **Pretty Woman** or be the object of an **Indecent Proposal**?

In most magazines you pick up, you can find at least one African-American woman, but usually she is a little light-eyed biracial girl who does little to represent women of color. Be gone with those tiny waisted, no-hip-having heifers. Bring on the models who range in color from caramel to dark chocolate. Then give them features familiar to Negro women. I'm talking about big booties, child-bearing hips, thunder thighs.

As a dark skinned girl, I was ridiculed. I can remember a time when one of my elementary school classes had a career fair. Like many other girls my age, I wanted to be an actress or a model. My classmates made it painfully clear that dark skinned girls are not considered pretty. They couldn't imagine why I would think that I could become a model. They suggested that I be a nurse or a teacher.

I was called names like "tarbaby" or "blackie." As a young girl I couldn't understand why some people of my own race would tease me about something I could not change. While a person of another race could see all the beauty I possessed — inside and out.

As women of color we have made progress: We are teachers, lawyers, doctors. We are elected to office. Who knows, maybe one day, we dark skinned women will be video hoochies, too.

zine articles, calling other sources for more background information. Some topics take more research than others, but most need a strong dose of outside information to strengthen their claims.

Introductions

Introductions make or break an essay. A weak introduction is not only the first view a reader gets of a writer, but poor introductions muddy up the trail, so students don't know what kind of evidence to use for support because their position is unclear. So we study how good writers begin their essays. I set this up ahead of time by copying introductions from a variety of sources. I show essays beginning with questions, dialogue, quotes, anecdotes, startling research, and I beg them never to begin with a dictionary definition, the quintessential essay cliché. (See the student introductions handout on page 77.)

One of the openings I use comes from an essay my former student, Joe Robertson, wrote during his senior year. In his essay, "Who Framed Rasheed Rabbit," Joe asks a series of questions to engage readers:

> Do you remember that cartoon with a mighty Black prince who looked like Denzel Washington? Remember? He rescued the lovely Black princess who looked like Halle Berry? Remember how the evil white wizard, an Arnold Schwarzenegger look-alike, got chased by an angry mob of bees? Me neither. Perhaps that's because African Americans aren't cast as heroes in cartoons.

Thao Vy, a graduating senior, opens her essay with conversation, a stage to launch her essay about the clash between Vietnamese immigrant parents and their children raised in the United States:

> "How do you expect to find a husband when you don't know how to cook?" my mom asks me.

> "I'll marry somebody who knows how to cook."

> "Well, if we were back in Vietnam, you would already know how to cook. Over here, you're so lazy."

"If you weren't so busy, maybe you could teach me how to cook. It's not my fault you don't have time to show me."

Conversations comparing what I would be like if our family still lived in Vietnam are common in my house.

Many of my students favor the conversation or anecdotal opening; I do, too. But it's a tricky lead because sometimes students get so wrapped up in the story that their essay gets lost. One student, for example, wrote a three-page lead into his four-page essay.

Mary Blalock, another Jefferson graduate, began her essay with a quote. Like the question opening, the quote introduction is a classic opening; it propels the writer forward in her essay:

I once heard a quote that made me laugh. It said, "Love is the history of a woman's life and an episode in a man's." It was the kind of laugh that happens when something isn't funny, when it's only true, and it hurts. It hurts because of the women I know, both young and old, who are bright, intelligent, and who have so much going for them, but they still value their relationships with men more than their relationships with themselves and other women.

Once I saturate students in essay openings, I ask them to write their own essay introduction. Volunteers transfer their openings to the board. We go through each one and talk about what the author needs to prove. This multiple exposure to introductions pushes students to use more imaginative openings than: In this essay I will tell you about . . . .

Conclusions

According to a Chinese proverb, "The beginning and the end reach out hands to each other." Students need to learn how to close their essays as well as open them. We look back at essays we've read and talk about the kinds of endings writers use: a summation of the points, a discussion of a potential solution to the issue raised, other questions that need to be answered as well as the original problem. We also look at the full circle conclusion that reaches back to the opening — perhaps Joe Robertson might come back to his original questions and suggest a solution: Why aren't there cartoon characters who look like Denzel Washington or Halle Berry? Until the media. . . .

Coloring

I pass out boxes of crayons — or one giant bucket of discarded crayons depending on school budget — and ask students to color in evidence and transitions in a common essay we've read. (See page 79.) I want them to see that essay structure can vary. Some essays have far more than five paragraphs; some have a thesis statement written out, while in others it's implied. Writers use all kinds of evidence from personal experience to examples from school, newspapers, movies, and books. Some use research. The coloring exercise visually demonstrates points I want to make in any kind of writing — from essay to poetry. Later, when they turn in their drafts, students repeat the coloring exercise with their own essays. Again, it helps them spot their holes.

If all of this seems repetitive, it is. I come at essay writing from many different directions — reading, writing, discussing, coloring, working in groups and individually — so that all my students understand. Unfortunately, I've never found a five-step Betty Crocker boxed essay recipe. Because students don't all learn the same way or enter my class with the same background knowledge or confidence, I need to teach essay writing rather than assign it. If they were lost when we discussed published essays, maybe they'll pick up something when they color in evidence and introductions. If they're not sure how to start, reading other people's openings might give them a way to enter their essay. If their support is weak, they might learn from coloring evidence on published essays or from their group work where other students brainstormed evidence.

> **In recent years I've tried to look more deeply at the roots of students' resistance to essay work. "Laziness" is a lazy explanation.**

Deadlines, Reality, and Response

I set a deadline date for the essays. I do this knowing that not everyone will have theirs completed. And I hear you clucking your tongues already. "How will they ever survive the 'real world' unless they learn to turn their work in on time? No one is going to hire and keep slackers."

I know. I know. But not everyone comes in knowing how to write essays. Perhaps in other schools or other teachers' classrooms everyone comes prepared, typed essay in hand. That's not been my experience.

I've heard teachers, myself included, talk about lazy students who just don't do their work. And certainly this is true at times, but in recent years I've tried to look more deeply at the roots of students' resistance to essay work. "Laziness" is a lazy explanation. There is always something more at work. Some students have had bad experiences writing essays, some have no experiences. Even before I taught untracked English classes, this was true. I try to "level the playing field."

Susan Lina Ruggles

A few — Khalilah, Rosa, Sarah, and Travis — have typed papers ready to read on the due date. Others write drafts that don't take off; some bring handwritten notes with an introduction and then confusion. Some don't have a clue. Sometimes, especially early in the year, students get stuck because they are still in the "one draft and then a grade" mode of writing. They fear beginning because as my daughter, Gretchen, told me when she was a sophomore in high school, "I know how I want it to be and when the words get on the paper, they aren't as good as the ones in my head."

I watch students in class. Some draft a line or two, pause, write another line, tear the paper out, crumple it and throw it away. Then they begin the process again and again. Like my daughter, they can't match the essay in their head to the one on paper. These are students I need to work with one-on-one. They need to learn William Stafford's famous maxim: "Lower your standards and write." Others put pen to paper and start. These are the writers who benefit most from my pre-writing work. They are comfortable writing, but use these strategies to move their writing to a higher level.

Some put their heads on their desks, defeated before they even start. These are usually students who have experienced too much failure in school. They were defeated before they came to my class. The head on the desk tells other students that they are too bored, too tired, too sick to write the essay; better to not try, than to try and fail. (I work with these students during class time, at lunch time, during break, after school or call them at home.) Some students work late, take care of siblings or their own children, cook meals for the family, rehearse for the school play, practice or play in a school game, and some don't do homework. This is life in my school, and I try to take advantage of knowing the reality ahead of time.

I start class read-arounds (see page 14 for a complete description of this activity) by getting a few people to volunteer reading their papers. These students benefit by getting the entire class's feedback — verbally and in written form. (See the Essay Response Sheet on page 80.) The class benefits by hearing how fellow classmates approached the assignment.

Then students, like Megan, Komar and Sokpha, who wrote part of their essays but got stuck, read their unfinished pieces out loud and get responses.

A Woman's Silent Journey
By Erika Miller

Am I fat? Look at my thighs. Oh God, they're huge, and my hips. Who's going to like me with this body? "Someday my prince will come," Cinderella hums in my ear. No prince will claim me as his bride. I'm too ugly.

Stepping on that scale in the second grade was the beginning of the end for me. Weighing in at 67 pounds was horrifying. As Tinker Bell looked into a hand mirror and realized her hips were too big in Peter Pan, I realized I was fat, enormous, and disgusting. At least that was the image Tinker Bell helped me paint for myself.

Four years later, I actually was overweight, and without an ounce of self-esteem. I was Seventeen magazine's nightmare and Disney's newest sidekick. Finally, after years of waiting, my belief that I was fat was validated by jokes and bullying by peers. I silently dreamed about being the skinny, blonde girl in cartoons or the curvaceous model gracing magazine covers.

A year later I was average in size, but I still held the self-conscious behaviors that were initiated in my seventh year. At this time I began my dieting lifestyle. The desire to be thin overtook my body. I kept my stomach in posture at all times, while I powdered my nose and applied lipstick. Instead of concentrating on having fun, my middle school and high school years were spent trying to achieve a perfect face and body.

The summer before my senior year, I discovered a diet that worked. It is called decreasing your food intake to what you need to survive and nothing more. In three months I went from 130 pounds to 103 pounds. People began commenting on how skinny I looked, and that I resembled a walking skeleton. The problem was, that I still looked 130 pounds to myself.

Soon I couldn't control my weight loss. I would wake up in the morning and weigh two pounds less than I had the day before. My hair became dry, my hands cracked and bled, and I lost my period for four months. I came to realize that something was wrong and began forcing myself to eat nourishing food.

I am recovering now, but why is this behavior normal in our society? Why are millions of women starving themselves to death? Has society made being thin this important? So important that women will die for the skinniest body? Why can't we be content with how we look?

The U.S. has an $80 billion diet industry. Companies are profiting off of our feelings of inadequacy. From birth, Disney taunts us with fairy-tale princesses who would die of anorexia if they existed. They win their men by fluttering eyelashes and innocent giggles (i.e., Snow White, Sleeping Beauty, Cinderella). The only prerequisite for princesses is beauty. And thus it is the only prerequisite for happiness.

By age 8, Mattel's Barbie takes over where Disney left off. This 42-24-32 woman would fall over if she was an actual person. But girls worship her body and dream about looking like her all the same. How can we let this happen? Eighty percent of all fourth-grade girls are on diets, according to a current poll. Why are 10-year-olds thinking about their weight, much less concerned about it? Could Barbie have something to do with this?

When Barbie gets old, Teen magazine places itself in adolescent girls' hands. Tall, thin women cover the pages and tempt girls with products to soothe their every need. What? Jimmy doesn't like you? Well, maybe it's because of that zit or those 10 extra pounds, or your dull hair. The list goes on and on. We, as women, are never good enough. Not good enough for men and not good enough for each other. We compare ourselves inwardly, while swearing our hips and thighs are the biggest to have ever walked the earth.

We need to change the way people think about women. We don't need to be sex objects who live to please men. Times have changed and are continually changing. We must no longer be dominated by male fantasies of what a woman should be, because we are all intelligent, wonderful people who have a lot more to offer than a slim body and a pretty face.

What points are they trying to make? What happened to the essay? How do they get unstuck? Again, this helps other students who can't see the direction of their essays, as well as students who didn't "get it." It is not uncommon for students to push through a blah draft just to "get it done," then when they hear their classmates' pieces, they find a new way to enter the essay to make it livelier.

After the read-arounds, we break into small groups or pairs and students read as much as they have completed and get a little help from their friends to push them to their next draft. In this first stage of response/revision, ideally students discover what's missing in their pieces. That night or after school in the computer lab, some students work on revisions. They add, delete, move, and edit until they feel satisfied with their piece. Others work on getting unstuck and others, I hope, work toward a draft.

Revisions

Revision is not just editing grammar and spelling. It's pushing for more evidence, cutting material that erodes or muddies key points, refining the argument. Here's another chance to engage students in a dialogue: "You write that you are angry about the new anti-immigration laws, but you don't explain the laws to the reader. What are the laws? Imagine you are writing to a friend who doesn't understand the importance of the laws. How will you explain the laws and their effects on immigrants? This is good where you give some examples from people you know, but can you tie it back to the laws? What do people who support the laws say? Can you talk back to their arguments?"

When students have amassed a chunk of writing, the abstract ideas of thesis and support are captured on paper. Here I find evidence of how each student processes information. If the student has completed two drafts, I can see the kinds of changes they knew to make. What did they add or change? What is still missing? Are there holes in their logic? Is there a pattern to their grammar and punctuation errors?

I diagnose the problem(s) and consider what each student needs to learn to proceed to the next draft. For some students it might be tightening language or using verbs more effectively. For others, like Rosa who wrote about the anti-immigration laws, it might mean explaining the situation more clearly, countering the opposition's arguments, reading more on the topic. For others it might mean starting again because they don't yet have a word on paper. With Akil, who

> **I find students take their writing more seriously and care more about fine-tuning and polishing it if they have real audiences.**

still didn't have a draft, I asked, "What makes you mad? You're never angry? Okay, you don't like it when store clerks follow you. That's a start. Why does that make you mad? How do you feel when that happens? Why do you think they follow you? Do they follow anyone else?"

This is also the most time-consuming part. I not only read each paper, I plan a strategy for each student. I often work individually with students. I don't mark every error. It would be too overwhelming for the student, but it would also waste my time. How much can a student learn in one draft? What is a reasonable goal: To spell "marble" correctly or to think through an argument? Students need both the technical skills of spelling, grammar, and punctuation as well as larger skills of argument and support. But they can't learn it all at once, so I pick one or two technical skills — periods, capitalization, semicolons, subject/verb agreement — that I teach individually, and I select one or two larger concepts to work on as well. I consider each draft, each new essay, part of a longer and larger learning process.

Publication: Beyond School Walls

Beyond just getting students to write, I want them to find an audience and attempt to publish their work — in small neighborhood or church publications, in the *Oregonian, Ms., Teen Voices, Calyx, New Moon, Ebony Men,* in our school newspaper or *Rites of Passage,* Jefferson's literary magazine. I also encourage students to think of non-traditional ways to publish. One student, Vinai, wrote about how few Asian-American books were in our library and how little teachers and librarians knew about these works. She published a flier for local libraries that included part of her essay as well as a listing of books by Asian-American writers. School librarians loved her work. Mary Blalock wrote about girls and body image in a newspaper format. She asked area middle-school teachers to distribute her "Girls' Bill of Rights" to young women in their classes. (See p. 75.) I find students take their writing more seriously and care more about fine-tuning and polishing it if they have real audiences.

Like good writing, good teaching is both messy and time-consuming. But to sit back at the end of the class period when those final typed drafts are stacked on top of rough drafts, filled with arrows and scribbles and Taco Time napkins, is as much a pleasure as sending out my own polished piece. Only in my classroom, there are no rejection slips, just tickets to the next draft. ■

A Bill of Rights for Girls

By Mary Blalock

WHAT'S WRONG WITH GIRLS?

If you look around at our world, it is not hard to find something that tries to tell you that as a girl, something is wrong with you. Girls are always told there's something wrong with them. TV and magazines seem to say that girls aren't any good unless they're thin and beautiful. It's hard to feel good about ourselves with these demands around us.

Recent studies show how adolescent boys differ from adolescent girls. They found that around the age of 11 (when puberty usually hits) girls begin feeling more insecure. 2,600 girls were asked how many of them agreed with the statement: "I'm happy with the way I am." In elementary school 60% of the girls agreed, but only 29% of the high school girls did. While boys are getting more confident, a lot of girls begin feeling bad about themselves and end up making bad choices.

Now it's time for girls to get some respect.

I wish that I had known about this when I was younger, but I had to go through a lot before getting on the right track again. Because there are a lot of things I wish I could have learned before. I've created a list of rights girls deserve to help you on your way to womanhood with confidence. There's already been a woman's movement, now it's time for girls to get some respect.

THE RIGHT TO LIKE YOURSELF

If you get into something that interests you, it helps you feel good about yourself. I like to draw and write, so when I'm feeling bad, I go into my room and draw a picture. There are lots of things that you can get involved in that can become a part of you. It will help you create a personality that you can be proud of.

Also think of things that you like and things that gross you out. What foods are yummy? What music is cool to you? What clothes do you like to wear? All this becomes part of you. Don't be ashamed if other people don't like your taste, or it isn't "cool." Like things because you like them, not because everyone else does. A lot of people like things because they have a name brand. All these names say is that it was expensive. There's nothing wrong with buying something just because you like it, not because it will be impress other people.

THE RIGHT TO LIKE YOUR BODY

This is a big subject with girls. It's almost impossible to avoid all those ads that try to tell us we need to be pencil thin and look like Cindy Crawford if we want to like ourselves. They are totally wrong! A woman's body is suppose to have fat on it so it can make babies, produce the right hormones, and just work right. The models in these ads have little girl bodies, even though they're women. It's rare for females past puberty to look like this, and it's not healthy to try. It's good for you to realize that, while these models are supposedly what we want to be, there are all different ways that people can look and they can all be okay. Take a look around you and compare what you see to what the media shows. You'll find that the world has a lot of different ways people can be beautiful.

THE RIGHT TO HAVE YOUR CAKE AND EAT IT TOO

Because the media create the idea that we're suppose to be skinny, there are a lot of girls dieting and getting involved in eating disorders. An eating disorder is when we start looking at food not only as just something we need, and something that tastes good, but as something bad. Though dieting is popular, I say "no way!" Food is something we all need so we can live and function like a normal person.

When we start dieting, we look at food as bad. I know from experience because when I started dieting, I got an eating disorder, lost too much weight and had to go to the hospital. It wasn't fun and I missed out on a lot of things. When you worry about dieting, you don't have time for fun. Dieting can also cause you to even want food more. Many people who try to diet, end up getting hungry or craving sweets and eat more than they would have usually. My advice to you is: accept your body the way it is and accept food as necessary. Don't try to diet, no matter what people say.

THE RIGHT TO GET ANGRY

I'm not saying that you should yell at people all the time, or get in fights, but there's nothing wrong with just getting mad. Usually when you feel this way, it's for a good reason and it's a signal that something isn't right. I'm sure a lot of people have told you "don't get mad" or "nice girls don't get mad" when you really were angry and you couldn't stop. But it's okay to get mad as long as you use words and express what you feel in a way that won't hurt anyone. It's okay to tell someone you're angry at them and try to work it out. If you just keep it to yourself, nothing will get resolved and you'll end up feeling bad. Don't turn the anger in on yourself either, that makes you feel even worse.

THE RIGHT TO FEEL PROTECTED

When we are little, we don't have to look out for ourselves because our parents do the job. But as we grow older we need to protect ourselves from dangerous things. Sometimes things may make you feel scared and weak. If someone is bothering you, it's good know how to defend yourself. Community centers offer classes in self-defense and martial arts.

These classes teach you how to feel strong and fight back if someone is trying to hurt you. Find someone who you can talk to about things that don't seem right and make sure they get worked out. It's hard to feel confident if you don't feel safe.

THE RIGHT TO DEVELOP YOUR BRAIN

Don't be a stupid-head; make sure you keep getting smarter. Sometimes we think people will think we're nerds if we know a lot of stuff. There's nothing wrong with being smart, it makes you a more interesting person. Don't accept things that people tell you, create your opinion about what you hear.

Read lots of books instead of watching TV. It's better for your brain and can be a lot cooler than some of the boring shows and commercials. You don't have to be a dweeb, just don't be dull when it comes to your brain. Tests and grades have nothing to do with how smart you are. I'm talking about learning how things work and how life works. You may not be very good in school but that doesn't mean you're not smart in other ways.

THE RIGHT TO BE YOURSELF AROUND BOYS

It's fun to flirt and get into relationships, but there's a lot of confusing things that go along with it. Just be sure that you don't get too dependent on boys to tell you that you're a good person. Never change yourself just so a guy will like you. If you change yourself, then they won't be liking the real you, only the show you put on. It's better to wait for a guy who will like you for who you are, then stay with one who doesn't. It's important to feel good about yourself, even if you don't have a boyfriend. Besides, boys aren't the only thing in the world and I'm sure you've heard the expression, "There are other fish in the sea."

THE RIGHT TO YOUR OWN ROLE MODELS

When we grow up, we get all these ideas about what a woman should be like. These aren't always positive ideas, so sometimes we have to find new places to show us what a woman is. Look around for women who you admire and ask them about their lives: how they became who they are. Take parts that you like about them and use them to create who you want to be. Don't try and be them, be yourself and walk along their path.

A PUBLICATION OF RETHINKING SCHOOLS

Introductions

Students from Jefferson High School wrote the following introductions. As you read over the sample openings, underline the thesis statement if it is stated, write it in the space below the introduction if it is implied. Also think about what evidence the student must provide in order to prove the thesis.

Questions

In his essay, "Who Framed Rasheed Rabbit," Joe Robertson asks a series of questions to engage his readers:

> Do you remember that cartoon with a mighty Black prince who looked like Denzel Washington? Remember? He rescued the lovely Black princess who looked like Halle Berry? Remember how the evil white wizard, an Arnold Schwarzenegger look-alike, got chased by an angry mob of bees? Me neither. Perhaps that's because African Americans aren't cast as heroes in cartoons.

Quote

Like the question opening, the quote introduction is a classic opening. Mary Blalock begins her essay with a quote that propels her essay forward:

> I once heard a quote that made me laugh. It said, "Love is the history of a woman's life and an episode in a man's." It was the kind of laugh that happens when something isn't funny, when it's only true, and it hurts. It hurts because of the women I know, both young and old, who are bright, intelligent, and who have so much going for them, but they still value their relationships with men more than their relationships with themselves and other women.

Jillana Kinney used an opening quote from an advertisement to capture her readers' attention in her essay on the role of overweight characters in cartoons:

> "Give us a week, and we'll take off the weight." "Keep the muscle, lose the fat!" scream TV and magazine commercials. Who wouldn't want to be thin in the 1990s with scrutinizing eyes and subliminal judgments from every passing stranger. Even animated cartoons are filled with prejudicial lessons for both young and old. Look at Porky Pig, Wimpy from Popeye, Baloo the Bear from *The Jungle Book* — all fat, stupid and for the most part, the losers in society.

Dialogue/Anecdote

The anecdotal opening is a small story that frames the topic of the essay personally. It can introduce characters, pose the thesis or dilemma that's central to your argument, and get you off to a fast start. The anecdote is a tricky lead because sometimes people get so wrapped up in the story that their essay gets lost.

Heather O'Brien uses a brief anecdote to make her point in her essay, "Self Inflicted Sexism":

> When I was in the fourth grade, my goal in life was to go to Harvard and become the first woman president. In the eighth grade, all I wanted was a boyfriend. How is it that my life could take such an abrupt turn?
>
> At the age of nine, it's still okay for girls to get dirty and want to learn to play the drums. By the time they reach twelve or thirteen, they're expected to be more interested in clothes than sports. Finding a date for the dance is more important than getting an A on the science project. Girls begin to worry about their looks and wonder how to become a model of grace and poise. Instead of reading *Discover* magazine, they invest their allowance in *Teen*.

Erika Miller used both a question and an anecdote in her introduction about the media's effect on young women's self-esteem:

> Am I fat? Look at my thighs. They're huge. And my hips? Who's going to like me with this body? "Someday my prince will come," Cinderella hums in my ear. No prince will claim me as his bride. I'm too ugly.
>
> Stepping on that scale in the second grade was the beginning of the end for me. Weighing in at 67 pounds was horrifying. Just like Tinker Bell when she looked into a hand mirror and realized her hips were too big in *Peter Pan*, I stepped on the scale and realized I was fat, enormous, disgusting. At least that was the image Tinker Bell helped me paint of myself.

Kaanan Yarbrough used his sisters' love lives to start off an essay on the book *Their Eyes Were Watching God:*

> After growing up in a house with three sisters, I noticed that girls can't distinguish the good guys from the bad. They dream of a prince, and he turns out to be a dog. Janie, from the novel *Their Eyes Were Watching God* by Zora Neale Hurston, is a character in a dream world waiting to be swept off her feet to happiness. Like my sisters, she has to meet a few dogs before she finds that prince.

Wake-Up Call

Chetan Patel sounds the alarm in his essay "The Nuclear Headache," where he exposes the federal government's plan to store nuclear waste on Native-American land:

> Fish with no eyes, fish with skin deformities, and fish with deteriorated fins and bones are being caught in the Columbia River. Soon these mutated fish will pop up all over the western United States. No joke. The government started a program to store nuclear waste on reservation lands volunteered by Native-American tribal councils.

Essay With An Attitude: CRITERIA SHEET

ASSIGNMENT: Write a persuasive essay which clearly states your opinion on a contemporary issue. Support your opinion using personal experience, anecdotes, statistics, evidence from every day life, novels, magazines, TV, movies, etc. In this essay, also focus on tightening your sentences and using active verbs.

CRITERIA: Attach this sheet to your essay.

1. **THESIS STATEMENT:** stated or implied. Write it in the space below.

2. **INTRODUCTION:** What kind of introduction did you use?

> Question
> Quotation
> Anecdote
> Wake-up call

3. **EVIDENCE:** Prove your point. Check which of the following types of evidence you used below. **On your essay — mark each type of evidence with a different color:**

> Personal Experience: Evidence from your daily life
> Anecdotes: Stories you've heard that illustrate your point
> Statistics/Facts
> Examples from novels, magazines, TV, movies
>
> Other_____

4. **CONCLUSION:** What kind of conclusion did you use?

> Summary
> Circle back to the beginning
> Possible solution
> Restate and emphasize thesis
> Further questions to think about

5. **TIGHT WRITING:**

> Active verbs
> Lean language
> Metaphoric language
> Sentence variety

6. **GRAMMAR, PUNCTUATION, SPELLING CHECKED AND CORRECTED**

On the back of this page, describe what you need to do to revise this essay:

Essay With An Attitude: STUDENT ESSAY RESPONSE SHEET

Your name_____

Writer's name_____

As you read your classmate's essay, respond to the following questions.
Make your feedback supportive and specific:

1. What kind of introduction did the writer use? Anecdote? Quotation? Question? Wake-up call? Did it capture your attention? What did you like? What could be improved?

2. What is the writer's thesis? Some writers may state the thesis directly or imply it. In space below, write what *you* think the thesis is. If you're unclear, say so.

3. What evidence was used to convince the reader of the writer's point? Make a list of several items: (Note: Some of these categories might overlap — just check all categories you think the writer used.)

    - Personal experience — evidence from the writer's life
    - Anecdotes — stories
    - Statistics/facts
    - Examples from novels, magazines, TV, movies
    - Other _____

    Does the writer convince you? Does the writer need more evidence? Be specific.

4. What kind of conclusion did the writer use? Summary? Circle back to opening? Possible solution? Restate and emphasize thesis? Further questions to think about?

    Was the conclusion effective? If not, what suggestions do you have for the writer?

Paul Barker/Deseret News

Acting for Justice

When my niece Kelly was seven years old, she developed odd tics — blinking her eyes rapidly, jerking her arms, then her legs, then convulsing her entire body. Grunts followed the tics. She attempted to make them sound like hiccups. At school she stood alone at recess; during lunch she ate alone. Kids tormented her, mimicking her sounds and movements. During all of her years of schooling, only one teacher stood up for Kelly. Her teachers believed her tics and noises were voluntary, so they punished her by placing her desk outside of the room. Some days they sent her to the principal's office.

When she was in eighth grade, my sister discovered that Kelly's condition had a name — Tourette's Syndrome.

How did this affect Kelly? She hated going to school. She feigned illness. Some days when she was unable to endure the teasing and isolation, she ran home. Eventually she dropped out of high school and spent years regaining the dignity that students and teachers stripped her of when she was a child. Kelly is not alone in her history. While most children don't have a medical condition that causes their isolation, too many children learn that any difference can make them a target.

Kids can be cruel, and their cruelty exacts a price from the victims. People experience acts of injustice daily. Sometimes these injustices occur in the form of an unkind comment about a person's weight, facial features, hair, language, ethnic or racial identity, gender, or religion.

But too often injustice is more severe. People are denied housing, jobs, fair wages, or a decent education because they differ from those with power. As both history and daily news has informed us: People are physically abused — sometimes even killed — because of these differences.

But kids don't have to be cruel; in fact, part of our roles as teachers and administrators in schools is to stop children from torturing others, but more importantly, educating them so that difference doesn't automatically mean outcast.

> **We can teach students about Frederick Douglass, Lucretia Mott, John Brown, Rosa Parks, and Dolores Huerta. But how do we teach them to stand up for the overweight girl sitting next to them in Algebra?**

We can teach students about Frederick Douglass, Lucretia Mott, John Brown, Rosa Parks, and Dolores

Huerta — larger than life heroes who struggled to end slavery and injustice — but how do we teach them to stand up for the overweight girl sitting next to them in Algebra? How do we get them to accept the gay math teacher down the hall? How do we get them to stop teasing a child who does not speak English as a first language?

It is not enough to uncover or reduce biases in our classrooms; we must act to stop them in the broader society. I developed this "Acting for Justice" unit for students to "practice" behaving as allies. In this lesson, students learn how to disrupt actions or words that stereotype or mistreat others as well as to become more aware of their own stereotypes.

This lesson deals with small-scale injustice where an ally can stop the abuse of an individual. But larger structures of exploitation and domination remain. Allies also need to work on bigger, society-wide change. Students must understand the need to struggle on both the personal and the societal levels.

Teaching Strategy:

1. I start the writing lesson by discussing "ally behavior." An ally is a person who stands up for someone when they face injustice. They intervene when someone is mistreated; they don't stand by and watch; they don't participate in the injustice, and they don't run away when someone else is suffering. I've found that it's helpful for me to demonstrate how I stop a person from telling a racist, sexist, or homophobic joke. Students can also talk about ways they have disrupted acts of prejudice or cruelty.

2. We brainstorm possible situations that might come up at school or in the neighborhood and then discuss how students might stop the mistreatment. For example, a girl wants to play basketball, but the boys say that girls can't play basketball: Girls slow down the game, and they can't shoot. A classmate is teased for wearing hand-me-down clothes. How would an ally behave in these situations?

3. When I first started using this activity, I developed "scenes" for students to act out because I wanted to get at injustices that I wasn't sure they would cover. Over the years, I discovered that it was far more powerful for students to write from their own experiences.

   I tell students that they are going to use incidents from their lives as improvisations to get a deeper analysis of discrimination and ally behavior. I ask students to list times they were the victim of an injustice or they perpetrated an act of injustice. They might also write about an instance of injustice that they witnessed.

After students make their lists, I encourage a few students to share their incidents. Mario wrote about store clerks following him because they thought he might steal clothes. Adam, an African-American student, shared that the counselor automatically placed him in a "regular" English class without checking his test scores or previous placement. Elena talked about how she tormented a boy in fourth grade as a way of getting "cheap laughs" from her classmates.

4. I ask students to write the story of the injustice and encourage them to include a description of where the story took place, a description of the people involved, and the dialogue of what was said during the incident. They might also include how they felt about the act and whether or not they were changed because of the discrimination.

Sharing Our Stories/Becoming Allies

5. I divide students into small groups so they can share their stories and remind them to listen carefully to each group member. After each person reads, the group does the following:

   • Discusses what can be learned from the story.

   • Asks the writer questions to get more details.

   • Shares any similar experiences from their own lives.

   • Reviews the stories they shared and discusses how someone could have intervened to stop the discrimination in each instance.

   • Decides which story they want to act out for the larger group.

6. Group members decide how to act out the scene. This is an improvisation: They choose character roles and decide how to act out the story, but they don't need to write down lines. I tell them to make sure one person in their group acts as an ally to interrupt the discriminatory behavior.

Acting for Justice

7. After students have had an opportunity to rehearse their scene, I bring the large group back together. I arrange the desks or chairs in "theater" style, so there is room for students to act out their stories. I tell students that they might feel uncomfortable in their roles as they act either as people who discriminate or as the victims, and that laughter is often a way that we release our discomfort; however, that

Tolerance

By Joe Stivers

The last hour of class on Friday seemed to last two. Derek moaned as he stared out the window at some kids who just couldn't wait. Out of all of the geometry teachers, out of all of the schools, why did I get him, Derek asked himself yet again.

Mr. Walker walked up to the board to demonstrate a problem. Derek's stomach cringed and his eyes darted around for some other distraction.

"Derek! I know that wall isn't that interesting. And by the looks of the last quiz, I think you should be watching the board anyway," the soft voice invaded Derek's recovery time.

Derek just gritted his teeth and looked at the board. He wasn't in the mood to have to stay after school today, especially with "The Queer." This nickname that most of the guys called Mr. Walker made Derek feel a little better, he just kept screaming it at Mr. Walker's back, only in his head, but it still made him feel a little better.

The hum of the bell outside in the hall signaled the end of another week for the students.

"Thank God!" Derek murmured to his friend Raymond who sat next to him.

"Derek, I'd like to talk to you, so if you could just stay in your seat, I'll be right with you," called Mr. Walker.

Raymond glanced at Derek with a smirk on his face. "The Queer strikes again, eh, Derek? Remember, don't bend over to pick up your pencil," whispered Raymond.

"Up yours, Ray. Wait for me, man. This shouldn't take long."

The class cleared out fast and Derek sat there, feeling uneasy. Derek's father had always "warned" him about Mr. Walker's "kind". "It's a disease," his father would say. "They're sick people. It could spread." Derek's stomach tightened up tighter at every step that Mr. Walker took towards him.

"Derek, I'm worried about your grade. I've checked your grades in your other classes, and you're doing great except for this class. Are you having difficulty understanding the work? I could arrange an after school tutoring session if you want. . . ."

"No! I mean, no, Mr. Walker. That won't be necessary. I'll do better. I have to go, Mr. Walker. I, uh, have to baby-sit."

"Okay, but I'm going to arrange a conference with your parents to see if we can do something about those test scores."

Derek just glared at the floor as he gathered up his stuff and headed out the door. The halls were empty except for a couple of teachers and students here and there. He could see Raymond at the end of the hall scribbling something on someone's locker. What a crappy way to start the weekend.

"So what's the story, Derek? You in love or what?" scoffed Raymond, not even bothering to look up from his handiwork.

"Screw you, Ray! He's calling my parents to make a conference. Jerk. I just want to get the heck out of his class. I didn't even know they let those people teach anyway."

"Don't worry, Derek, it's Friday. Let's just go get something to eat and see if we can get into some trouble."

Raymond's easy approach to life and its responsibilities made Derek feel better. Raymond always cheered Derek up. He was a good friend to have. He was upbeat and positive. He loved to joke around, but he was as serious as a heart attack when it came to school work.

Monday morning came and Derek felt relieved and pissed off, just because it was Monday morning. Everybody had on their morning scowls as they walked to their first class. Everybody except the teachers. Derek wondered if they knew how much the students hated that.

Derek walked into the cafeteria, bag of chips and a can of Arizona in hand, and started searching for Raymond. He spotted him across the large green room putting lettuce in one of the new kid's bag. Derek smirked and headed towards him.

"Ray, you're such a punk. One day it's going to catch up with you."

"Well, until then it's fair game. Did your boyfriend call your parents this weekend?"

"No, maybe he forgot or something. Why, are you getting jealous or something?"

A small commotion in the entrance of the cafeteria interrupted their typical male repertoire. Mr. Walker had entered the cafeteria. A few students stopped eating to stare. Others bent their heads close together whispering and smirking. But Mr. Walker walked in, got his food and walked out like he was oblivious to everything going on. Derek couldn't figure out if Mr. Walker didn't notice people's reactions to him, or if he just didn't care. Raymond and Derek finished eating and headed to class just in time to be late enough to interrupt the teacher while he was trying to explain something. The teachers wondered if the students knew how much they hated that.

After hanging out at Ray's house a couple hours after school, Derek headed home to find his mother with her "you're-this-close-to-being-grounded" face on.

"Hey, what's for dinner Mom?"

"Geometry homework. We haven't had that in a while, huh dear?"

"Oh man! Did he call?"

"Did who call? Were we expecting him to call? No, couldn't have, because I know if you were expecting him to call, you would have said something to me or your father. Me and your dad have to go see him tomorrow after school. In light of our inconvenience you will be looking at either the back of your door or a geometry book until you can get your priorities straight, understood? And by the way, I ordered pizza. I'll call you out when it gets here."

Derek stalked back to his room. He wasn't as mad as he thought he would be. It was bound to happen, but that wasn't to say he was just perfectly at ease with his new predicament. "Out of all of the geometry teachers, out of all the school, why did I get him?" Derek asked himself yet again.

The next day in class Mr. Walker acted like everything was normal. He went on teaching like he always did, ignoring the snickers and smirks, acting like he was having the time of his life. And Derek passed the class time like he always did, looking out the window or watching Raymond pull another one of his acts to keep himself busy.

"Derek! Derek!" Raymond hissed trying to get Derek's attention away from the window. "So how long are you grounded for?"

"For as long as it takes me to get my grade up in here. My parents are coming in today after school so they all can devise a plan to crush my spirit."

"Well have fun. Man, I'd pay big to see the reaction on your old man's face when he sees a queer. I can already tell it's going to be a Kodak moment."

Derek wasn't allowed to attend "the sentencing" as he had begun to call it. All he could do was sit in his room and imagine how his dad was going to react, but he wondered to what degree his dad

would take it. Maybe his dad would actually make the school transfer Derek out of Mr. Walker's class. Derek heard the car pull up and he went out to receive his sentence. With his dad involved, Derek knew he wouldn't be in too much trouble.

"So what's my punishment?" Derek asked as his parents walked into the living room.

"I think you've already been punished enough Derek. I can't think of any punishment worse than being stuck in a room for 45 minutes with that fairy," Derek's father said as he eased casually into his lazy boy chair and searched for his remote.

"Bingo!" Derek thought to himself.

"Jay! We talked about this in the car ride home. Mr. Walker is a teacher and it is none of our business what goes on in his bedroom!" Derek's mom pulled off her raincoat, hung it in the hall closet and made her way towards the kitchen.

"It concerns us if his bedroom habits show up in the classroom and start messing with my kid's head. Stinking faggot! Back in my day the school system would have showed that homo how to teach, how to teach right out of his ass! Next thing you know, they'll have some Jew or nigger trying to teach, stealing our jobs."

"I said enough Jay! I don't want to discuss this anymore."

Both Derek and his mother were shocked at his little speech. Derek's father had ranted about homosexuals before, but he had never shown this side. Derek felt truly betrayed. What made his ears sting and took his breath away was the "nigger" remark. Derek had always seen Ray as a friend first, then Black. But his own father had made his friendship with Ray seem dirty. They had been born at the same hospital, spent every summer at the same camp; even their girlfriends were a couple of sisters. Now Ray's color was just thrown into Derek's face. No longer an innocent friendship, but to his father, something ugly, a weed.

All Derek could think was why. Why Dad? What's the matter with Ray? He's like my brother, and now you say he isn't fit to be in my class, let alone my life. Derek walked down the hall into his room. Sleep didn't come easy that night, but tears did.

Without saying a word to his parents, Derek left for school the next morning still wounded from the night before. Derek couldn't focus on anything, just those few words that had made him see his father in a new light. Derek went into the cafeteria for breakfast and sat down with Ray. He slowly drank the milk and looked at the sausage suspiciously.

"Hey Derek. So what did Mr. Walker say last night?" Ray said as he filled the salt shaker with sugar.

"I don't know. I wasn't allowed to go."

"Damn, you must be in bigger trouble than I thought! What did your dad say?"

The sting came back. The hurt was renewed. How could his dad be so wrong about another person? Derek thought hard on that. His dad was wrong about Ray, so why couldn't he be wrong about Mr. Walker? His dad didn't know Mr. Walker. He didn't know about all the extra stuff he did for the class

like the day he made popcorn balls into geometric shapes and if you guessed the right shape, it was yours. His father didn't know about the pies and styrofoam models he made so the students could "see" geometry. Hours of setting up computer programs for a 10-minute demonstration because a student couldn't understand a certain concept. He stayed hours after school to help them. You could see how much he loved what he was doing by just watching him teach.

"It doesn't matter Ray. It doesn't matter what my father said. Let's get to class. I need help on my geometry homework; we have a test on Tuesday."

---

doesn't mean that we think discrimination is funny.

8. As each group improvises its story, the rest of the class watches and take notes to capture any great language that they might want to use in a story. I encourage them to think about the following questions:

- What was the discrimination?
- How effective was the disruption/ally behavior?
- What else could have been done?
- Have they ever been in a similar situation where they acted for justice? What happened?

After each group presents its scene, students discuss the questions listed above. Sometimes it helps for the "actors" to stay on stage, so that the audience can ask them questions, "How did you feel when Stella called you a name? What caused you to disrupt the injustice? How did you feel afterwards?"

Stepping Into Fiction

9. After all groups perform at least one improvisation, I ask students to write an interior monologue from one character's point of view. An interior monologue captures the thoughts and feelings of a character as they are engaged in a situation. It may be a character they portrayed or observed. (See "Promoting Social Imagination Through Interior Monologues," page 134.)

10. As students read their monologues, they often excavate the emotional territory these pieces triggered. How do people feel when they are laughed at? Excluded? How do they feel when

they gather the courage to stand up for someone else, when they fight back against ignorance and hate? Why don't people act even when they feel morally compelled to interrupt? Who gets hurt?

This would also be a time to explore the difference between intervening on a personal level and working for change at a national/international level. Encourage students to talk about movements they know about. (This activity is a good one in units that examine other social movements for justice — from the ending of slavery in the United States to the ending of apartheid in South Africa.)

11. To move to fiction from the monologues, I ask the class to become an audience to help develop the story line. Joe Stivers' piece, "Tolerance," (see page 83) started as an interior monologue from the main character's point of view. He is angry that his teacher is gay. Joe, my student, didn't know where to go with this story. After he shared his interior monologue, his fellow students gave him suggestions. He worked in bits and pieces over time. He struggled with the ending until he made the main character's father homophobic. It took him most of the quarter and many revisions to get there.

Justin Morris went inside a difficult character in his story "Maurice" (see next page). What made this young man act the way he did? Justin worked through his interior monologue to discover an answer to his question.

One student, a biracial girl who hid her African-American identity from the class, told me in private that she cried after watching the cruelty of her classmates in middle school, but she was so afraid that they'd turn on her that she never helped anyone out. "They had teased me about my facial hair. I was afraid that if I helped the boy they were teasing that they would remember my hair and start laughing at me again."

I was surprised at how many of my students shared instances when they tormented others. I was equally surprised at how few intervened to help when someone was hurt. But I also learned that students felt conflicted and unhappy about their role in hurting others. Students need the tools to confront injustice. Acting in solidarity with others is a learned habit.

In the introduction to *The Power in Our Hands*, Bill Bigelow and Norm Diamond write that to "teach is to be a warrior against cynicism and despair." When I remember my niece Kelly, whose Tourette's Syndrome caused her to become a constant target, I know that we must all become warriors against cynicism and despair. We must all act for justice; we must act for each other. ■

For Further Reading

Bambara, Toni Cade. "Raymond's Run," in *Gorilla, My Love*. New York: Random House, 1972.

Coville, Bruce. *Am I Blue? Coming Out from the Silence*. New York: Harper Trophy, 1994.

Houston, Jeanne Wakatsuki. "Shikata Ga Nai," in *Farewell to Manzanar: A True Story of Japanese-American Experience During and After the World War II Internment*. New York: Bantam Books, 1973, pp. 10-11.

McKnight, Reginald. 1992. *A Different Kind of Light Shines on Texas*. Boston: Little, Brown & Co., 1992.

O'Callahan, James. "Orange Cheeks," in Greer, Colin, and Kohl, Herbert (Eds.), *A Call to Character: A Family Treasury of Stories, Poems, Plays, Proverbs, and Fables to Guide the Development of Values for You and Your Children*. New York: Harper Collins, 1995.

Wong, Jade Snow. 1995. "Fifth Chinese Daughter," in *A Call to Character*. (See entry above.)

Maurice

By Justin Morris

Maurice was obnoxious. If you wanna get down to it, he was a guy's guy. Not very much of a people person. You know the type: He'd call a girl out of her name in the blink of an eye, and he'd cuss you out if you looked at him the wrong way. Most of all he never . . . I mean he never . . . ever . . . showed any kind of emotion. Every school has a Maurice. He comes in different shapes, colors, sized, and genders. But one Mother's Day assignment meant the reshaping of Maurice's life. I was there, and I'll never forget it.

I remember seeing him in the hallway before, in-between, and even during class. There he was: a rolled up magazine (VIBE) in his left hand, a bag of Doritos (Nacho Cheesier) in his right, and his Walkman stuck in his jacket pocket. His friends were crowded around him, while his head bobbed rhythmically back and forth, left and right, to the tape in his Walkman. He'd say something now and then to one of his friends or he'd say something smart to a girl who'd be walking by. Mostly he was absorbed in his music.

I could tell that Maurice was putting up a front. I'm not gonna speak for everybody when I assume a lot of people knew exactly what Maurice was all about. Nothin', I mean, playing the role of a tough guy seemed so natural to him, you just knew there had to be a compassionate side hidden inside. Somewhere. Just think about some of the guys that you see, or know, in high school who act so tough. You just know they're so full of it. Something was going on inside of them to keep them so alive with distrust and vulgarity.

He stood almost 6 feet tall, he was mixed (he looked it), he sported close cut curly hair that was covered by a baseball cap facing forward. He was one of those skinny dudes who wore baggy clothes, and he always had his signature headphones that were either glued to his ears or permanently draped over his neck, cranked up at the loudest volume imaginable. You never saw Maurice without his Walkman.

He was the reason why I went to third period English. He was the reason many people went to third period, I think. Not because it was an easy class (it wasn't) and not because it was fun (it had its moments). It was because Maurice never sat on a desk like the rest of us. That would mean admitting that he was at least half-human. Sometimes he arrived 10, 20, even 40 minutes late. On top of that, it would take him the remaining class period to get settled down.

Our teacher wasn't the least bit intimidated by Maurice. In fact, I think that she was the reason why he even bothered showing up to class. She often leaned back in her chair while Maurice was standing somewhere running his mouth. She wasn't being passive, in fact, she was letting Maurice have his outlet. He had so much built up energy, she made a choice to allow him to vent some of it out in class. It was either that or let him fight it out.

Maurice and our teacher, Mrs. ___ played off of each other like a comedy team. They were Grumpy Old Men except one of them was a woman. She treated him like an old friend, which is better than the way some of the other teachers treated him. I had a class with him last year. Mr. Marx, U.S. History, would give Maurice referrals every day.

"Go to the deans," he'd say.

"Go ___ yourself, man," Maurice would reply. I always liked the way Maurice talked. He talked like he walked; kinda slow, but you knew he was getting somewhere.

What bothered Mrs. ___ the most was the fact that there was more to Maurice than met the eye. She was forever telling the class how gifted of a writer he was, but he had yet to share some of his pieces in class. He spent a significant part of the class period whispering and laughing with Little Homie, who was almost always slouched in the chair next to him (when Maurice decided to take a seat). Little Homie was always sleepin', and mostly always high, but on the rare occasion he was awake and sober, he made trouble with his partner Maurice.

"Yo man, women are like cows, dammit! There's no other way around it," Maurice said. This was his reply to a discussion we were having on Women's Rights. None of us were shocked, believe me. His remark earned moans of approval from the guys and a deafening smack of teeth in unison from the girls.

Mrs. ___ said, "Not all girls are like that, Maurice, just the ones you go after."

"Naw, man, it ain't even about that. Damn—" He wasn't upset. He was actually smiling just knowing that Mrs. ___ was trying to clown him.

"What about your mom, or . . ." Mrs. ___ was interrupted by the ringing of the bell. Little Homie's eyes peeled open slowly. He rose out of his chair and began to stagger aimlessly into the hallway as usual. Sunday was Mother's Day, our assignment: Write a tribute to our mothers.

The next day about 20 minutes into class about five poems have been read. The current poem is mushy and way too sentimental. It mentions flowers ready to bloom and endless loads of crap. I yawn, and Mrs. ___ gives me THE LOOK. Maurice is shifting uncomfortably in the desk next to me. I read my poem about the time my mother took me to see **Ghostbusters** on my birthday years ago.

Immediately afterwards, Maurice gets up out of his desk and walks out the door. This is his way of asking if he can go to the bathroom. Ten minutes later I'm aching for a smoke. I pass a note to Mrs. ___ asking if I can go to the bathroom. She passes it back to me saying, "No."

I ask her, "Why?"

She says, "Maurice hasn't returned with the pass." Ah-ha.

"Maurice didn't take the pass, " I say. She gives me permission and I'm out the door.

Take a left and push open badly painted double doors. I reach in my pocket for my smokes. The back hallways are unusually dark. The faint smell of marijuana lingers. I round the corner when I hear a sniffling. Someone is up ahead. I walk a few steps closer and I see a faint outline of a guy. His baseball cap is on the ground in front of him. I slow down my step until I'm right in front of the guy. I return my cigarettes to my pocket.

"Are you okay?" I ask this without hesitation. I'm freaked out. Next to him on the floor is a crumpled piece of paper that was once folded. I bend down next to him and he looks up at me with sad, wet eyes.

"Not really," he says. I'm guessing that he recognizes me. Maurice and I have talked only a couple of times. Nothing special. It's dead silent except for his sniffling. I wish I had a Kleenex so he could blow his nose.

"Hey, is this your poem?" I ask.

He doesn't answer. He just looks at me with a vacant expression.

"Can I read it?" I ask hesitantly. It's not like me to meddle in another man's business like this, but I felt like I had to do something. He nodded his head.

His poem was called "Mother." It was about his mother speaking to him from her grave, telling him how much he loves her and misses him. Mrs. ___ was right, he was a good writer.

"I'm sorry to hear about your mom, Maurice. That's gotta be tough. . . . I don't know what to say. . . . When did she die?"

"You don't have to say anything. Not to me, not to anybody, OK?"

"Aw, I ain't gonna tell nobody. I'm not like that."

"Good," he said. And with that he put himself together. He took the poem from my hands and started back towards the classroom. He turned around and quickly said, "Thank you," before walking up the steps and walking through the badly painted double doors. I couldn't move. I didn't know what to do with myself. It made me sad to see the look on his face.

When I returned to class, I saw Maurice at his desk just sitting there. Everybody else was busy talking about their plans for the weekend.

Maurice reached in his coat pocket and put his headphones over his ears. His poem was folded neatly before him on his desk. Our eyes met for a brief second. Little Homie woke up and nonchalantly wiped the drool from his chin. Maurice turned his head away from my gaze and began to stare out the window, up at the sky.

Writing the College Essay:
Creating A Vision of Possibility

Over a decade ago, 25 seniors sat in my Contemporary Literature and Society class and discussed their futures. We had just celebrated Sheila's 18th birthday and prom and graduation could be viewed on the horizon. After blowing out her candles, Sheila said, "I am soooo happy to have made it to 18 without getting pregnant. I am the first woman in my family to graduate from high school. And the first woman to make it to 18 without a child." Several other students joined in with similar stories.

Sheila's story was not uncommon in my classrooms. Many of my students were the first in their family to graduate from high school. Many were the first to attend college. Some already had children.

> **While most parents want their children to go to college, if they haven't gone themselves they might not know how to help their children prepare or apply.**

Although my family situation differed in some ways from my students', there were similarities. I remember my fear that I would not graduate from high school. Mom left for work before I got up for school. She was too tired at night to ask about homework or even cook, much less initiate discussions about my future. I usually ate dinner at my older sister's home. Although I was the youngest child in my family, I was the first to attend college. My oldest sister joined me during my freshman year.

As a junior/senior English teacher, I understood the overwhelming sense of awe and fear that college can inspire. I attempted to give my students the help I needed when I was a high school senior.

The Culture of College

For many students, there is no culture of college in the home. While most parents want their children to go to college, if they haven't gone themselves they might not know how to help their children prepare or apply. My student, Trisa, articulated this after we visited a more affluent high school in the suburbs. One of her "ahas" about the difference between our schools was summed up in her quote, "At West Linn, students didn't ask each other if they were attending college, they asked each other where they were going. Attending college was a given." In homes where no one has gone to college, the difference between *if* and *where* is a big one.

My mother supported my entrance into college, but we didn't have a clue how much money it really cost or how to apply. Mom had never set foot on a college campus, but she'd harbored the dream of becoming a teacher when she was younger. Either we didn't have college counseling in my high school or I wasn't perceived to be college "material," because no one at Eureka High helped me think about where I might want to attend. I did apply to several University of California campuses because I'd visited a friend's sister at Berkeley, and I pumped her for information. The University of California at Santa Barbara accepted me, but after the burning of the Bank of America in nearby Isla Vista and campus riots in '69, Mom thought Redwood Community College would be a better choice. Her thinking was, "A college is a college." My students struggled with similar problems. The choices overwhelmed them, and even the application fees seemed excessive.

One of my students who was the first member of her family to attend college said, "I don't know what changed for me this year. Now I get good grades. I

88

A PUBLICATION OF RETHINKING SCHOOLS

Cleo Photography

job. A significant number of my students lacked the credits to be juniors or seniors when they entered my untracked classes, so when I started in on college, they rebelled. Justifiably so. They were sick of school, and they didn't want to study for the SATs or write college essays. But I believe it is essential to give students a vision of their life after high school; in fact, it was crucial to their success in my class that they established an attainable goal and direction for their life after Jefferson. Without that vision and goal, it was too easy to sleep in, watch daytime soaps, and forget about homework.

How I talked with students about their future was crucial. On one occasion I spoke with my class about college and I inadvertently put down working-class jobs, "You don't want to push a broom or pump gas the rest of your life. That might be okay when you're young, but you don't want to make a career out of it."

Nyke got mad. "Hey, my dad owns a janitorial service. He pushes brooms, mops, and vacuum cleaners every night. That's how he puts the food on our table, and I don't see anything wrong with that." Nyke was right, and I felt ashamed. His words recalled the disparaging remarks some of my teachers made about jobs that required physical rather than mental labor. Thanks to Nyke, I remember both of our fathers and speak with students about the dignity of work.

want to do my work. I stay for academic clinic. I get my homework done." But I knew what had changed. One day during the previous summer while Natalie and her parents visited family in Seattle, her father drove her to the University of Washington, a beautiful campus. They ate lunch, toured the campus, and he spoke of his desire for her to attend a four-year college. Through that visit, Natalie's father helped her see college as a possibility.

Resistance: Is College the Only Option?

Let me set the record straight: I don't think college is the only option for students. But most students will need post-secondary education to get a living wage

But I also talk about options. Most students do harbor some kind of secret vision of their future, some spark from childhood or some current passion that they'd like to transform into their future work — whether it's becoming a hairstylist or working as an ecologist trying to save the salmon runs. For Angie, it was a love of animals that made her want to become a veterinarian. Teaonshae didn't want to go to a four-year college, but she cut and styled hair on her front

Granny's

By Alyss Dixson

The house seems smaller than I remember it, the chain link fence overgrown with grass, its wheat-like stalks protruding out over the sidewalk. The rest of the yard is mostly dirt, except for the windy cement path leading to the front door. The entranceway is a mixture of dust and water, with footprints leading in and out of the house from the 15 or so little kids Granny's always got running around, wild and screaming.

On the concrete patio in front sit the usual gang of drunken male cousins, whistling at any woman unfortunate enough to walk by. As usual they're trying to impress one another with their respective plans for the future. A sudden gust of wind brings the smell of beer, and cigarette smoke blowing across the yard. It mixes with the smell of greens and chicken coming from the house.

The rank odor of pee, courtesy of three generations of children sitting on the living room carpet, greets me in the dining room as I come through the door and perch on the edge of a worn wooden chair, one of the remnants from a once elegant dining set. The floor's still covered in the same flower-'n-square pattern I remember from the last time I was here nine years ago. The only difference being, now there's dirt in the corners of the room, and ants crawl freely, unmolested, across the floor. The middle is still white, the pattern showing clearly, although I notice the plastic covering from the linoleum has long since peeled away.

Strange how none of this bothered me that last visit. Then I felt at home among the boxes and books stacked everywhere. I was one of the wild banshees running around, screaming at the top of my lungs, hair flying everywhere, dirty clothes, and muddy bare feet. Having spent the first four years of my life in Los Angeles with my grandmother, the late night sirens, drunken old men, and seemingly endless, "Did you hear what happened to so-and-so? He got arrested!" were normal, common occurences.

Granny sits in her arm chair, secure in a nest of just-washed clothes, gossiping with all the female cousins, most of whom are drunk and pregnant, or have a small child sitting on their laps. As regal as any queen, she grabs another shirt to fold, reaches between her legs to pull out a pair of underwear.

Still talking she yells at Jake to "get his Black ass in here and eat somethin' before it's all gone," 'cause she's, "not cookin' nothing else."

Getting out of my chair, I turn and wander into the kitchen. Hoping to find something to do, I feel like an intruder, unwanted and hopelessly "white" after my years in Oregon. I hear M.C. Hammer coming from the back bedroom and go to investigate. I find one of my cousins named "Foots" imitating M.C.'s dance steps bare-foot on the rough wood floor. We're standing between the two bunk-beds that are crowded against the walls, facing each other, and I ask him to teach me how to dance. He just sort of laughs and says sure, launching immediately into the "Roger Rabbit," the bane of my existence. Jerking like an idiot and feeling not only like a white girl, but an Oregon white girl at that, I finally tell him I have to go check and see if my dad is ready to go yet.

I find him in the living room with Granny and my cousin Rose; the others have left, gone outside to joke and laugh with their friends. I notice a certain uneasiness in my dad. He's perched his full three-hundred pound frame on the edge of the chair and looks like he's being interrogated. Beads of sweat stand out along his hairline. His eyes dart around the room, careful not to rest on any one thing, afraid to look condescending, aloof.

Rose is sitting on the couch that's along the far wall, pregnant belly rising up in front of her. The baby's father is in jail, and Rose is an ex-drug abuser, like everyone else in the family. I'm skeptical about how much of an ex-abuser she is because at times she loses her grip on reality, to say the least.

The wall opposite the couch is lined with baby paraphernalia: crib, stacks of Pampers boxes, baby clothes and toys, old suitcases, and picture albums. The windows have long since been covered over with junk. Joining Rose on the couch, I look at the huge TV set pushed up against the wall. I remember watching **The Magic Flute** and **Scooby Doo** as a child on that same set. Now it's used as a table, pictures of grandchildren and great-grandchildren propped on top.

Rose grabs my hand and leads me to the front bedroom, all the while giggling about what she wants to give me. The room is a jumble of army cots, clothes, shoes, children, and odds and ends picked up in 64 years of life. Taking my hand she slips a large gold ring onto my finger. "I got it offa base head for five bucks, you like it?" she breathes, eyes wide. I shake my head yes, and start to take it off. "You can have it," she says, all at once quiet, reminding me of the cousin I remember from childhood, when I was everyone's baby and had to be fussed over, hair combed.

My dad calls me out of the bedroom and stands hitching up his jeans over by the front door. Granny gets up to go into the kitchen and fix two big plates of food for us to take home. Despite her bulk, or perhaps because of it, she seems tired. Her shoulders are sloped and her smile isn't quite as ready as I remember it. My dad tells me he's going outside to talk with a couple of cousins out there. I follow Granny and tell her "it's alright I can do it." But she just smiles and says, "No, baby. Grandma'll fix you-all a plate."

I give her a hug and watch as she begins to pile greens onto a ceramic plate. I guess all those years in Oregon have changed us; now I feel above this, repulsed even. I'm torn between the love I have for my grandmother and anger at the family that's put her in these circumstances. I want to shout at them, tell them all to just leave her alone. Ask them if they can't see what they're doing to her. She's spent the last fifty-some-odd years of her life doing for others. First with her younger brothers and sisters, then with her own children, now with her children's children and any strays picked up along the way. When does she get her turn to rest, to come home and not have someone yelling, "Granny what's for dinner?"

I sigh, and Grandma turns around and asks me what's the matter. I tell her, "nothing," but there are tears in my eyes, which I wipe away quickly, making some complaint about all the smoke in the house. From outside my dad calls me, telling me to, "say good-bye to Granny so we can git." I give her another hug and kiss, and say good-bye, walking out the door.

I'm almost to the gate when Granny calls me, "You forgot your plate, sweetheart." I take it from her and get in the car, she waves at me, and calls out "Granny loves you, baby'" as we pull away. I wave back and think, "I know Grandma, I love you, too."

porch every weekend and all summer long. Keith, who drew my wrath for the cartoon characters that disfigured my desks, wanted to be a graphic artist. Lurdes hoped to be a lawyer who helped immigrants. Yuliis doodled dress designs and aspired to become a fashion designer. And Nicole wanted to write plays that dealt with social issues.

Helping students articulate these dreams not only pushed them to write college or scholarship essays, it helped them create goals for themselves that pulled them out of bed or off the couch and into my classroom.

Creating the Desire: Bringing Back Former Students

Like most public schools, Jefferson opened its doors in September before college students made their way back across the country or down the street. I took advantage of that and invited my former students in for a talk. Usually I created a panel that included students who attended local, Black, community, small and large colleges all over the country. I wanted my current students to listen to Jefferson graduates talk about their experiences.

While they did talk about classes, cost, grades, scholarships, they also talked about campus food, football games, marching bands, campus traditions, bugs, heat, homesickness, and what they wished they would have taken care of when they were juniors and seniors. Olivia, who had a full ride at a state college, talked about how she tried to spend an hour a day in the library during her senior year finding scholarships. She also encouraged all students to visit the campus prior to attending: "I didn't know I would smell manure all day and hear cows and pigs all night." Harold agreed. "Until I went to college, I'd never been some place that didn't have sidewalks." And Sekou talked about the opening traditions at Morehouse College in Atlanta that both welcomed him and made him feel a part of a rich history.

Laughter ricocheted off the walls of C-12 on these days as students shared their experiences. Because these panels had become a tradition, many of my former students called me and volunteered to come back and talk once they were "grown." But more than laughter and sharing, my former students created the sense of possibility and desire in my current students. They had known Harold when he blocked the stairs between B floor and C floor. In fact, they'd known Harold when he claimed to be a gang

> **I decided to take my students on field trips to local college campuses hoping to create a hunger for those green spaces, those ivy-covered walls, for an education. But I wanted more than a walk around campus. I wanted students to attend a class so they could see that the "academy" was not out of their reach.**

member at middle school. If Harold or Tony or Renee could go to college, so could they.

Campus Visits

Billie Letts, in her novel *Where the Heart Is*, captured my fears and doubts when she described the main character's first day at college:

> *Novalee had never been on a college campus before and she was sure everyone who saw her knew it. She tried to look like she belonged there, but she didn't figure she was fooling anyone.*

I too was awestruck, but if I hadn't visited Claythel Burke at University of California at Berkeley, I may not have overcome my fear that I didn't belong. I decided to take my students on field trips to local college campuses hoping to create a hunger for those green spaces, those ivy-covered walls, for an education. I wanted them to see themselves on a campus — just as Natalie's father had when he took her to visit University of Washington.

But I wanted more than a walk around campus. I wanted students to attend a class so they could see that the "academy" was not out of their reach. Two of the most successful attempts to bring my students to a campus happened because of my college professor friends. Tony Wolk, an English professor at Portland State University, agreed to teach my students a writing lesson on campus. When we arrived, he passed out chocolate chip cookies he'd baked for them and treated them to an outstanding lesson using dreams as an entry to a piece of writing.

Once when I had a grant to support my vision, I took students to University of Oregon — a two-hour bus ride away — where they met with my Writing Project mentor, Nat Teich, and some former Jefferson students who attended the university. Nat's class focused on metaphors in poetry. Students connected. They knew they belonged. This was their strong suit. He had also arranged tours around the campus.

Why Would They Want to Know About Me?

When faced with sample college essay forms asking them to write about significant life events, my students balked. Few of them believed that they had done anything worth writing about or that someone else would want to read. Sure, I loved their stories and poems, but I taught at Jefferson. Why would a college admissions officer want to read about their life? They hadn't traveled or earned straight As. They were sure that their lives were not significant enough to write about. As soon as I asked them to list significant experiences or accomplishments, I could feel the whine rising up across the room even before Ayanna raised her hand. "Ms. Christensen, I haven't done anything. I haven't gotten good grades. I never went anywhere. I haven't accomplished anything."

Ayana had barely finished before Ted headed for me with his head down and tilted, the way he carried it when he had his "I can't do this" frown on. And Terressa was a pile of hair and fumes under Rosa Parks' poster.

Getting these students to write college essays acknowledging their skills was like steelhead fishing in the Columbia: no fish. They didn't see their incredible resilience, their ability to see through people's agendas, to spot phonies within seconds. They discounted the richness of their lives, the stories they had heard growing up, their grandmothers' wisdom. They didn't count the gifts they brought daily to my life. Why should they? In a society that prizes money and all it can buy — expensive clothes, cars, homes, high SAT scores, travel to foreign countries — many of my students didn't measure up in the traditional sense, but they had the skills our society sorely needs: compassion, heart, the ability to see through lies and deception, as well as the skill to wrestle any point to the ground.

Writing the Essay

"All the college will know about you are numbers: your Social Security number, grade point average, and test scores. You need to make them see you as an individual," I told my students. "This is your chance to tell your story, to jump up off the page and let them know what they'd be missing if they didn't let you attend their school or give you money to attend school."

Typically, we work through two pieces — a special person essay and an incident that shaped them —

92

Saxophone
By Dyan Watson

I sat on the floor and assembled my saxophone. As I adjusted the reed, I searched for a song I could play. Just as I was about to plunge into a blues standard, my Japanese sister handed me a book turned to a famous folk song. While I played, my Japanese host family sang along, covering my sight-reading bloopers. I couldn't believe it! Here I was in Japan, a 16-year-old playing a Japanese folk song on the alto saxophone — an instrument known for swing and bee-bop.

That night, as I tossed on my mat, I gloried in what took place. We had "jammed" together. Few words were spoken, yet we understood each other clearly. Music proved to be the universal language.

In the years ahead, I want to create that scene over and over. I want to teach others how to communicate with music and with other media. As a teacher, I want to help my students break down the barriers between Blacks and Asians, Americans and Japanese, and others as well.

As a musician, I have learned that music is more than just a pastime — it models the way we can live together as people. As a Black youth, I realize the importance of learning to accept others' differences without losing my own identity.

Each of us is part of a symphony. In a good symphony each instrument knows its own strengths and weaknesses. Every instrument has limitations: the euphonium can only go so high, the clarinet so low. But when the two instruments merge a powerful range is present, resulting in music that entices ears to come and listen.

To create great music, each instrument must give a little. When playing with a flute, a trumpet shouldn't play full capacity or it will trample the gentle sounds of the flute. The trumpet must soften enough for the flute to be heard. The trumpet will still be identified as a trumpet. It has just shared itself with the flute.

Working hard to harmonize without drowning out anyone is what cultural diversity is all about. It is about sharing my culture's history and myself with others while they share their history and themselves. It is about broadening our understanding of people with different backgrounds by participating in intercultural activities such as study abroad.

When I traveled to Japan, I was the stranger. I was clumsy with chopsticks. I felt awkward taking my shoes off when I entered a home. Using the correct greeting presented a constant challenge. After a week, I began to adapt — things no longer seemed strange to me. Instead, they were just different. Being totally emerged in Japanese culture helped me appreciate the differences instead of mocking them. From crossing the street to saying hello, I learned to accept and sometimes treasure the differences between our cultures. I also discovered many similarities.

I came back to my high school determined to know more. I wanted to match what I learned from my Japanese family with what Asian-American authors wrote. I read personal accounts of the Japanese-American experience — connecting the lives of the Japanese I had met with those who were American born. I wanted to see how the cultural values of their motherland affected second and third generations.

Participation in this cultural experience pushes me to be open-minded to others from various backgrounds. When I become a teacher, in my classroom, I want my students to attain these same goals. I want them to know that by harmonizing, we will understand and appreciate each other more — allowing us to become better musicians — better people, who compose great symphonies.

The Children's Prayer Group

By Chetan Patel

Dressed only with a sheet folded like dothu, I stood on stage and read in my native language, Gujarati, about the importance of strong family relationships. I finished and when the curtains came down, I hurried off the stage as a group of three girls took their position for a dance. Fifteen minutes later, I was back on stage, singing about the life of Narsinh Mehta, an old Indian saint. As I looked out on the audience filled with faces that looked like mine, I sensed how after six years, I had helped to establish Indian culture in the youth. These were a few of the many activities performed by the Children's Prayer Group during last year's Diwali. It had been our largest and finest celebration of the Hindu New Year.

Six years ago, it wasn't like this. I watched episodes of **Mahabharata** with my mother, but never understood a word of the ancient Hindu epic. Each episode was in Gujarati, a language I had forgotten in my childhood. Sure, I could say things like, "She went outside," or "Give me some food," but I couldn't hold a conversation or read a single world. People would call me a dorjivo to my face, thinking I didn't know they were saying I was stupid. The worst part was watching my grandfather's eyes burn as he scolded me for not caring about the importance of the past. It's not that I didn't care; I take great pride in my Indian culture.

But learning about India meant learning about Hinduism, another title I claimed but knew nothing about. All the Hindu scriptures were in Gujarati. It was as if my culture was behind a locked door, and language was the key I needed.

I tried to avoid learning Gujarati. I checked out books and encyclopedias, trying to comprehend what it meant to be Hindu. But the books weren't meant to be read by a 12-year-old. The only thing I learned was that I believed in hundreds of different gods — only a small part of the religion.

My parents were too busy working to teach me Gujarati. People in the Indian community, especially older members, grew sick of ignorance shown by children my age who had the same problem. One day, my friend's grandfather, Ramanbhai, decided to form the Children's Prayer Group, dedicated to teaching first generation Indian children about their past, including Hinduism and Gujarati.

Thrilled, I marched with my brother and sister every Sunday at noon to Ramanbhai's house. He told us of Prince Rama and his victory over Ravana, and the reason we are vegetarians — a question I'd always asked my father, but never received an answer for. He taught us ancient prayers and told us to respect our parents by telling them jai Shri Krishna every morning before leaving for school. We soon started to read and write in Gujarati. The only problem was that only a few children from the Indian community attended.

It was a cold November day when Ramanbhai told us about an idea he rolling around in his head. "This Diwali let's celebrate with a party. When I lived in Zambia, we had a big celebration." His plans were set into motion and we thought of a clever way to get Indian children to attend. Most kids thought Indian functions were boring, but it was going to be different this year. We ordered 20 pizzas for dinner, just for them. Although we only sang two songs, hundreds of people showed up for the celebration, including many children. The following Sunday, new faces were present at our meeting.

Six years later, our group size has tripled since its creation and our Diwali celebrations now include dances and plays. My life changed in those years because of the program. Now I can understand what's happening when my mother watches an episode of **Mahabharata** and more importantly, I've regained my Indian identity.

otherwise known as the "aha" moment essay. After reading through numerous college and scholarship applications, I found these two were anchors my students could use. I called them the interview suit or the basic black dress. They wrote and honed two of the essays and then changed them if they needed to answer a slightly different question.

Significant Person Essay

Sometimes I didn't even say we were writing a college essay, because it sent students into immediate panic and anxiety. Their vision of a college essay is a list of their achievements: paragraph after boring paragraph of their accomplishments. Instead we'd just write the piece as part of another unit we were working on.

The easiest essay to tuck in without their knowledge was the special person essay. For example, when we read *Their Eyes Were Watching God* (1978), we discussed how Janie's grandmother influenced her, then we wrote an essay about someone who was important in our lives. When we studied the Abolitionists during Literature and U.S. History, we talked about "moral ancestors" — people who weren't related to us, but whose social conscience and engagement set a standard we wanted to live by — and we wrote about them. Around Thanksgiving, we wrote essays about people we're thankful we have in our lives. Sometimes the "Sweet Learning" lesson (see page 23) acted as the essay's starter dough. Later, students could dig these pieces of their portfolios to clean up as a college essay.

But sometimes I hit the essay straight on— usually by busting their stereotypes of a college essay. We'd read "Granny's" by Alyss Dixson, an essay that helped buy her a ticket into Yale (See page 90). Typically students say, "That's not a college essay. You can't write about ants and urine when you're trying to get into college." Students needed to see that they didn't need to make themselves sound like Dick and Jane from the old first-grade readers. They needed to sound like themselves, to share the world that they come from.

I began by asking students to make a list of people who had influenced them. They may or may not have known this person. It could have been a coach, a parent, a grandparent, a person in their church or summer camp, a person they admired, but didn't know — a moral ancestor. Next to the person's name, they wrote how the person touched them, why they were

important. We shared the lists to percolate ideas for each other.

Once they'd chosen a person, we did a series of quick-writes. First, I asked students to describe this person: "Tell me what they look like, let us hear him/her talk, give you advice. Brainstorm details about the person: Do they wear an apron? Smell like Old Spice? Run their hands through their hair? Push their glasses up on their nose?" I usually did a visualization at this point (see page 28) as it helped students dive into the piece and retrieve memories.

For the next quick-write, I asked them to describe an incident with the person that illustrates why the person influenced them. I gave them an example of Ray Cetina, my principal at Grant Elementary School in Eureka, who created a science club that met at 7 in the morning and invited all students to attend. For Mr. Cetina, we were all "talented and gifted." We all deserved special programs. His sense of equality and expectation shaped my life as a student and a teacher.

Sometimes, obviously, students wrote about people they hadn't met. I asked them, "What has this person accomplished that makes you admire them? Be specific. Not "they are great and courageous," but she fought cancer, he helped get kids off the street, she was the first woman tap dancer to make it big. Go into detail. You will need to cut back later, but get it all down now."

Then I brought it back home. "From this person's accomplishments what did you learn that you will take with you into your future? In other words, tie this person's achievements to your future goals."

The quick-writes were a jumble — like pieces for a quilt that needed a unifying pattern to hold them together. I told students, "Read back over your quick-writes and think like a storyteller — get down scenes, dialogue, make the person come alive. Play with each part. Write fast. Be bold. Keep all drafts — even the ugly ones, they might have a line or two that can be saved. Fit this all together once you get all of the details. Write first. Piece later. If you get stuck, look back at the student models for a way out."

The "Aha" or Incident Essay

The second essay was much more difficult to write and explain, partly because it asked students who hadn't even lived two decades to inventory their lives and then scrutinize them for a moment where they had a vision of the possible. This paper was like a

> Helping students articulate their dreams not only pushed them to write college or scholarship essays, it helped them create goals for themselves that pulled them out of bed or off the couch and into my classroom.

A Lesson in Passion

By Chelsea Henrichs

"If I came to see you, I'd ask for my money back! I've paid. Give me something to watch! If you're going to dance, dance." The tiny, dark woman says over the banging of the piano. We all laugh, but I take what she says and store it away. Her words make me push myself harder. I am the fairy queen. I am Juliet. I start to lose myself in this character that I have created for her. I imitate her gracefulness that I know dazzled audiences, though she's never told me. I watch her and I see where I hope to get. I want to be beautiful and powerful at the same time. I want people to want to watch me dance.

I first met Elena Carter when I was a sophomore, and she choreographed a piece for the Jefferson Dancers. I was an understudy for a part that was flirtatious and fast. The need to please her and pull her style of ballet out of my body was a challenge. My love for ballet grew stronger after each rehearsal with her. In her ballet class during my junior year, I learned not only about ballet, but also about passion.

Elena's passion comes from the country where she's still a citizen: Mexico. Even though her father was an American, she is Mexican, and she is very proud of her country. Elena's passion soared when she was a member of the Dance Theater of Harlem.

As a senior, I've gotten the chance to be a teacher's assistant for Elena's Ballet II class. In the small studio overlooking the football field, I've witnessed Elena's teaching. With shouts of "zam" and "yes," she brings out the passion in her students. She uses humor and paints pictures with her words. "Ashley, you are giving me skim milk. I want egg nog with whiskey!" Elena pushes her students to reach their limit, to tell a story with their bodies and faces. She teaches that ballet is not just a series of steps, but reaching your audience, even if the audience is just her.

When I leave Jefferson in June, Elena will be one of the teachers who I carry in my heart. She encouraged me to let go of my inhibitions and to remember that ballet is about passion. She showed me how to make a move "more," to have "volume," and to push myself to the edge. Elena taught me through example, not only of her life, but in the way she carries herself. She stands out in a crowd. She taught me to be a dancer.

heat-seeking device, finding the student's heart: What matters? What's important? Why? What might they want to spend their lives doing? When was the moment they knew that?

I changed my major three times during college — from math to marine biology to literature. And after I graduated I started a master's program in Medieval Literature, switched to law school, and ended up a teacher. So I know that the flash of illumination I had in fourth grade when my chicken died and I dissected it did not turn out to shine a light on my future career. But learning to find and define those moments that shape us can make us see our gifts and our potential.

When Andrew Kafoury wrote about his love for theater, the authenticity of his voice, the depth of his experience on and behind the stage came across.

> I love acting. I love putting on costumes and becoming creatures I am not. I love my skin sweating as bright lights send heat soaking through my body. I love getting to know my cast, watching the drama behind the drama. I love the quick change, the black out, the dry ice and stage combat! I love cranky stage managers and quiet co-stars. I love watching ego-stricken actors fall into decline while a new face emerges from the shadows. I love the monster special effects that steal the show, and that oh-so-precious moment when you, the actor, send the audience head over heels with laughter. I love the call sheet with my name on it, and the director who calls to say I'm perfect for the part. I love the shows that I wish would go on forever, and even the ones I can't stand till they're over.

> I love sitting backstage, exhausted from the matinee, and knowing in another two hours I'll go out there and do it again. I love to play the bad guy, and I love getting that killer role I've always wanted. Hell, I love it when they toss a spear in my hand and say, "Go stand in the corner." I love classical and contemporary, tragedy and comedy, romance and swashbuckling! I live for the moment when I run on stage for curtain call, and the applause gets just a little bit louder. I love the smooth feeling of

steady memorization, and those intense moments when something unexpected happens, like an actor not showing up two minutes before curtain, so the stage hands have to make a split second decision because, damn it, man, the show MUST go on.

To get students started on this piece, we once again began by reading student essays. They saw the range of illuminating moments that Jefferson graduates described from Dyan Watson's playing saxophone in Japan (see page 93) to Chetan Patel, who attends University of Chicago, learning about his heritage. (See page 94.) The model essays explored the sweep of possibilities.

Before we read the pieces, I asked students to imagine they were members of the admissions committee at a college. We played through scenarios: Who would they want on their campus? Would diversity be important? Would it be an asset? Would they only let in people who could afford it? Were they looking for valedictorians? What other skills would they look for? Would they want people who spoke one language? The same language?

I wanted students to question the way things are, to create a sense of possibility. In some countries post-secondary education is a right. Students and their families are not forced to mortgage their homes and their futures to attend college. How would that change admissions?

After this preparation, I told them to jot notes on what they learned about each student as they read their essays. What did the piece make clear about the student that their GPA and SAT scores might not? Would this be a person they'd want on their campus? Why or why not? What skills would this student bring to the school that might not be traditionally prized?

Students began to see how the essays made the writer come alive through their stories. I made the point that they could write a resumé that lists their achievements, but only through story and essay could they give the admissions committee a ticket into their lives.

Rather than a recitation of facts, I wanted students to create the scene, so we could see them on the street, in the room, on stage. I used a visualization to push them into the scene. I asked them to remember a particular moment or to freeze one frame of an incident. Where are they? What does it look like? Smell like? Who else is there? What are they saying? When they opened their eyes, I asked them to capture the scene. Chelsea Henrichs wrote:

> *"If I came to see you, I'd ask for my money back! I've paid. Give me something to watch! If you're going to dance, dance." The tiny, dark woman says over the banging of the piano. We all laugh, but I take what she says and store it away. Her words make me push myself harder. I am the fairy queen. I am Juliet. I start to lose myself in this character that I have created for her. I imitate her gracefulness that I know dazzled audiences, though she's never told me. I watch her and I see where I hope to get. I want to be beautiful and powerful at the same time. I want people to want to watch me dance. (See page 96 for the complete essay.)*

Eric Mashia opened his essay with a scene from a middle school classroom:

> *I was in Mrs. Klein's seventh grade English class. We sat in a circle telling what we wanted to be when we grew up. I remember Sara said, "I want to be a police officer." Good luck I thought. If she saw someone fighting, she would run the other direction. Then there was Nathan who hoped to become a professional football player. If he could make it being four-foot seven and weighing less than one hundred pounds then the saying, "You can become whatever you want to" really is true. But then came my turn. I said, "I want to be the next Montel Williams, a male Oprah Winfrey."*
>
> *As middle schoolers we were into the newest news. Who was going with Demetria or Lameka, and who just got beat up in the fight yesterday. My quest for scooping news led me to write for my school newspaper at Jefferson High School.*

Teaonshae started her essay with a scene of her doing hair on the front porch of her house. Ayanna opened with a story about a teacher who believed in her as a way of edging into an essay about wanting to become a teacher herself.

Writing college essays was not easy — not only because students still needed work on their writing skills, but more importantly, because some students needed to discover there was room at the "academy" or the institutions of higher education for them. Their frustration was more often about the distance between what they thought colleges want and their assessment of their lives.

Certainly, not all of my students attended post-secondary institutions. Many started, dropped out, started over. And one unit — even with college visits, panels of graduates, and college essays — cannot

> **They can write a resumé that lists their achievements, but only through story and essay can they give the admissions committee a ticket into their lives.**

overcome the gap between the class differences between those who wonder *where* they will go to college and those who wonder *if* they will go to college. The long tongue of the road towards equality is neither certain nor easy, but as teachers we must continue to travel it. ■

References

Hurston, Zora Neale. *Their Eyes Were Watching God*. Urbana, IL: University of Illinois Press, 1991.

Letts, Billie. *Where the Heart Is*. New York: Warner, 1995, p. 292.

The Politics of Language

Teaching Standard English: Whose Standard?

When I was in ninth grade Mrs. Delaney, my English teacher, wanted to demonstrate the correct and incorrect ways to pronounce the English language. She asked Helen Draper, whose father owned several clothing stores in town, to stand and say "lawyer." Then she asked me, whose father owned a bar, to stand and say "lawyer." Everyone burst into laughter at my pronunciation.

What did Mrs. Delaney accomplish? Did she make me pronounce lawyer correctly? No. I say attorney. I never say lawyer. In fact, I've found substitutes for every word my tongue can't get around and for all the rules I can't remember.

For years I've played word cop on myself. I stop what I'm saying to think, "Objective or subjective case? Do I need I or me here? Hmmm. There's a lay coming up. What word can I substitute for it? Recline?"

> **People of diverse backgrounds are mixed together and when they come out they're supposed to look like Vanna White and sound like Dan Rather. The only diversity we celebrate is tacos and chop suey at the mall.**

And I've studied this stuff. After all, I've been an English teacher for over 20 years. I've gone through all of the Warriner's workbook exercises. I even found a lie/lay computer program and kept it in my head until I needed it in speech and became confused again.

Thanks to Mrs. Delaney, I learned early on that in our society language classifies me. Generosity, warmth, kindness, intelligence, good humor aren't enough — we need to speak correctly to make it. Mrs. Delaney taught me that the "melting pot" was an illu-sion. The real version of the melting pot is that people of diverse backgrounds are mixed together and when they come out they're supposed to look like Vanna White and sound like Dan Rather. The only diversity we celebrate is tacos and chop suey at the mall.

Unlearning "Inferiority"

It wasn't until a few years ago that I realized grammar was an indication of class and cultural background in the United States and that there is a bias against people who do not use language "correctly." Even the terminology "standard" and "nonstandard" reflects that one is less than the other. English teachers are urged to "correct" students who speak or write in their home language. A friend of mine, whose ancestors came over on the Mayflower, never studied any of the grammar texts I keep by my side, but she can spot all of my errors because she grew up in a home where Standard English was spoken.

And I didn't, so I've trained myself to play language cop. The problem is that every time I pause, I stop the momentum of my thinking. I'm no longer pursuing content, no longer engaged in trying to persuade or entertain or clarify. Instead I'm pulling Warriner's or Mrs. Delaney out of my head and trying to figure out how to say something.

"Ah, but this is good," you might say. "You have the rules and Mrs. Delaney to go back to. This is what our students need."

But it doesn't happen that way. I try to remember the rule or the catchy phrase that is supposed to etch the rule in my mind forever, like, "people never get laid," but I'm still not sure if I use it correctly. These side trips cost a lot of velocity in my logic.

Over the years my English teachers pointed out all of my errors — the usage errors I inherited from my mother's Bandon, Oregon dialect, the spelling errors I overlooked, the fancy words I used incorrectly. They

Rick Reinhard

find Fred doodling pictures of Playboy bunnies. When I sat down and asked him why he didn't write, he said he couldn't.

I explained to him that in this class his writing couldn't be wrong because we were just practicing our writing until we found a piece we wanted to polish, in the same way that he practiced football every day after school, but only played games on Fridays. His resistance lasted for a couple of weeks. Around him other students struggled with their writing, shared it with the class on occasion and heard positive comments. Certainly the writing of his fellow students was not intimidating.

On October 1st, after reading the story, "Raymond's Run" by Toni Cade Bambara (1972), about trusting people in our lives, Fred wrote for the first time: "I remember my next door neighbor trusted me with some money that she owed my grandmother. She owed my grandmother about 25 dollars." Fred didn't make a lot of errors. In this first piece of writing it looked like he had basic punctuation figured out — except for the odd capitals in the middle of the sentence. He didn't misspell any words. And he didn't make any usage errors. Based on this sample, he appeared to be a competent writer.

However, the biggest problem with Fred's writing was that he didn't make mistakes. This piece demonstrates his discomfort with writing. He wasn't taking any risks. Just as I avoid lawyer and lay, he wrote to avoid errors instead of writing to communicate or think on paper.

When more attention is paid to the way something is written or said than to what is said, students' words and thoughts become devalued. Students learn to be silent, to give as few words as possible for teacher criticism.

did this in good faith, in the same way, years later, I "correct" my students' "errors" because I want them to know the rules. They are keys to a secret and wealthier society and I want them to be prepared to enter, just as my teachers wanted to help me.

And we should help kids. It would be misleading to suggest that people in our society will value my thoughts or my students' thoughts as readily in our home languages as in the "cash language," as Jesse Jackson calls it. Students need to know where to find help, and they need to understand what changes might be necessary, but they need to learn in a context that doesn't say, "The way you said this is wrong."

When Fear Interferes

English teachers must know when to correct and how to correct — and I use that word uneasily. Take Fred, for example. Fred entered my freshman class unwilling to write. Every day during writing time I'd

Valuing What We Know

Students must be taught to hold their own voices sacred, to ignore the teachers who have made them feel that what they've said is wrong or bad or stupid. Students must be taught how to listen to the knowledge they've stored up, but which they are seldom asked to relate.

Too often students feel alienated in schools. Knowledge is foreign. It's about other people in other times.

> ## HEY! GO BOY!
>
> By Thieson Ngyuen
>
> Hey! Go boy!
> Don't let people disrespect you.
> When I can't read I feel sad too.
> They make fun about mistakes
> The pronunciation that I shouldn't make.
> But what else can I do?
> When I started English later than you.
> Hey! Go boy!
> Just try your best.

At a conference I attended, a young woman whose mother was Puerto Rican and whose father was Haitian said, "I went through school wondering if anyone like me had ever done anything worthwhile or important. We kept reading and hearing about all of these famous people. I remember thinking, 'Don't we have anyone?' I walked out of the school that day feeling tiny, invisible, unimportant."

As teachers, we have daily opportunities to affirm that our students' lives and language are unique and important. We do that in the selections of literature we read, in the history we choose to teach, and we do it by giving legitimacy to our students' lives as a content worthy of study.

One way to encourage the reluctant writers who have been silenced — and the not-so-reluctant writers who have found a safe but sterile voice— is to ask them to recount their experiences. I sometimes recruit former students to share their writing and their wisdom as a way of underscoring the importance of the voices and stories of teenagers. Easton Rochelle, a student in my senior writing class, brought in a few of her stories and poems to read to my freshmen. Rochelle, like Zora Neale Hurston, blends her home language with Standard English in most pieces. She read the following piece to open a discussion about how kids are sometimes treated as servants in their homes, but also to demonstrate the necessity of using the language she hears in her family to develop characters:

> "I'm tired of washing dishes. Seems like every time our family gets together, they just got to eat and bring their millions of kids over to our house. And then we got to wash the dishes."

> I listened sympathetically as my little sister mumbled these words.

> "And how come we can't have ribs like the grownups? After all, ain't we grown?"

> "Lord," I prayed, "seal her lips while the blood is still running warm in her veins."

> Her bottom lip protruded farther and farther as she dipped each plate in the soapy water, then rinsed each side with cold water (about a two second process) until she felt the majority of suds were off.

> "One minute we lazy women that can't keep the living room half clean. The next minute we just kids and gotta eat some funky chicken while they eat ribs."

> . . . Suddenly it was quiet. All except my little sister who was still talking. I strained to hear a laugh or joke from the adults in the living room, a hint that all were well, full and ready to go home. Everyone was still sitting in their same spots, not making a move to leave.

> "You ought to be thankful you got a choice."

> Uh-oh. Now she got Aunt Macy started. . . .

After reading her work, Rochelle talked about listening to her family and friends tell their stories. She urged the freshmen to relate the tales of their own lives — the times they were caught doing something forbidden, the times they got stuck with the dishes, the funny/sad events that made their freshman year memorable. When Rochelle left, students wrote more easily. Some. Some were afraid of the stories because as Rance said, "It takes heart to tell the truth about your life."

But eventually they write. They write stories. They write poems. They write letters. They write essays. They learn how to switch in and out of the language of the powerful as Rochelle does so effortlessly in her "tired of chicken" piece.

Sharing Lessons

And after we write, we listen to each other's stories in our read-around circle where everyone has the opportunity to share, to be heard, to learn that knowledge can be gained by examining our lives. (See page 14 for a complete description of this activity.) In the circle, we discover that many young women encounter sexual harassment, we learn that store clerks follow Black students, especially males, more frequently than they follow white students, we find that many of our parents drink or use drugs, we learn that many of us are kept awake by the crack houses in our neighborhoods.

Before we share, students often understand these incidents individually. They feel there's something wrong with them. If they were smarter, prettier, stronger, these things wouldn't have happened to them. When they hear other students' stories, they begin to realize that many of their problems aren't caused by a character defect. For example, in Literature and U.S. History, a young man shared a passionate story about life with his mother, who is a lesbian. He loved her, but felt embarrassed to bring his friends home. He was afraid his peers would think he was gay or reject him if they knew about his mother.

After he read, the class was silent. Some students cried. One young woman told him that her father was gay and she'd experienced similar difficulties, but hadn't had the courage to tell people about it. She thanked him. Another student confided that his uncle had died from AIDS the year before. What had been a secret shame became an opportunity for students to discuss sexual diversity more openly. Students who were rigidly opposed to the idea of homosexuality gained insights into their own homophobia — especially when presented with the personal revelations from their classmates. Those with homosexual relatives found new allies with whom they could continue their discussion and find support.

Sharing also provides a "collective text" for us to examine the social roots of problems more closely: Where do men/women develop the ideas that women are sexual objects? Where do they learn that it's OK for men to follow women or make suggestive remarks? Where is it written that it's the woman's fault if a man leers at her? How did these roles develop? Who gains from them? Who loses? How could we make it different? Our lives become a window to examine society.

Learning the "Standard" Without Humiliation

But the lessons can't stop there. Fred can write better now. He and his classmates can feel comfortable and safe sharing their lives or discussing literature and the world. They can even understand that they need to ask "Who benefits?" to get a better perspective on a problem. But still when they leave my class or this school, some people will judge them by how their subjects and verbs line up.

So I teach Fred the rules. It's the language of power in this country, and I would be cheating him if I pretended otherwise. I teach him this more effectively than Mrs. Delaney taught me because I don't humiliate him or put down his language. I'm also more effective because I don't rely on textbook drills; I use the text of Fred's writing. But I also teach Fred what Mrs. Delaney left out.

I teach Fred that language, like tracking, functions as part of a gatekeeping system in our country. Who gets managerial jobs, who works at banks and who works at fast food restaurants, who gets into what college and who gets into college at all, are decisions linked to the ability to use Standard English. So how do we teach kids to write with honesty and passion about their world and get them to study the rules of the cash language? We go back to our study of society. We ask: Who made the rules that govern how we speak and write? Did Ninh's family and Fred's family and LaShonda's family all sit down together and decide on these rules? Who already talks like this and writes like this? Who has to learn how to change the way they talk and write? Why?

We make up our own tests that speakers of Standard English would find difficult. (See p. 113.) We read articles, stories, poems written in Standard English and those written in home language. We listen to videotapes of people speaking. Most kids like the sound of their home language better. They like the energy, the poetry, and the rhythm of the language. We determine when and why people shift. We talk about why it might be necessary to learn Standard English.

Asking my students to memorize the rules without asking who makes the rules, who enforces the rules, who benefits from the rules, who loses from the rules, who uses the rules to keep some in and keep others out, legitimates a social system that devalues my students' knowledge and language. Teaching the rules without reflection also underscores that it's OK for others — "authorities" — to dictate something as fundamental and as personal as the way they speak. Further, the study of Standard English without critique encourages students to believe that if they fail, it is because they are not smart enough or didn't work hard enough. They learn to blame themselves. If they get poor SAT scores, low grades on term papers or

> As teachers, we have daily opportunities to affirm that our students' lives and language are unique and important. We do that in the selections of literature we read, in the history we choose to teach, and we do it by giving legitimacy to our students' lives as a content worthy of study.

essays because of language errors, fail teacher entrance exams, they will internalize the blame; they will believe they did not succeed because they are inferior instead of questioning the standard of measurement and those making the standards.

We must teach students how to match subjects and verbs, how to pronounce lawyer, because they are the ones without power and, for the moment, have to use the language of the powerful to be heard. But, in addition, we need to equip them to question an educational system that devalues their life and their knowledge. If we don't, we condition them to a pedagogy of consumption where they will consume the knowledge, priorities, and products that have been decided and manufactured without them in mind.

It took me years to undo what Mrs. Delaney did to me. Years to discover that what I said was more important than how I said it. Years to understand that my words, my family's words, weren't wrong, weren't bad — they were just the words of the working class. For too long, I felt inferior when I spoke. I knew the voice of my childhood crept out, and I confused that with ignorance. It wasn't. I just didn't belong to the group who made the rules. I was an outsider, a foreigner in their world. My students won't be. ■

Reference

Bambara, Toni Cade. *Gorilla, My Love*. New York: Random House, 1972.

For Further Reading

Delpit, Lisa. "The Silenced Dialogue: Power and Pedagogy in Educating Other People's Children." *Harvard Educational Review*, (58)3, 1988, pp. 280-98.

Shor, Ira. *Freire for the Classroom*. Portsmouth, NH: Heinemann, 1987.

Shor, Ira, and Freire, Paulo. *A Pedagogy for Liberation*. South Hadley, MA: Bergin & Garvey, 1987.

Rick Reinhard

Reading, Writing, And Righteous Anger:
Teaching about Language and Society

Several years ago, I attended a literature workshop where we read a chapter from Olive Burns' novel *Cold Sassy Tree* (1984). The workshop was wonderful, full of useful techniques to engage students in literature: a tea party, text rendering, writing from our own lives using an innocent narrator as Burns does. Great methodology. And strategies I use with almost every unit I teach. But the entire workshop ignored the issues of race, class, and gender that run like a sewer through the novel — from the "linthead" factory workers, to the African Americans who work as kitchen help, to the treatment of women. The workshop explored none of this.

For too many years in my teaching career, I also ignored the social text. I thought it was sufficient to talk about setting. I hadn't been taught anything different. Saying the novel was set in the South during such and such a period was enough.

But it's not enough. Not questioning why the "lintheads" and the African Americans in the novel were treated differently, not exploring the time Grandpa blamed Grandma for not bearing him a son allows readers to silently accept these practices as just. Young women internalize the idea that they must be beautiful and bear sons to be loved. Working class students learn that it is their fault if they are poor like the lintheads in the novel. When I taught literature without

examining the social and historical framework, I condoned the biased social messages students absorbed.

Today, I attempt to teach students to question the basic assumptions of our society that legitimate inequality — whether based on nationality, race, class, gender, or any manifestation of these, like language or dress. For example, why were the "lintheads" — as the factory workers were called — poor? In a society that has so much, why do some starve while others get fat? Why do women have to conform to conventional standards of beauty to be loved?

In most units of study I use a basic format:

- A question which provokes the examination of historical, literary, and social "texts."

- The study and involvement of students' lives.

- The reading of a variety of texts from novels to historical documents to first-person narratives to movies, speakers, role plays, and field trips.

- A final project that opens the possibility for students to act on their knowledge.

This kind of teaching is big and messy. It combines the reading and writing of poetry, fiction, essays, historical documents and statistics, lots of discussions, read-arounds (see page 14 for a complete description of this activity), days of writing, responding, and revising student work.

This kind of teaching takes time. We can't race through a half dozen novels. I'm forced to make difficult choices about what I include and what I leave out. Often one novel will provide the center, or core, and I'll surround it with other texts, role plays, videos, improvisations, museum visits, or speakers.

The Question

In my Contemporary Literature and Society classes, we explore the question, "How is language political?" Why language? Because language is about power. And critical literacy is about "reading" and uncovering power relationships in the world. Whose language or dialect has power? Whose doesn't? Why not? What happens if someone has a Mexican or Vietnamese accent? A British accent? How does language benefit some and hurt others?

> **When I taught literature without examining the social and historical framework, I condoned the biased social messages students absorbed.**

Through the study of language, students look behind the social hierarchy that ranks some languages as standard and others as substandard. We ask: Whose papers get corrected for language errors and whose are judged correct? How might that affect students' feelings about themselves? Their language? Their family? We ask: Who scores high on SATs and who doesn't? We stop pretending that grades, achievement, high test scores are based only on a meritocracy where everyone started out equal. We look at how some privileges, like high SATs, might look like they are earned, but really have been inherited based on social class or race or gender. We look at pieces of literature, we read studies, we examine our own lives as we search for answers to the question: How is language political?

We also look at how language is embedded in culture. Language isn't just about subjects and verbs; it's about music, dance, family relationships; it's about how we view the present and the future. We read Jack Weatherford's study of native languages (1991). What might a language full of nouns tell us about a culture? How about a language full of verbs? A language with no past tense? No future tense? A language with no word for "read" or "write"? A language with six words for love?

Students' Lives at the Center

To teach students to read and write and think critically about the "word and the world," as Paulo Freire phrases it (Shor and Freire, 1987), means to engage them in a study of their lives in relation to the larger society.

It is important for students to write about their lives even when they are studying the politics of language because their lives are part of the text of the class. Their experience with language helps us understand how society creates hierarchies that rank some languages as "standard" and others as "substandard"; some as "educated," others as "ignorant."

Bringing in students' language is more than a feel-good gesture, more than erasing the shame that comes when one's language is considered inferior. What Lois Yamanaka (undated) writes about Pidgin, I could have written about my home language, and many of my students could write about their linguistic heritage — from Ebonics to Spanish to Vietnamese:

> *Our present day Pidgin, Hawai'i Creole English expression — labeled the language of ignorant people, substandard and inappropriate in any form of expression, written or oral — has retained its stigma of poverty, racism and powerlessness from the early days of the plantation system.*

> *For me, writing my poems and stories using Pidgin has been a very painful process. I cannot begin to tell of the importance of this language whose speakers have been "systematically and institutionally duped into believing that we have no literary value or voice."*

As we discuss language and culture, students write pieces about themselves, their homes, their family sayings, their language. We do what Yamanaka urges. We remember our homes without censoring:

> *Language is power. A so-called bastard language is charged with its own rage and energy. . . . I will never move away from Pidgin. . . . Why would I move away? I tell young writers to use their ears and their sounds because sounds sometimes come with such clarity, and not everyone can render them in words. If you can do it in Samoan, Armenian, Filipino, or Vietnamese, do it. I tell my students to clean their ears, listen, and render sound. . . . I will say it again — and I have come a very long way in believing and knowing this — it is impossible to ban the sound of one's memory.*

I want students to hear the cadences of home and cherish them. I encourage them to use their "home language" as they write stories and poems. We read, for example, Toni Cade Bambara's short stories and excerpts from Sandra Cisneros so they understand

106

Susan Lisa Ruggles

how to mix home language and "Standard English." The following excerpt from Pam Clegg's story, "My Nerves Wasn't All She Got On" tells about getting in double trouble — first, for her messy room, and then for talking back to her mother:

"Pamela!"

What she want now? Dog, every time I start watching TV she always wants to call.

"Pamela, git up here now!" Mama yelled down the steps.

I knew it. She always gots to go upstairs in our room.

"Ma'am?" I said when I entered the room.

"Didn't I tell you to clean this closet and this room? It look like a pig sty. How can you live in this mess?"

"Mama, this ain't my stuff. It's Tracy's. I cleaned my part of the room."

"Girl, how you gon' tell me this is Tracy's stuff when I'm looking at the clothes I bought you scattered around this room and thrown in this closet?"

"Mama, that's not..."

"Girl, what is this? Now you tell me I didn't buy this for you." She held up a pair of pants that she bought me for school that year. Then she turned and looked in the closet. "Oh, my Lord. Girl, you

got all these good clothes up here just balled up and look at this." She pulled out an ugly brown skirt and showed it to me. I didn't want that thang in the first place. Dog, I wish she would just leave. She always worrying about our room. . . .

Pam's story, published in the 1989-90 *Rites of Passage*, Jefferson's literary magazine, always brings about great sounds of laughter from students. Most of us can relate to the dirty room scene, but for many students the sound of Pam's voice also reminds them of the voices in their homes.

When writing his college essay about a change he made, Alejandro Vidales used home language as a way of presenting and honoring where he comes from:

Growing up in the city of San Diego was hard for me. Both of my uncles had been gang members. My older uncle, José, was in with the 18th, but he lived in L.A. so I didn't see him much. My other uncle, Martín, was a Vato Loco, and he lived with my grandma and me. The only role model I had was my uncle. Man, he was bad, and I wanted to be just like him! The way he talked, walked, even the way he smelled. He was smooth. I remember going cruising with him. "Hey, man, I wanna be como tu when I grow up. I'm going to have more rucas than you. I'm going to be their Latin lover, rolling in my candy apple green low rider with a big Aztec Warrior painted on the hood. I'm going to be the coolest Cholo in San Diego."

Finding the Inside

By Mira Shimabukuro

"When you go to China" I told her, "you don't even need to open your mouth. They already know you are an outsider. . . . They know just watching the way you walk, the way you carry your face. They know you do not belong.

"My daughter did not look pleased when I told her this, that she did not look Chinese. Oh, maybe 10 years ago she would have clapped her hands — hurray — as if this were good news. But now she wants to be Chinese, it is so fashionable. How can she think she can blend in? Only her skin and her hair are Chinese. Inside, she is all American."

- Lindo Jong, in **The Joy Luck Club** by Amy Tan.

When I was in seventh grade being ethnic was the thing to do. My dad is Okinawan, born in Hawaii and that year I let everyone know my Asian-ness. Sushi was in, and I boasted my father's seaweed rolls which would show up in my lunches on occasion. I ate with chopsticks wherever I could, denouncing the forks I was handed in Chinese restaurants I patroned with my Caucasian mother. When a friend came in one day wearing a hapi coat and asked me what the characters meant on the back, I quietly said I did not remember, kicking myself under the table for not keeping up with my Japanese lessons.

That summer I went to Hawaii to visit numerous relatives, and people who I was sure I shared blood with even though I had no idea how. If I asked Dad, it took half an hour for him to remember and then another half an hour for him to explain it to me so that I could even begin to understand. All his relatives were close - even fourth cousins by marriage.

We stayed with Shi-chan auntie on Maui. There I met my twin third cousins, Stacy and Tracy Okohama. They were a year older than I, but we ended up spending all of our time together. We went to the beach, helped Auntie make rice crackers and kimpiro and went on long drives in the back of my second cousin's pickup. One of those evenings I learned what Lindo Jong had tried to explain to her daughter.

It was a beautiful night. Sunsets in Hawaii can't be beat and the black-orange sky proved to be no exception. We were coming back from a visit to Auntie Sue's pineapple farm where she had shown me how to tell when the pineapple is ready for picking. Stacy and Tracy were discussing where different cities were on the mainland when they suddenly slipped into words I couldn't understand.

"Where you stay now, Mira, eh?" Stacy nodded at me.

"With Auntie, you know that."

"No where you stay now?" she repeated. Tracy started to giggle.

"What do you mean?"

"She don't understand, Stace," Tracy laughed.

"Come on, tell me."

"You no speak Pidgin?"

"I don't know," I said. "Is that like eakingspay-isthay-ayway?"

Tracy and Stacy howled, rolling around in the truck.

"What you say? No dat's Pig Latin," they said trying to sit up.

They decided to speak heavy Pidgin the rest of the night. Shi-chan auntie would give them the old "stink-eye", as they called it, but they kept on anyway. When my dad was in the room, he giggled at their words and my other cousins would try to smother their laughs. I alone could not understand. And they knew. At home I had paraded around in front of my friends. The Hawaiian expert. It was in my blood, and to me that counted. I had lived on the mainland all my life and my cousins knew this, even before we met, but tonight they felt it and so did I.

Later in **Joy Luck Club** Jing-Mei Woo talks about visiting family in China. As a child, she had thought of herself as Caucasian and all her friends agreed. She thinks back to her mom, so different from Lindo, and her words. "Someday you will see," said her mother. "it is in your blood, waiting to be let go."

Not until Jing-Mei meets her half sisters does she understand.

"And I now see what part of me is Chinese. It is so obvious. It is my family. It is in our blood. After all these years, it can finally be let go."

I'm now standing at my father's wedding reception. Shi-chan auntie is showing me photos of Stacy and Tracy's graduation. Their smiles are barely seen under the layers of leis on their shoulders. They are happy, seemingly breathless that they have made it. I know they are not thinking of that night as I am now.

The wedding photographer calls us over. It is time for the big family photo. I scoot in next to Dad and put my arm around him. Behind me, Auntie Sue, Shi-chan and all the others crowd in. I am most certainly not the Hawaiian expert now. The generations surround me, half-Pidgin, half-mainland. Say cheese, he says behind the camera and we do. It is now that I see what part of me is Asian, what part comes from Hawaii. It is too obvious. It is my family. It is in our blood. I now can let go of that night.

My uncle would hit me on the head and laugh, "You don't know what it's really like to be a Cholo — always running from the police, watching your back. You don't want to be a Cholo because once you're in, you can't get out."

When he told me these things, I didn't care, I just thought he didn't want me to be cool like him. Every morning I would wake up, put on my khakis and creased shirt that my abuelita *ironed the night before. My black shoes were so shiny I could almost see myself in them. I slicked back my hair so much that my* abuelita *would say, "Parece que te lambio una vaca."[1] Then I put on my hair net and headed out the door.*

My observation over the past decade is that students write more freely when they use words and phrases of their home. Home language is the link for many students that starts the words flowing.

Bringing students' languages, ancestors, sayings from their homes into the classroom validates their languages, culture, and history as topics worthy of study. It says they count; their language is part of a history that most textbooks ignore, or worse, label as incorrect. Speaking their languages, telling their stories breaks the pattern of silence and shame that "correction" without historical and linguistic context breeds. How else can we understand our society and our world if we don't bring in the lives of the people living it? As Lois Yamanaka wrote, "With language rests culture. To sever the language from the mouth is to sever the ties to homes and relatives, family gatherings, foods prepared and eaten, relationships to friends and neighbors. Cultural identity is utterly akin to linguistic identity."

Of course, I also have the responsibility of teaching students how to write in "Standard Edited Written English" because that is the "cash language" valued in our society. As my former student Khalila noted when she returned from college to speak to my class, "No one asks you to write poetry in college. They want essays and they want them correct."

Reading the Word and the World

During this unit we read literature from diverse perspectives: "Wild Meat and Bully Burgers" a short story by Lois Ann Yamanaka (1996) about the politics of Pidgin in Hawai'i, *Pygmalion* by George Bernard Shaw (1914) about the politics of English in England, "How to Tame a Wild Tongue" by Gloria Anzaldúa (1987) and "Achievement of Desire" from *Hunger of Memory* by Richard Rodriguez (1992) about the politics of English for people whose home language is Spanish. We also read a segment of *Brothers and Sisters*

by Bebe Moore Campbell (1994), "From Africa to the New World and into the Space Age," the first chapter of Geneva Smitherman's book *Talkin' and Testifyin': The Language of Black America* (1997), and the Ebonics issue of the journal *Rethinking Schools* (Perry and Delpit, 1997).

We read these pieces, talk back to them, examine how the characters feel about themselves, their families, culture, and race. As they read, I ask students to take notes on their readings, to think about why one language is standard while the rest struggle under labels of "lazy," "incompetent," or "broken," to think about whose languages are in those categories and whose aren't. I encourage students to "talk back" to these readings, to imagine they are in a conversation with the writer.

For example, when responding to Smitherman's article, "Black English/Ebonics: What It Be Like?" in the Rethinking Schools issue on Ebonics, Kesha wrote, "I used to think that Ebonics meant we couldn't speak proper English, that we were dumb. I'm glad we learned the true history [of how Ebonics came from Africa]." Later, reading the same piece, she noted, "Reading these articles and watching the video [*Black on White: The Story of English* (1986)] made me realize that the words I speak and the way I speak came from my African people. I felt pride."

> **Bringing students' languages, ancestors, sayings from their homes into the classroom validates their languages, culture, and history as topics worthy of study. It says they count; their language is part of a history that most textbooks ignore, or worse, label as incorrect.**

Ebony wrote, "People don't understand Ebonics, so they call it ghetto or slang. They need to learn the history." Saqualla noted, "A lot of us who speak Ebonics are ashamed of our talk because the society we live in expects something different, looks down on us." Responding to the quote, "Attitudes shape expectations and a teacher's expectations shape performance," Niambi wrote, "This is so true. A kid can tell if they are being treated as if they are stupid, and many times feel they must be if a teacher says they are."

Our discussions on these articles and pieces of literature spark heated debates. After reading Rodriguez's "Achievement of Desire," students argued about the need to leave their culture and language behind in order to succeed. They compared Rodriguez to Esther in Campbell's *Brothers and Sisters* — people who move

[1] Translation: "It looks like a cow licked your head."

up, "act white," and leave their culture and their people behind. Students asked each other: Should LaKeesha, a young mother with a desire to get off welfare and become a bank clerk, get the job even if she speaks "nonstandard English"? How much are we willing to change in order to get ahead? Is speaking Standard English acting white? Does everyone have to code-switch on the job? Kesha asked, "Why we always gotta be the ones who have to change?" Goldie asked, "Why can't we be the standard?" and Masta asked, "Who made the standard? Who died and made them the standard makers anyway?"

There are no easy answers to these questions. Brandon argued that it was economic suicide to think that a person who spoke nonstandard English could make it in the marketplace without learning the cash language. Licy defended people's rights to retain their home language without the social stigma.

I also nudge my students to see if any of the characters' lives parallel struggles they face. When students read a book that is as foreign to their lives as Shaw's *Pygmalion*, one of the ways they can engage in the reading is by finding similarities to their own lives, linking Eliza Doolittle's struggle with English in England and the world of my student Alejandro, who crossed the border with his grandmother and a coyote when he was five. Even noncritical reading theory acknowledges that students must be engaged in a text to read it.

Later when students complete critical essays on one

Grandma's Kitchen

By Alisha Moreland

We gathered together in Grandma's kitchen. We gathered in the name of food. In Grandma's domain she was the director and we were the employees. Grandma would lift her chubby hands, one on her hip, the other in the air — "I want you to get da eggs fo' the co'nbread. Alisha, I want you to make the macaroni." We all moved and were guided by THE HAND, Grandma's hand. There was a melody in her kitchen; it kept us moving. Her kitchen contained a rhythm that made our souls dance.

"Them black-eyed peas soaked and ready to go, Grandma."

Grandma turned and gracefully swayed her finger. "Put 'em in that there pot with the ham hocks." The kitchen soon filled with the delicious scents of soul food. Food from our roots, food that made being Black wonderful. Food that spoke to us. We gathered together in the name of food. It is what makes us Black.

Food created an environment for us to use language unique to Grandma's household. I could tell when Grandma had overexerted herself. She'd wipe beads of sweat from her brow. Her food spoke. Her actions spoke.

Looking back on my experiences in my grandma's kitchen, I realized how crucial they were to my development. I am talking about the things that constitute Blackness. My language, tongue, vernacular, vocabulary were Grandma's kitchen. Food was the rhetoric. I know "co'n bread." I am intimate with "black-eyed peas." Language went beyond vocal.

Language is complex. It is the foundation of a culture. It dictates actions, lifestyle, social and economic status. It is powerful. In Grandma's kitchen food spoke for itself. It moved us, directed us. When Grandma spoke, she was as Black as she wanted to be. I have seen the influence of language. Grandma's kitchen immersed me in it. She nurtured me in the language common to our household.

I became aware of the authority of language when I became independent of Grandma's kitchen. Outside of her kitchen, I was kicked, hit, knocked down, cut, bruised, beaten, brutalized, and raped by a foreign authority — Standard English. The only language I had known was the language of Grandma's kitchen. But it became unacceptable when time and age forced me to move beyond my comfort zone.

The summer of 1993, my seventh-grade year, I was selected to go on a trip to Mt. Adams. I had only heard of Mt. Adams on television and from white kids whose parents were enviromentalists. I was elated. "Grandma, I'm goin' to Mt. Adams. My teacher picked me to go."

"That's good. Who you going with?"

"I guess I'm going with them kids from West Sylvan."[1]

"Well, have fun, Baby. Huh, Mt. Adams. I'll say."

I left the following week. We met at the West Sylvan campus. As soon as I arrived, I knew I was in for a change. I observed the people I was going to conquer Mt. Adams with. We all had one thing in common: We were seventh graders.

I looked past the fact that all the other kids were white. Their physical attributes didn't concern me. It was their social attributes that inadvertently ostracized me.

---

1 West Sylvan Middle School is a predominately white school that mostly draws from a wealthy West Hills neighborhood in Portland.

or more of the texts we've read during our unit on the Politics of Language, they write about their lives as well. Alejandro and Hecmarie compared their difficulty learning English when they came to the states, and the taunts they faced, with Eliza's endeavors to learn "proper" English. As Alejandro wrote in his literary essay:

> When I came to this country and started school, it was a new experience. When I arrived in my classroom all the kids stared at me. I had hair like the white kids, but I was darker than them. I was not Black though. I was in between.
>
> I was constantly made fun of because of my accent. It seemed funny to my classmates and all the stereotypes in the cartoons would make them say stuff to me like "Arriba! Arriba!" This really aggravated me. Like Eliza. I wanted to be respected for who I was. If it meant changing, I was willing to do it. I had to teach people who I was and make them respect me. In the process, I had to beat up a couple of kids. But even though I changed, I remembered where I came from. Eliza didn't.

Denedra compared the disruptive role of alcoholism in Eliza's life and the abuse of alcohol in hers. Djamila and Jason discussed the difficulty of going "home" that Eliza and Richard Rodriguez suffer after they've become educated and their own struggles to belong in two communities: Hawaiian/mainland for Djamila and urban African-American/suburban African-American for Jason. Alisha Moreland

---

"Hi, my name is Jennifer. What's yours?"

"I'm Alisha."

Jennifer flashed a smile. "I'm so excited to be here. We get to do some cartography and examine the nitrogen/phosphorous levels in streams."

"I thought we was going to Mt. Adams so we can hike."

Jennifer corrected me, "You mean to say, 'I thought we were going to hike.'"

Hurt and angered, I lashed back, "No, I meant to say what I said." Jennifer took this as a cue to dismiss herself from my presence.

On the long bus ride, Jennifer made fun of me with her friends, "She talks like a dumb fool. Funny like. Ha! Ji! Ji! Ha!"

The joke was on me. I sat by myself in the back of the van and talked to myself, "They ain't no betta' than me. I'm just as good as them." My thoughts were my only form of encouragement.

We arrived at the mountain. The van became saturated with "Wow!" "Awesome!" I bellowed out the first thing that came to my mind when I saw the snow-covered peak, "That's tight."

Silence fell on the van. All eyes were on me. Jason snarled at me, "Where did you get your language from? Tight is not used in the proper context. There is nothing tight about the mountain."

Anger got the better of me, and I snatched the back of his shirt. "Don't tell me what ain't in context."

"Look, Felicia, Alisha, or whatever your name is, you can't even speak properly. 'Ain't' isn't a word. But you wouldn't know this because you 'ain't' smart." The kids on the bus leveled into laughter.

I sat in the back of the van by myself. I tried to think of something positive inside, but couldn't find any morsels of encouragement. Jason had managed to steal them from me.

If they only knew. If those kids only knew that their putdowns cut and bruised me. When they criticized my speaking patterns, they were talking about the place I rose from, the only place I knew. They were reprimanding Grandma's kitchen, the cornbread and black-eyed peas of my home. They were telling me that the love and nurturing I received wasn't good enough. Grandma's kitchen language was love and compassion. According to these kids, my foundation was cracked and unsturdy.

Grandma used the word "ain't" all the time. The word flowed out of her mouth as smooth as water sliding over rocks. Now the word had become tainted.

I am from Grandma's kitchen. Jason and his friends temporarily broke me. Through the cracks I learned an uncharitable lesson: The way you speak dictates who you are. That means you can be as articulate as Bill Clinton or Ron Herndon[2] and have no substance.

I may not have been able to articulate ideas in Standard English in seventh grade, but I had substance. I knew love, compassion, giving, and caring. Grandma's love, time and commitment gave me substance. I have learned to speak and write Standard English, but I must tell you I would choose substance over Standard English any day.

Grandma's kitchen is the reason I am here. Her language recipe will be a part of every kitchen I'm in. It's what I know and love.

---

[2] Ron Herndon is the leader of Portland's Black United Front and a strong, vocal advocate for school equity.

described the safety of her grandmother's kitchen and the harsh reality of the world. (See page 110.)

Taking the Lessons
Beyond the Classroom's Walls

Creating a critical literacy classroom means teaching students to read and write. But instead of asking students to write essays that demonstrate a close reading of a novel, or engaging in a literary evaluation of the text, critical literacy creates spaces for students to tackle larger social issues that have urgent meaning in their lives.

As DeShawn demonstrates in the opening to his essay, these pieces can reflect the struggles students deal with daily:

> I was born Black, raised Black, and I live Black. But now that I have achieved a job outside the general Blackness, some say I'm white because of the language I choose to speak at work. Have I put my culture behind me in order to succeed?

Kaanan Yarbrough wrote his essay to an audience of teachers. He came alive to the study of Ebonics and the struggles around it in Oakland, California. He began to understand his problems with spelling, grammar, and writing might have been influenced by home language. But he also came to see that if his teachers understood more about his "home language" they might have helped him more:

> Teachers should be able to teach students Ebonics if they want. People need to accept it. Ebonics is going to be here forever. You can't take a whole language and get rid of it. Teachers who don't know about Ebonics should learn about it so they can build better relationships with kids. Teachers would understand what kids are talking about when they speak Ebonics.
>
> When I went to school, teachers didn't really teach me how to spell or put sentences together right. They just said sound it out, so I would spell it the way I heard it at home. Everybody around me at home spoke Ebonics, so when I sounded it out, it sounded like home and it got marked wrong. When I wrote something like, "My brother he got in trouble last night," I was marked wrong. Instead of showing me how speakers of Ebonics sometimes use both a name and a pronoun but in "Standard English" only one is used, I got marked wrong. So when my teachers graded my papers, they would either put a lot of corrections on my papers or just give me a bad grade. They didn't

> **When students are "steeped" in evidence from one of the units, they begin to write. I want them to turn their anger, their hurt, their rage into words that might affect other people.**

know where I was coming from.

> People are going to speak and write how they hear things from home. Kids should be able to get taught both, but just know when to speak "proper" and when not to. Like when they go to a job interview, they should speak proper, but when they are at home, they should speak Ebonics. Teachers should teach kids when and where to speak Ebonics.
>
> I feel you can't take a part of someone's history and heritage away from them. In school they teach us about a lot stuff that never happened, like when they say that Christopher Columbus discovered America. They might as well teach kids something that's real, like Ebonics, and help kids out.

Moving Beyond Classroom Walls

When students are "steeped" in evidence from one of the units, they begin to write. I want them to turn their anger, their hurt, their rage into words that might affect other people. We talk about potential audiences and outlets — from parents, to teens, to teachers. Students have written pamphlets for parents to "teach" them about how to use cartoons and videos carefully with their children (see p. 45), and articles about anorexia for middle school girls (see p. 73). Khalilah wrote a piece about the politics of color (see p. 70). Joe sent his cartoon essay off to *Essence* magazine because he wanted African-American males to take note of how they are "dissed" in cartoons. Tammy wrote about the prejudice against "fat" people in our society. In our language arts classrooms, audience shouldn't be a pretend someone out there. We need to find ways for students to express their real concerns about the world to real people.

Sometimes their writing addresses the outrage that comes when they understand that they didn't need to feel the pain or shame that their "secret education" drilled into them. During the follow-up to our unit on the politics of language, students read a chapter from David Owen's book *None of the Above* (1985) called "The Cult of Mental Measurement." (See "Writing the Word and the World," page 58, for a more in-depth discussion of this book.) In this essay, Owen describes the racist past of the SATs and also points out how race continues to be a factor in these kinds of standardized tests today. Students are outraged by their discoveries. A few years ago, Frank rallied the class to go on strike and refuse to take the SATs. After a long debate, the class decided that their strike might hurt them more than it would hurt ETS. Several students vowed that they would not apply to any school that used the SATs as an entrance requirement.

But we did find a way to demystify the tests and use our knowledge to teach others about our outrage. I asked students to analyze each of the verbal sections of the SATs. We examined the instructions, the language, the "objectives" of each section. We looked at how the language and culture of the SATs reflected the world of upper class society. After examining each section and taking the tests a few times, I asked students to construct their own tests using the culture, content and vocabulary of Jefferson High School.

After students complete the test and our unit on language, we take our tests and knowledge up to Ruth Hubbard's education classes at Portland's Lewis and Clark College. Sometimes we find other professors at local universities who welcome my students in as teachers for a day. My students "give" the pre-service teachers the JAT and ask them to imagine that it is a high stakes test that will determine their future — what college they get into, scholarships they'll have access to. After the tests, students discuss the issue of testing and language. In this way, my students have a real audience whose future teaching practice will hopefully be enlightened by their work. They see that what they learn in school can make a difference in the world, and so can they.

Language arts teachers need to explore more than the best practices, the newest techniques in our profession. We need to explore and question the content as well. Too often, critical literacy is seen as valuable in inner city schools or schools where students of color represent the majority of the student body, but it is deemed unnecessary in schools where the majority of students are of European descent.

I'd argue that critical literacy is urgently needed in these schools as well. Students must learn to identify not only how their own lives are affected by society, but also how other people's lives are distorted or maligned by the media and historical, literary, and linguistic inaccuracy. ■

References

Anzaldúa, Gloria. "How to Tame a Wild Tongue," in *Borderlands/La Frontera: The New Mestiza*. San Francisco: Spinsters/Aunt Lute, 1987, pp. 53-64.

Black on White: The Story of English [videorecording], a BBC-TV co-production with MacNeil-Lehrer Productions, in association with WNET. Chicago: PMI/Films, 1986.

Burns, Olive. *Cold Sassy Tree*. New York: Dell, 1984.

Campbell , Bebe Moore. *Brothers and Sisters*. New York: Putnam, 1994, pp. 194-199.

JAT - Jefferson Achievement Test[2]

Each question below consists of a related pair of words or phrases, followed by four lettered pairs of words or phrases. Select the lettered pair that best expresses a relationship similar to that expressed in the original pair.

1. Tony: Play::
a) Broadway : Annie
b) Oscar : Tom Hanks
c) Brandon : Soccer
d) Howard Cherry : sports.

2. New Growth : Perm ::
a) press : straight
b) weave : long
c) corn row : braid
d) nails : fill

3. Ranfal : Lowrider ::
a) Ben Davis : shirt
b) Mexico : cold
c) Mexican : brown
d) Cuete : gun

4. Red Beans and Rice : Play ::
a) corn and tortillas : run
b) song : dance
c) mozzarella : cheese
d) sonata : musical

5. Dancebelt : Boxers ::
a) shoes : socks
b) student : teacher
c) leotard : leg warmers
d) prison : freedom

[2] Not all of these fit the SAT question model. The point is to get students to understand the relationship between tests, culture, and privilege. This is just one vehicle to learn that lesson. Answers: 1) The correct answer, according to Jefferson students, is d: Tony is the award given for plays. At Jefferson the Howard Cherry is awarded for excellence in sports. 2) The correct answer is d: When hair gets "new growth," it needs a perm. When nails get new growth, they need a fill. 3) The correct answer is a: A ranfal is a type of lowrider. Ben Davis is a type of shirt. 4) The correct answer is c: "Red Beans and Rice" is a the name of a play. Mozzarella is a kind of cheese. 5) The correct answer is d: A dancebelt is worn by a male dancer to keep his "privates" in place. Boxers are loose fitting underwear; thus, the difference between a prison and freedom.

Owen, David. *None of the Above: Behind the Myth of Scholastic Aptitude.* Boston: Houghton Mifflin, 1985.

Perry, Theresa, and Delpit, Lisa (Eds.). "The Real Ebonics Debate: Power, Language, and the Education of African-American Children." *Rethinking Schools,* 12(1) [entire issue]. Milwaukee, WI : Rethinking Schools, Fall, 1997.

Rodriguez, Richard. *Hunger of Memory: The Education of Richard Rodriguez.* Boston: Godine, 1982.

Shaw, George Bernard. *Pygmalion: A play in five acts.* Harmondsworth, England: Penguin, 1914.

Shor, Ira, and Freire, Paulo. *A Pedagogy For Liberation: Dialogues On Transforming Education.* South Hadley, MA: Bergin & Garvey, 1987.

Smitherman, Geneva. *Talkin' and Testifyin': The Language of Black America.* Boston: Houghton Mifflin, 1997.

Weatherford, Jack. *Native Roots: How the Indians Enriched America.* New York: Crown, 1991, pp. 195-213.

Yamanaka, Lois. *(1996).Wild Meat and Bully Burgers.* New York: Farrar, Straus & Giroux.

Yamanaka, Lois. (undated). *The politics of Pidgin.* Promotional material. New York: Farrar, Straus & Giroux.

Resources

Baca, Jimmy Santiago. "So Mexicans are Taking Jobs from Americans." In Daniels, James (Ed.), *Letters to America: Contemporary American Poetry on Race.* Detroit: Wayne State University Press, 1995, p. 29.

Crawford, James. *Hold Your Tongue: Bilingualism and The Politics Of English-Only.* Reading, MA: Addison-Wesley, 1992.

Dorfman, Ariel. *The Empire's Old Clothes: What the Lone Ranger, Babar, and Other Innocent Heroes Do to Our Minds.* New York: Pantheon, 1983.

Dunbar, Paul. Laurence. "We Wear the Mask." In Miller, E. Ethelbert, *In Search of Color Everywhere: A Collection of African-American Poetry.* New York: Stewart, Tabori, & Chang, 1994, p. 72.

Espada, Martín (Ed.). *Poetry Like Bread: Poets of the Political Imagination from Curbstone Press.* Willimantic, CT: Curbstone, 1994.

Jordan, June. "Nobody Mean More to Me Than You and the Future Life of Willie Jordan." In *Harvard Educational Review,* 58(3), August 1988, pp. 363-374.

Lyon, George Ella. "Where I'm From." In Blum, Joshua, Holman, Bob, and Pellington, Mark (Eds.). *The United States of Poetry.* New York: Harry N. Adams/Times Mirror, 1995.

McDaniel, Wilma Elizabeth. "Who Said We All Have to Talk Alike" In King, Laurie (Ed.), *Hear My Voice: A Multicultural Anthology Of Literature From The United States.* Menlo Park, CA: Addison-Wesley, 1993.

Walker, Alice. *The Color Purple.* New York: Washington Square, 1982.

Cleo Photography

The Tea Party:
Enticing Reluctant Readers to Read

On the day we begin a new book, I bring cookies and juice to sweeten the learning. I type out five roles for main characters in the book. I color-code cards for easy identification. For example in James Welch's *Fools Crow* (1987) all of the Fast Horse cards are blue, Yellow Kidney cards are yellow, and so on. I try to find enticing passages from the novel to use in these roles, or I write a piece from the character's point of view. I want to create intrigue and questions as well as to familiarize students with the characters before they begin reading. I write the role in first person, so students can more easily get into the character's head. In Zora Neale Hurston's novel *Their Eyes Were Watching God* (1991), Nanny's card reads:

> *Grandma/Nanny: I didn't want Janie taking off and getting pregnant like her mother before her. I wanted more for her. That's why I told her she should marry Mr. Logan Killicks so she could have something for herself. I'm the one who told Janie that I didn't want menfolks, white or Black, making a spit cup outta her. A Black woman can't have much in this world, but before I die I'm gonna make sure Janie's got something.*

I give each student one of the five character cards. On a separate paper, they write down the character's name and key pieces of information that other people

in the class should know: Who they are related to, what their problem is, what has happened in the past that they are worried about. (See the sample worksheet on page 118.) After students write key points about the passage, I instruct them to write some questions or thoughts they have about their person. They don't have much information, so they often have a lot of questions. For example, "What happened to Nanny to make her so bitter?" or "Does Janie love Logan Killicks?" Sometimes I propose a topic I want them to write about as if they are the character. In *Their Eyes Were Watching God,* I ask students to jot down what their character might write about love from their character's point of view.

Getting to Know You: The Tea Party

Then students, in their character roles, get up, walk around, and introduce themselves to other characters. In Hurston's novel, I include roles for Nanny, Tea Cake, Janie, Joe, and Logan. Students must find the four other characters and write down key information about them before returning to their seats. After they've recorded the information on each of the characters, I ask them to formulate questions they want to find out more about as they read the novel. Because some of my more devious students find ways to cut their work short, I tell them that they have to talk to the other characters, not copy their cards.

We share their questions as a way of prompting the reading. After the tea party for *Their Eyes Were Watching God*, the class asked the following questions: Who were the men in Janie's life? Who treated her like a mule? Why do people talk about her? How did Tea Cake teach Janie to love? Why was Nanny so negative? How did Janie do Logan wrong? What is a spit cup and what happened to Nanny that made her think like that?

Sometimes I ask them to draw a diagram of how they think the characters are related to each other. Students share their models on the board or overhead and explain their reasoning. After a tea party on August Wilson's play *The Piano*, for example, one student put the piano in the center of a web and each character in a wheel around it. He explained that the piano seemed to be the center of each character's problems.

> **I've witnessed too many students fail because they are poor readers. When we hand students texts or readings, we have to stop expecting that all students come with the tools they need.**

Raising Questions about Society

Because novels and history too often marginalize people of color, women, or working class people, I create roles to highlight that problem if it exists in the reading or the history we're studying. For example, if a minor character, like a maid or "house man," is invisible in the story, I "invite" this person to the tea party. Before class, I ask a dramatic student to take the "invisible" person's role. I give them the card to read, then during the tea party, I ask them to help me serve tea and cookies. After the rest of the class has discussed the characters they met, this person stands and says something like, "I wasn't invited to your tea party. . . ." and then goes on to explain who they are and what part they play in the book or history.

End of Unit Activities

Whether I am enticing reluctant students to read novels or provoking them to read between the lines of historical texts, the tea party provides an entrance into the new novel or historical study. But I have occasionally used this strategy at the end of a unit when students have conducted research or read novels on their own in literature circles.

For example, after researching people who resisted or worked for the abolition of African-American slavery, one of our culminating activities was a tea party. Students created cards on the abolitionists/resisters they studied — Sojourner Truth, Frederick Douglass,

William Lloyd Garrison, Nat Turner, the Grimke sisters, and more. During the tea party, students collected information on the methods these historical figures used in their struggles to end slavery: uprising, writing, speeches, etc. Using this information, students wrote a paper comparing resistance strategies and advocating for the tactics they felt were most effective.

After a literature circle where students chose to read historical novels or autobiographies written by African Americans — including *Beloved* by Toni Morrison, *Narrative of the Life of Frederick Douglass* by Frederick Douglass, *Kindred* by Octavia Butler, *I, Tituba, Black Witch of Salem,* by Maryse Condé, or *Middle Passage* by Charles Johnson — students in each group created character cards for their novel. Their goal was to entice other students to read their novels as well as share historical information from the book.

In the introduction to *Rethinking Our Classrooms* (1994), the editors wrote, "A social justice classroom offers more to students than do traditional classrooms and expects more from students. Critical teaching aims to inspire levels of academic performance far greater than those motivated or measured by grades and test scores. . . . [O]nly by systematically reconstructing classroom life do we have any hope of cracking the cynicism that lies so close to the heart of massive school failure, and of raising academic expectations and performance for all our children."

How does the tea party do all that? Students can succeed if a teacher is willing to find the strategies and lessons that hook them instead of pushing them out. As a high school teacher I've witnessed too many students fail because they are poor readers. When we hand students texts or readings, we have to stop expecting that all students come with the tools they need. Let's take the time to teach students reading and writing skills instead of bemoaning the fact that so many come unprepared. ■

References

Bigelow, Bill, et al. *Rethinking Our Classrooms: Teaching for Equity and Justice.* Milwaukee, WI: Rethinking Schools, 1994.

Hurston, Zora Neale. *Their Eyes Were Watching God.* Urbana, IL: University of Illinois Press, 1978.

Welch, James. *Fool's Crow.* New York: Penguin, 1987.

Tea Party Roles
Thousand Pieces of Gold

LALU NATHOY/POLLY: This book is the story of my life — a Chinese girl smuggled into the United States to become a prostitute in a mining camp. Although my father called me qianjin, his thousand pieces of gold, he ended up selling me to bandits for two bags of seed. Through my wit and grit, I survived slavery, prostitution, and Chinese Exclusion laws, and yes, I was a prize in a poker game.

CHEN: Don't judge me too harshly for becoming a bandit. You might call me cruel, picking up young girls and selling them into prostitution, giving my own wife to a gang of outlaws, stealing from hard-working farmers, but what is a man to do when life deals him the wrong hand? I worked hard. Fate brought a famine that changed all of our lives.

JIM CHEE: Did I love Lalu? You'll have to read the book to find that out. I sold my strength to a company that contracted labor. A healthy Chinese man cost anywhere from $400 to $1000. I worked six bitter years to pay my debt. Yet this country still won't let me own land or vote. Gold Mountain? Not for the Chinese.

HONG KING: Yes, it's true that I bought Lalu as a slave. I don't call her Lalu. Her name is Polly, and she's my caged bird. She shouldn't complain. I give her plenty to eat and nice clothes to wear. I even let her mine the gold in my saloon floors. In return, she makes me rich. Have I done any worse than her own father who sold her for two bags of seed? I came to this country with nothing. Now I am rich.

CHARLIE: I can make tin cans dance with my gun, and I can shake the blues out of you with my fiddle, but can I make Polly love me? Like Hong King, I'm a saloon owner and a gambler, and I'd risk my life to make sure that Polly doesn't end up deported back to China or swinging from a rope when the anti-Chinese fever comes to town. Is my game good enough to win Polly?

Tea Party Roles
Their Eyes Were Watching God

JANIE: This book is the story of my life with three men. All I wanted was a man I could love and respect who didn't treat me like a mule. People have always had their mouths on me: talking about my hair and what I wear. But believe me, I am a woman who's going to teach you something over the next few weeks.

NANNY: I didn't want Janie taking off and getting pregnant like her mother before her. I wanted more for her. That's why I told her she should marry Mr. Logan Killicks so she could have something for herself. I'm the one who told Janie that I didn't want menfolks, white or Black, making a spit cup outta her. A Black woman can't have much in this world, but before I die I'm gonna make sure Janie's got something.

LOGAN KILLICKS: Janie says I look like some ole skullhead in the graveyard. It's true. I am a great deal older than Janie, but I'm an upstanding man in my community and I own 60 acres. I want a nice looking wife to fix me dinner, maybe help me around the place. I like Janie's long black hair and pretty face. But the woman done me wrong.

JOE STARKS: I told Janie when I first met her that I planned on being a big man. And I kept my promise to her. Everyone looked up to me. I built our town, got streetlights, a post office, a grocery store. I made us the lord and lady of our town. I put Janie on a pedestal where all the townfolks wouldn't be able to touch her. But did I satisfy Janie?

TEA CAKE WOODS: Okay. From Chapter One you hear about me. I'm a sometimes worker, sometimes gambler who is a great deal younger than Janie. She might be 40, but she is still a beautiful woman, the song of my earth. Yes, I asked Janie to pick beans by my side. I am love and laughter and talking in rhymes. I taught Janie how to love.

Tea Party

1. Read your role.

2. Write the passage or key points about your character in the space below.

3. Write some questions or thoughts you have about your character after reading the description.

4. Write about each of the other four characters you meet at the tea party. Write notes as the person introduces him or herself to you.

    *1st Character name:*_____
    Description:

Tea Party continued

2nd Character name:_____

Description:

3rd Character name:_____

Description:

4th Character name:_____

Description:

5. In the space below, draw a diagram, graph, tree, picture, or some kind of
   visual representation that shows the connections between the characters.
   Feel free to add other words into your creation.

6. Write an explanation of your "visualization."

7. Write four questions that you have about the characters or the book.

8. Write three predictions about the book or the characters.

 A PUBLICATION OF RETHINKING SCHOOLS

Jean-Claude Lejeune

Celebrating
The Student Voice

Lawson Inada, a Japanese-American poet and professor of literature at Southern Oregon State College, came to my Literature and U.S. History class one year. His visit was one of those lucky circumstances: The class was in the middle of a unit on the history of education and one of the poems he pulled from his new book *Legends from Camp* was about a classroom experience. When Lawson read "Rayford's Song" (see next page), Bill Bigelow and I realized it was an opportunity for students to remember and explore their own history as students.

In "Rayford's Song," Inada remembered one of his classrooms in the 1930s in Fresno, a town in California's San Joaquin Valley where many people of African, Chinese, Filipino, Japanese, and Mexican descent worked in the fields and canneries. "Our classroom was filled with shades of brown," he recalled. "Our names were Rayford Butler, Consuela and Pedro Gonzales, Susie Chin, and Sam Shimabukuro. We were a mixture. The only white person in the room was our teacher. Our textbooks had pictures and stories about white kids named Dick and Jane and their dog, Spot. And the songs in our songbooks were about Old Susanna coming 'round the mountain and English gardens — songs we never heard in our neighborhood."

Some of the songs mentioned in the poem may not be familiar to today's students. "Old Black Joe," for example, is a Stephen Foster song written in 1860 that attempts to create nostalgic memories for the days of slavery.

"Rayford's Song" arouses strong emotions in students because it speaks to how schools sometimes dampen our hopes and expectations. Many of us have experienced the loss of our voices, our songs, our stories as we travel through schools. We've been told that we are not important, our people are not worth studying, or our language is "wrong." Inada's poem dares to speak about that silencing.

RAYFORD'S SONG

Rayford's song was Rayford's song,
but it was not his alone, to own.

He had it, though, and kept it to himself
as we rowed-rowed-rowed the boat
through English country gardens
with all the whispering hope
we could muster, along with occasional
choruses of funiculi-funicula!

Weren't we a cheery lot —
comin' 'round the mountain
with Susanna, banjos on our knees,
rompin' through the leaves
of the third-grade music textbook.

Then Rayford Butler raised his hand.
For the first time, actually,
in all the weeks he had been in class,
and for the only time before he'd leave.
Yes, quiet Rayford, silent Rayford,
little Rayford, dark Rayford —
always in the same overalls —
that Rayford, Rayford Butler, raised his hand:

> "Miss Gordon, ma'am —
> we always singing your songs.
> Could I sing one of my own?"

Pause. We looked at one another;
we looked at Rayford Butler;
we looked up at Miss Gordon, who said:

> "Well, I suppose so, Rayford —
> if you insist. Go ahead.
> Just one song. Make it short."

And Rayford Butler stood up very straight,
and in his high voice, sang:

> "Suh-whing a-looow
> suh-wheeeet ah charr-ee-oohh,
> ah-comin' for to carr-ee
> meee ah-hooooome. . . ."

Pause. Classroom, school, schoolyard,

neighborhood, the whole world
focusing on that one song, one voice
which had a light to it, making even
Miss Gordon's white hair shine
in the glory of it, glowing
in the radiance of the song.

Pause. Rayford Butler sat down.
And while the rest of us
may have been spellbound,
on Miss Gordon's face
was something like a smile,
or perhaps a frown:

> "Very good, Rayford.
> However, I must correct you:
> the word is 'chariot.'
> 'Chariot.' And there is no
> such thing as a 'chario.'
> Do you understand me?"

> "But Miss Gordon. . . ."

> "I said 'chariot, chariot.'
> Can you pronounce that for me?"

> "Yes, Miss Gordon. Chariot."

> "Very good, Rayford,
> Now, class, before we return
> to our book, would anyone else
> care to sing a song of their own?"

Our songs, our songs were there —
on tips of tongues, but stuck
in throats — songs of love,
fun, animals, and valor, songs
of other lands, in other languages,
but they just wouldn't come out.
Where did our voices go?

Rayford's song was Rayford's song,
but it was not his alone to own.

> "Well, then, class —
> let's turn our books to
> 'Old Black Joe.'"

— Lawson Inada

TEACHING STRATEGY:

Text Rendering

- Ask students to reread the poem and underline the words, lines, or phrases that strike them for some reason — perhaps because these seem important to the poem, maybe because students like the sound or maybe because line relates to something in their lives: e.g., "Where did our voices go? . . . I must correct you. . . . One song . . . . One voice."

- Tell students that they are going to create an oral group poem with the words, phrases, or lines they've selected. Each student can say his or her addition to the oral poem when there is a pause. They might want to use some of the devices of poetry and song — repeating a line or word, echoing.

Sometimes students like to experiment with the call and response more typical in sermons. Encourage students to call out lines or words to form the new poem, in what might be described as the literary equivalent of an improvisational musical composition. To give students the idea, have eight or ten students come in front of the room and experiment as an example.

Sometimes it takes a few times to get this going. Have patience. It's worth it. As students reread the poem, they come to new understandings about the piece. Sometimes I have students begin singing "Swing Low, Sweet Chariot" as background to the poem — or I play a recording of the song softly while we read the poem.

Reflections on the Poem:

- Ask students to write for five or ten minutes about the poem. They might want to describe how the poem made them feel, their reactions to the poem, or memories that the poem evoked. There are no wrong answers.

- After students have written, begin the discussion. Some students might want to read their responses while others might want to use theirs as a springboard for contributing to the class talk about "Rayford's Song."

Student Writing

- Inada speaks of schools silencing students, but he also speaks more broadly about whose lives are included in the curriculum and whose are excluded. Ask students to write about a time when their voices were silenced or they felt their history or stories were silenced or left out of the classroom. They might want to write this as a story or a poem. (See "The Music Lesson" on p. 124 and "His Story" on p. 123. Also see "Elements of Fiction," p. 29, and "Narrative Criteria Sheet," p. 36.)

Read-Around/Collective Text

- Ask students to take notes as they listen to their classmates' papers. They might note how people felt about being silenced, who was silenced, who silenced them, and how they responded. After all the students have read who want to read, ask them to review their notes, think about the stories/poems and write a paragraph or two on the ideas that emerged from the stories. They might want to mention specific people's stories. See p. 14 for more thoughts on using the read-around as a teaching strategy. ■

Reference

Inada, Lawson, *Legends From Camp*. Minneapolis, MN: Coffee House Press, 1993.

HIS STORY
By Masta Davis

Sittin' in the class,
the only spot of color in the place.
We're talkin' about history,
but mine's gone without a trace.
I turn the pages looking for color
at a vigorous pace.
Ahh.
Stop and it slaps me in the face.

Pictures of Africans,
sardines packed in ships.
Damn!
It looks like I'm gettin' ripped.
Ooops!
Here's King.

They always got the brotha'
who had the Dream.

I turn the page and reached
the end?
Slavery ain't how my history began.

Lies, fibs, and mistruths must be corrected.
It's time for my people to be honored and respected.

The Music Lesson
By Sarah Stucki

I don't remember the words that were spoken or if there were any, but I'll always remember his face. His tears. His sobs.

The choir room was extraordinarily noisy. The excitement of a new day was rushing through everyone. There was so much energy in the air. Enough to make lights shine and fires to start miraculously on their own. It was the perfect day for a complete disaster.

Mr. Dunn, the bald, squatty man, lined us up how we sang. The good ones were in the middle, bad ones on the sides, and, of course, his star, his daughter, Brittany, right in front even though she was tall and made it difficult for anyone to be seen behind her.

"All right, class, quiet down." He spoke in his fake, confident voice, the voice that made people squirm and their blood boil.

"Let's begin with scales. Ready and. . . ." He tapped his baton on the music stand. He gripped it as though it held all the power in the world, his power that decided our self-esteem.

"La la la la la la la la la la." We were running through the non-thought containing notes. Clearing our throats to reach the high ones. Quietly bowing our heads for the low ones. Laughing when we made a mistake because we knew we were horrible. So did Mr. Dunn.

"Ha ha ha ha." Loud laughter burst from someone to the left of me. I turned to look and see who it was. My face turned red. It was Mark. My crush on him was given away by my bright face. Suddenly, a loud tapping. I whirled around to look at Mr. Dunn pounding on the music stand for us to stop with our scales.

"Who was laughing just now?" His veins stuck out of his stubby neck. Silence. "Who was it?" He struck the stand with his baton. His eyes searched the risers for the guilty party. The person for whom the lecture would be worthy.

I felt his eyes pass over me. I was afraid for Mark because I just knew that Mr. Dunn would figure out it was him. I guess it didn't help much that 59 out of 60 choir students were staring straight at Mark.

"Mark Hubble." His voice boomed throughout the auditorium. "What was so funny. Mr. Hubble? Why don't you share it with the class?" He stared at Mark with a smirk on his face. Mark just stared at his feet. "Excuse me, Mark, are you deaf? What was so funny?"

A mumble came from Mark's serious face. "Nothing," he said.

"Nothing, huh? Well, if it was just nothing, then why don't you come and show us how well you can sing?" He made this statement as though he were a god. "Come on, Mark. Stand here and sing your scales for the class." He pointed to the front of the music stand.

Mark was a good guy. He obeyed his teachers. He was never mean at all. He was "fortunate" to be at our school because he was from a reservation in Arizona. So, of course, he went to the music stand and stood before his peers. Us.

"You may begin now," Mr. Dunn spoke bluntly. The piano player began the run through the notes as Mark whispered the scale. "Sing louder, Mark, we can't hear you." Mark sang a little louder. Tears began to fall from his eyes. "Mark, you can sing louder. We heard you loudly before when you were laughing." Mark was crying harder now. Sobs began escaping from him.

He was very embarrassed, and I didn't blame him for crying. I would have too if Mr. Dunn had treated me like Mark, and I feel today that the only reason he was so mean to Mark was because Mark was Native-American.

Mark never finished those scales that day, and he never came back again. I don't blame him for that either.

A PUBLICATION OF RETHINKING SCHOOLS

Poetry

Poetry: Reinventing the Past, Rehearsing the Future

Poetry needs to dust its knees and hurry to the nearest basketball court to shoot a little hoop, grab one of its rusty medals and use it for a hopscotch marker, jump rope on a crowded asphalt playground, scrawl graffiti on bathroom walls, get off the shelf and into the lives of kids.

Poetry is held too sacred, revered a bit too much to be useful. Someone lied to us a long time ago when they whispered, "Kids hate poetry." Kids might hate the poetry that rustles in old pages and asks them to bow and be quiet when they come into a room. They might hate reading poetry unlocked only by the teacher's key and writing poetry that's delivered up like the New York Times crossword puzzle, but give them poetry that presses its ear against the heartbeat of humanity and they're in love.

> **Poetry is held too sacred, revered a bit too much to be useful.**

Poetry allows students to crawl inside their own lives as well as the lives of literary and historical characters, where they can emphathize with the Tainos' anger and despair when Columbus "discovered" America, the determination of the striking miners in Pittston, or the triumph of Celie at the dinner scene in Alice Walker's *The Color Purple*. Through poetry kids can give voices to people whose voices usually don't find ways into classrooms or textbooks, including their own.

Poetry and Literature: Personalizing the Connections

Literature does more than provide an account of the lives of its characters — it offers students a chance to peer into the society of a given time period. Earlier in my teaching career, I bypassed opportunities to read this social history and concentrated instead on the elements of fiction. I did this in good faith because I wanted to develop my students' skills and their love of literature, so they would be lifelong readers. But I didn't prepare them to "read" the real world, to decipher the texts that bombard them daily. Now I see reading as a chance not only to rediscover the past, but to teach students to "read" the untold stories in the daily news as well. In literature, as in history, many voices have been silenced — women's, African Americans', Latinos', Native Americans', Asian Americans'. Poetry and other kinds of writing that let students respond on an emotional level to society can be a vehicle to excavate these untold stories.

Because poetry melts students' understanding into a "raw core of feeling," as Sonia, a senior in my Contemporary Literature and Society class said, it also develops children's abililty to empathize with others. In Portland, Oregon, violent, racially motivated crimes have become part of the social landscape. I attribute this, in part, to the view of people of color as "other," to the inability of too many folks to "walk in another's shoes." This is, of course, a very partial explanation for a complex problem, but when the literature that students read — *Huckleberry Finn, To Kill a Mockingbird*, and other "classics" — ignores or stereotypes women and people of color, our students begin to develop one-dimensional portraits of "others" in our society. The poetry that students write

Jean-Claude Lejeune

from the point of view of literary characters can be an entry into the concerns of people who come from different cultural or socioeconomic backgrounds.

After reading *The Color Purple*, for example, students in my Literature and U.S. History class chose one of the characters and wrote a poem from that character's point of view. (See page 134 for the complete lesson.) Don Pendelton wrote in Celie's voice:

> *I am Celie.*
> *I am the cold hard black floor*
> *everyone walked on.*
> *People have stained me and laughed*
> *but I stayed solid under them*
> *and did not squeak.*
> *I am the floor now*
> *but once you go downstairs*
> *I become the ceiling.*

After he read his poem, the class discussed it. His poem opened the analysis of Celie. Instead of simply imposing our questions on the class, Bill Bigelow and I raised our concerns in the context of the students' insights. "How is Celie like the floor? Why is she stained? What does that mean? What events caused that? In what ways did she stay solid? How does

Don's image of Celie change at the end? Why? What brought about the change?" The ending was hopeful — not only about Celie, but about life. It suggested that people can change. What circumstances are necessary for change to occur? Don's metaphor gave us an opening to discuss Celie.

Many of the young men in the class chose to write with women's voices. Through their writings they began to explore the lack of power these women, especially Celie and Squeak, feel in the beginning of the novel. They hooked into their own feelings of fear and helplessness and, we hoped, developed a greater understanding of contemporary women's issues.

Many female students also explored Celie's character through a list of details either from her life or from language "stolen" from Alice Walker. Stephanie Hale remembered Celie as the "'sure is ugly' child/ who was given away/ with a cow" and "put under a man." Ednie Garrison said she was "Sold to marriage/ Sold to life/ Sold to love/ Sold like agates to children/ Sold to a man." Gina wrote that she was "unsightly trash/ tossed to the side of the room. . . . The girl whose life held no worth."

The language these young women used was threaded with the words of commerce — "given," "sold," "worth," which provided an opening for Bill

CELIE
By Lila Johnson

I am a record
on your shelf
the one
dressed
in dust and age
full
of cracked songs
you play
when you are blue
the one
pushed
behind the others
cool black jackets
smooth golden sounds
the one
your liquor-heavy fingers
find
on days
your red water eyes
don't know the difference
just an old record
you play me
when you are blue

I was the quiet you destroyed,
replaced with bulldozers.
I was the children playing in the sun,
chased away, replaced with apathetic workers.
I was the land stolen, for which you gave
nothing,
replaced with nothing.
I was the Olinka people.

Omar made links with the Native American unit we studied earlier in the year. When we asked students to write these poems, we said, "Find your passion. Twist and manipulate the assignment until you can find something you care about." Assignments written only for the teacher are bland and uninspiring. Omar took us at our word. He was less interested in the dynamics between the men and women in the novel than he was in the fate of the Olinka. During class discussion, a poem like Omar's allowed us to recall the Cherokee Trail of Tears and to link the colonial justifications of the British in Africa with Andrew Jackson's similarly racist attitudes toward Native Americans — people he derided as "savages" and "children of the forest." But it also offered an opportunity to think whose story is untold when we read about new land developments, new malls, or new housing tracts. Whose land was taken?

The discussions that follow student poetry are simply more engaging than those in which Bill and I provide all the questions and answers. What struck them, what moved them in the novel, is focused and concentrated into a poem — the heart of their interaction with the book. Class discussion peers into this heart and reads it. Students are more involved because they had a hand in shaping the content of the discussion.

Not every aspect of the novel will be revealed in the students' poetry, perhaps not every character will be written about. But Bill and I wove in important points that escaped the students' lines and discussed missing characters in the context of those who were present. Mr. _____, for example, was rarely if ever, written about. This omission alone gave us an opportunity to raise a number of questions.

The poem can serve as a rough draft, or an outline, for an essay. Once they've found their "passion," students can translate it into another form. Getting students to write poetry is not enough. They must learn to extend their metaphors, to articulate the flashes of insight they found in their poems. Don can use his floor/ceiling metaphor as a framework to describe Celie's change. Ednie and Stephanie can write about the objectification of women. Omar can use his poem to pursue a comparison of the treatment of the Olinka

and me to a discussion of women as commodities. In this transaction women without beauty were "trash" who must be "given away." The poems became a lens through which we could focus on how women are valued, not only in *The Color Purple*, but in our society. Sometimes the poems were masks for the students' questions about their own worth or value as women.

While most students write from Celie's, Harpo's, Sofia's or Shug's lives, a few, like Omar Hanson, take on the Olinka people:

OLINKA
(The Olinka people were a West African tribe in Alice Walker's novel, *The Color Purple*. The Olinka, like indigenous tribes throughout the world, were pushed off their land for the sake of profit.)

I was the roofleaf plant you killed,
replaced with rubber.
I was the village you plowed over,
replaced with asphalt.

128

and Native-American tribes. "The essay just grows out of the poem," Sonia said.

Getting students to write poetry is obviously not enough, nor is it the only strategy we use to discuss the novels, stories, and autobiographies read in class. But it is a valuable method that can help students develop empathy for the "others" in our society whose stories don't find their way into the novels stored in our textbook rooms. And in the process, students discover poetry as a tool of communication.

Poetry into History:
Blowing Life into a Dry Skeleton

History is the tale of the winners. Poetry helps students hear the rest of the story. What's untold? Students reinvent history by writing through a real or imagined character from the past. They live, at least momentarily, the lives of the people they create, and by doing so they come to a greater understanding of the struggles those people engaged in.

Instead of viewing history as a dry skeleton of facts to be memorized, students become aware that those "facts" were the choices made by or imposed on people at the time. Those "facts" were the result of struggles won or lost by those whose lives were affected by the outcomes. This is important. When we, students or teachers, see history as inevitable, we become passive and accept the status quo. By giving voice to historical characters, students not only see the possibility of the past being different, but they also learn to see the future as unwritten, a field of possibilities, the outcome dependent, in part, on their actions.

When I talked with students about why poetry should be used in history, Mira, a student in the Literature and U.S. History class, said, "Poetry made history come to life. When we wrote after *Hearts and Minds*, I was there. I was a soldier. I identified with what was going on. I felt their feelings. I got more involved. This wasn't just history. This was life. Poetry helped me examine why the war happened because I got inside the people who witnessed it."

Rachel Knudsen "witnessed" the war from the point of view of a pilot from the documentary film *Hearts and Minds* (1974) during a unit on Vietnam. Rachel used the poem to solve a puzzle: How could men produce the bloodshed she witnessed in the film? How could they talk about people as targets? How could they become immune to the suffering their planes leave behind? In her poem "I Flew a Plane," she tried to understand the emotional distance the pilot creates between himself and his victims: People become machines — "metal heads" and "machine arms." If the pilot denied their humanity, then he couldn't feel the pain of their deaths. He was the "technician" who "only flew the plane." War became a video game, and

Too often schools don't teach students how to handle the explosive feelings that come with adolescence. By writing and sharing the "raw core of feelings" that create havoc in their lives, they can practice a more effective way of handling their emotions.

he was a champion player. In the following poem Rachel "stole" the language of Randy Floyd, the now-repentant bomber pilot in the film who says, "I never saw their blood. I never heard their screams. I never felt their pain. I only flew the plane."

> *Flying high over*
> *the patchquilt*
> *of an unknown country*
> *leaving exploding shells*
> *behind me,*
> *I never saw their blood.*
> *I never heard their screams.*
> *I never felt their pain.*
> *Flying low over*
> *burning huts*
> *torched by green men*
> *with metal heads*
> *and machine arms,*
> *leaving corpses*
> *in bomb craters*
> *that I,*
> *the technician,*
> *created.*
> *I never saw their blood.*
> *I never heard their screams.*
> *I never felt their pain.*
> *I only flew the plane.*

Instead of becoming the pilot, Keely Thrasher wrote to the pilot — telling him what he missed after he dropped the bombs:

> *. . . You didn't smell the flesh,*
> *Caught in a barbed wire,*
> *Torn like an old rag,*

> ## Getting students to write poetry is not enough. They must learn to extend their metaphors, to articulate the flashes of insight they found in their poems.

Soft brown skin heated to black. . . .
You didn't taste the blood,
Mixed with dirt and rice,
Staining the walls of the huts
Splashed on the faces of young girls. . . .

Keely saw the devastation the soldier left behind, but she wanted to forgive him. She felt the enormity of his guilt and understood how hard these deaths would be to live with. She ended her poem:

You must have missed those things.
If you hadn't you would have turned back,
Picking up every shell you dropped,
And putting a bandage on every scrape you caused.

Margo Gay's confusion over the war poured into the present as she tried to understand a co-worker who was a veteran:

If I touched what was left
of your fingers
would they split open
and gush images to me?

Would I see the dead
of Vietnam —
thanks to you?

Would I see the heroin and
alcohol you found
your comfort in?

If I watched long enough
would I see what I
didn't know before —
A gentle man
always kind,
instead of this rough exterior
always pushing me away?

Louie, I don't want you
to be a murderer
because I haven't known
you long enough to
let that slide.

Margo used her poem to explore questions she had about Louie. Before the war, was he a "gentle man/ always kind/ instead of this rough exterior/ always pushing me away?" Was the heroin and alcohol an escape from the deeds he committed in Vietnam? She wanted to know more, but she was afraid to learn too much because she wasn't sure she could "let [murder] slide."

The poems are not a substitute for information. Students need to investigate why the war happened. The emotional intensity students invested in these poems would be impossible without that knowledge. In addition to reading numerous first-person accounts and historical documents chronicling the involvement of France and the United States, they participated in a role play Bill Bigelow (1995) created, taking the parts of Viet Minh cadre and French government officials. They also read Bobbie Ann Mason's *In Country* (1985), selected poems from Yusef Komunyakaa's *Dien Cai Dau* (1988) and Vietnamese poetry from the anthology *Of Quiet Courage* (Chagnon and Luce, 1974). Perhaps the most difficult and ultimately most powerful assignment asked them to interview veterans. Students' anger and angst were fueled with knowledge.

After Rachel, Keely, Margo, and their classmates read their poems, we discussed reasons for the anger, the guilt, the withdrawal, the "rough exterior" of the soldiers. The poems became prompts to explore the lives we invented. Why was it necessary for soldiers to dehumanize the enemy? What happened to the veterans after they returned home? Margo was reluctant to let Louie "slide." Was this a common reaction when soldiers came back from the war? How did these men and women learn to live normal lives again after their experiences?

Still, poetry is not social analysis. Students' poems won't help them figure out why Truman and Eisenhower sided with the French against the Viet Minh or why the United States created South Vietnam after the 1954 Geneva Accords. However, the poetry will draw students into the pathos of Vietnam by depicting the human consequences of those decisions. And by humanizing the war, students may care enough to join our investigation into its causes.

Or they may not. What made this experience intense and good also raised problems. Through their poems students lived with their characters. They were emotionally attached to the soldiers or the peasants

PHOTOGRAPH, 1969
By Katy Barber

This is my mother
lifting her hair long
like a low whistle
off of her neck
These are her fingers
caught in the tangles
of brown and gold caught in
silver earrings
This is my father
reaching through the lens
to touch the edge
of a new family
to touch her opening belly
under her full dress

This is existing
before I exist

This is me growing up
against their lives
him watching for a sharp
breath from her
her looking out
onto the boarder of birth
this is bumping us into three

interest in analyzing our own lives: What gives us ful-fillment? What are our common problems — divorce, loneliness, loss, drug and alcohol abuse, shame — and how can we confront them? How can we help each other confront them?

Mira Shimabukuro told me, "Poetry helped me get rid of pain. It got things out. Helped me deal with my problems. My poem, 'Her Wedding Day,' where I talk about my mother getting remarried, I've been dealing with since I was five. I worked through that pain when I wrote the piece. Learning to write poetry is not about technique, it's about wrestling with your life." In class, we wrestle together — and try to build a collective text that both heals and illuminates.

Class read-arounds are filled with students coming to terms with their parents' divorces. In the poem, "Saying Goodbye," Katy Barber addressed her father:

> My mama washed
> your clothes for twenty-one
> years and now you want
> me
> to show you how to operate
> that washing machine hidden behind
> the basement stairs show you
> as if her hands weren't good
> enough her elbow grease
> not greasy enough her sweat
> not clean enough show you
> as if forty-eight isn't too old to start
> My mama washed your clothes
> for twenty-one years
> and now you fold your own or bribe
> your good son Matt with a trip
> to Powell's or flowers for his Rachel
> as if a gray beard signaled you
> to learn to take care
> of yourself as if you would do without
> her as if you meant to say goodbye
> with a spin cycle and a box full
> of powdered detergent

they created. They could be reluctant to leave the arena of feelings and move into the world of analysis. That's the seduction of poetry. When Bill and I began edging toward the kinds of questions I've listed above, student groaned, "Can't we just write? Do we have to talk about it?" The poetry worked. Sometimes too well.

Personal Poetry:
Wrestling With Your Life

Just as poetry helped students imagine the pain and struggles of the Vietnamese and the characters in *The Color Purple,* it can also provide an opening for us, students and teachers, to investigate our own lives. Through the writing and sharing of poetry, we can probe our wounds and try to discover their roots, we can share our joy and learn that like the characters in history and literature, we don't have to suffer or struggle or laugh alone. With luck, we can develop an

Katy's voice crackled with anger. Her father learning to operate the washing machine, a duty her mother performed for 21 years, provoked Katy's wrath. This was not about unlearning sex roles; this was about leaving. When Katy shared, others added their stories, "Yeah, when my dad left. . . ." or "Catch this, the dude. . . ." The pain students nurtured privately was shared. They learned: They are not alone.

> **When students begin to take measure of the part society plays in their problems, they can use that knowledge to explore their problems more thoroughly instead of immediately blaming themselves.**

The characters differed. The leaving differed. The pain remained common ground.

The dance of acceptance and rejection is repeated throughout school. Students practice feeling okay about themselves without buying designer jeans, they discover how it feels to fit under someone's shoulder, to get a part in a school play and lose a best friend on the same day. Too often schools don't teach them how to handle the explosive feelings that come with adolescence. By writing and sharing the "raw core of feelings" that create havoc in their lives, they can practice a more effective way of handling their emotions. They discover the comfort of finding an accepting group who listens sympathetically and often identifies with their troubles.

While I don't believe that poetry will stop drug and alcohol abuse, I do think we need to teach students effective ways of dealing with their volcanic emotions. Poetry is an effective beginning.

Poetry also provides an opportunity to explore the social origins of some of the problems students face individually. In the following poem, "Playing the Fool," Masta Davis wrote a poem of a direct address to gang members in the community:

My brotha'. My brotha.
Why don't you get for real?
Out there on the street tryin' to make a deal.
Selling stuff that would kill yo' mother.
While the other man laughs in your face, under cover.

Ohh, so you making mo' money here
than anywhere?
Hope you enjoy it
'cause you ain't goin' to be alive next year.
What can I do so that you brothas will see?
Slangin' and bangin' ain't the way, you gotta believe.

Look at us. Killing over colors.

Damn y'all some ignorant brothas.
Doin' the shit the Klan did 30 years back.
Look at you, a brotha killing another Black.
The Ku Klux Klan ain't gotta worry about a thang.
We killin' ourselves off real clean.
Shootin' and sellin' to dope fiends.
Look at y'all. You have destroyed our dreams.

Through Masta's poem, we could discuss why young people turn to the Crips or Bloods. Instead of wringing our hands, we began to reflect on their growth: What conditions exist that push kids into gangs? Masta's poem provided evidence for our talk: What other options do students have? Who is working in their neighborhood? Who has money? Who drives fancy cars and wears the latest brand of tennis shoes? Who doesn't? How is a person's value measured in our society?

When students begin to take measure of the part society plays in their problems, they can use that knowledge to explore their problems more thoroughly instead of immediately blaming themselves. For example, young women who feel the necessity of dieting, bingeing, and purging, or not eating can be exposed to the role that advertising plays in eroding their self-esteem.

School life is often alienating. Students sit in rows, they're told not to talk to the people around them. In the five minutes between classes, they don't have time to be "real" or to find out much about each other. When the bell rings, students are usually asked to put their lives aside and get to work. Writing and sharing their own lives begins to confront this alienation. Their interactions with each other are part of the content of the course.

Nicole Smith-Leary, a senior, said, "When I hear Mira or Rachel read, I think, 'Hey, they have the same feelings I do. Even though they were brought up differently, even though they're Asian and white and I'm Black, we've experienced some of the same things. They teach me about humanity.'"

And through the writing and sharing of their lives, students practice for the future. Students' histories are the texts we study. These "texts," together with the methodology — sitting in a circle, students and teachers both sharing; students calling on and questioning each other — all help students rehearse to become more active and critical participants in their world. They learn to expect more: a voice in shaping a discussion and the curriculum more generally, a dialogue about their grades, an opportunity to read and study about people like themselves, purposeful work in a community of learners.

They begin to sense that they don't have to accept life as it presents itself. Some learn to object to the inequities they find in school — and in the world. Katy Barber, for example, attended a well-known and distinguished private college after she graduated from Jefferson High School. She continually challenged her professors: Where were the women writers? Where were the African-American writers? The Asian-American writers? Where were the assignments linking their lives to the course, to contemporary world problems? Finally, disgusted with the school's lack of responsiveness, she left that school. Today, she has her doctorate and is still concerned with issues of inclusiveness and social justice.

Of course, it oversimplifies the complex weaving of literature, history, social analysis, writing, and classroom discourse to claim that poetry alone allows Katy or her peers to resist the society they find themselves in. But poetry is one of the strands in the weaving — a vital one.

References

Bigelow, Bill. "Role-playing the Origins of U.S. Involvement," in *Social Education*, 52(1), 1985, pp. 55-57.

Chagnon, Jacqui, and Luce, Don (Eds.) *Of Quiet Courage.* Washington, DC: Indochina Mobile Education Project, 1974.

Komunyakaa, Yusef. *Dien Cai Dau.* Middletown, CT: Wesleyan University Press, 1988.

Mason, Bobbie Ann. *In Country.* New York: Harper & Row, 1985.

Sexton, Anne. "Love Song," in *The Complete Poems.* Boston: Houghton Mifflin, 1981, pp. 115-116.

Walker, Alice. *The Color Purple.* New York: Washington Square, 1982.

TO THE COACHES OF THE YEAR
By Bobby Janisse

To the coaches of the year
With your raises and numerous job offers
bought not by your pain and sweat,
but by the sweat of your little army
who you lead into battle
like a general.

But do you fight?
No, you stand there with your whistle hung around your neck,
yelling out commands,
"50, 20, up, down,"
depending on how you feel that day.

"All for one and one for all,"
you say,
but when you get your wage increase,
what are the legs that support your table receiving?
Huh?
Nothing, but a pat on the back
and a certificate of participation.

When you win your championship,
they ask, "Where are you going next?"

But no Disneyland this year, my friend.
It's 50, 20, up, down for you.

And this time the whistle dangles from our necks.

Promoting Social Imagination Through Interior Monologues

Written with Bill Bigelow

Jean-Claude Lejeune

One of the most important aims of teaching is to prompt students to empathize with other human beings. This is no easy accomplishment in a society that pits people against each other, offers vastly greater or lesser amounts of privileges based on accidents of birth, and rewards exploitation with wealth and power. Empathy, or "social imagination," as Peter Johnson calls it in *The Reading Teacher*, allows students to connect to "the other" with whom, on the surface, they may appear to have little in common. A social imagination encourages students to construct a more profound "we" than daily life ordinarily permits. A social imagination prompts students to wonder about the social contexts that provoke hurtful behaviors, rather than simply to dismiss individuals as inherently "evil" or "greedy."

Imagining Thoughts of Others

One teaching method Bill Bigelow and I use to promote empathy, and return to unit after unit, is the interior monologue. An interior monologue is simply the imagined thoughts of a character in history, literature, or life at a specific point in time. After watching a film, reading a novel, short story, or essay, or performing improvisation skits, the class brainstorms particular key moments, turning points, or critical passages characters confronted. During a unit on the Vietnam War, we watch the 1974 documentary *Hearts and Minds*. The film (available in many video stores) weaves interviews with U.S. soldiers and Vietnamese with newsreel footage of the war and unexpected scenes of daily life in the United States. Student suggestions included writing from the points of view of

134

an American pilot who has become critical of his role in the war, a North Vietnamese man whose entire family has been killed in a bombing raid, a Native-American Marine who was called "blanket ass" and "squaw" by commanding officers, and a Buddhist monk who solemnly lectures the United States on the futility of trying to conquer Vietnam.

Sometimes students choose to write from the situations we brainstorm, sometimes they don't. The monologue technique gives structure to the assignment, but the freedom to write from anyone's point of view allows students to mold the piece to the contours of their lives and interests.

Deanna Wesson chose to write her interior monologue as a poem. She picked a quote from a soldier who said, "We're taught to obey our government. I would have to go if I were called." She wrote:

> *It doesn't matter*
> *that I would be going against*
> *all the values by which I've lived my life.*
> *It doesn't matter*
> *that I would break all of God's commandments.*
> *It doesn't matter that I would have to murder and torture*
> *innocent human beings*
> *It doesn't matter*
> > *that this war has been caused*
> > *by my own government*
> *It doesn't matter*
> > *that I have no idea why we're fighting*
> *It doesn't matter*
> > *that my government is poisoning*
> > *soldiers with Agent Orange*
> *It doesn't matter*
> > *that my "enemies" are fighting only*
> > *for the right to govern themselves.*
> *It doesn't matter.*

Using the soldier's words as a jump-off point, Deanna explores how she might feel if she were in the soldier's place. Throughout the poem she also uses other information she learned during the film.

> *The monologue technique gives structure to the assignment, but the freedom to write from anyone's point of view allows students to mold the piece to the contours of their lives and interests.*

In our classroom circle, students read their pieces aloud and give positive comments on each other's work. Listening to the collection of writings offers students an intimate portrait of the social consequences of the war. We feel, rather than observe from a distance. These portraits provide us a way to talk about the film without writing typical discussion questions. The issues embedded in the text are viewed through a more personal lens. The different lives that students imagine and their different interpretations give us opportunities to explore the film or reading more thoroughly.

As is true anytime we wonder about other people's lives, our monologues are only guesses, at times marred by stereotype. But the very act of considering, "How might this person experience this situation?" develops an important "habit of the mind" and draws us closer together. We write the monologues along with our students and can testify at the startling insights and compassion that can arise. Usually, we — students and teachers — tap into our own well of pain, pride, sorrow, confusion, and joy. Although we may never have experienced war, we know the pain of losing a family member or friend; we have experienced the difficulty of making a tough decision. Likewise, we have felt joy. From these shared emotions we can construct a piece that allows us to attempt a momentary entrance into another person's life.

In our Literature and U.S. History class, we read "A Jury of Her Peers" by Susan Glaspell, a 1917 story about rural women's lives. In the story, Minnie Wright, who lives on an isolated farm, strangles her

---

I WENT LOOKING FOR JEFFERSON
By Aaron Wheeler-Kay

And I Found . . .
All The Nations Of The World
   Wrapped In Baggy Jeans
     Sweat Shirts
      Braids.
Closed Minds Slowly Opening
Like Doors Under Water.
Jefferson Is Our Wetstone;
The Blade Is Our Mind.

VIETNAM:
NO SCISSORS TO THE TRUTH
By Meg Niemi

They sent Dad back
in an army green
Ziplock Freezer Bag
the kind Mama
shells sweet peas in
and stocks in the ice box
as a reminder of
sunnier days.

They sent him as
a reminder,
a token of the war
that his 3-month-old child
would spend the rest
of her life
trying to thaw.

There were no scissors
to cut through to
the truth
They even made sure
he was double sealed
for our protection —
leaving a number
as his only identity.

If Mama had shaken that bag
to spill the truth,
would he have rattled
like those summer sweet peas
shaken from a pod —
would I have heard
Sunday talk
of Kentucky catfish,
Jesus Bugs
and days 'in country'?

husband in desperate retaliation for his strangling her bird, the creature that brought her the only moments of joy in an otherwise bleak life. We suggested students might begin their monologue or poem with "Write that I. . . ."

Maryanne assumes the persona of Minnie Wright and tries to imagine what in her life would lead her to commit such a horrid crime:

> Write that I was young,
> tender like the gardenia blossom . . .
>
> I know that you think
> I killed my husband,
> my keeper, protector.
>
> I stayed in that house, broken
> chairs beneath me, husband on top
> pushing his fury through me . . .
>
> Please don't forget the bird.
> You must tell them about its voice.
> It was strangled.
> We were strangled.

Interior monologues tap other people's pain, but they also tap people's hope. After watching *The Killing Floor*, about the World War I Black migration to Chicago and union organizing in the stockyards, Debbie wrote an interior monologue from the point of view of Frank, a Black worker recently arrived from the South:

> I sit and listen to the unfamiliar air of music drifting in through my window. Crickets had made music in the South, but never in a tune like this one. I want Mattie to hear this new music. The sound of white men's feet on the dirt avoiding our Black bodies on the sidewalk. Oh, to share the sounds of coins clinking together as I walk.

As students read their pieces aloud in the circle, we ask them to take notes on the "collective text" they create, to write about the common themes that emerge, or questions they're left with. Or we might pose a particular question for them to think about. For example, after we watched the film *Glory*, about the first regiment of African-American soldiers who fought in the Civil War, we wrote a dictionary definition of the word "glory" on the board and asked students as they listened to each other's interior monologues to notice: "Where is the 'glory' in the film

Glory?" Students' own writings and observations became different points of entry to explore the many contradictions in the film and the events it depicts. For example, Eugene wrote, "In our class reading it was commented that there was mostly pain and not much glory. I think that their pain was their glory, the fact that they were willing to be martyrs. They were fighting for a freedom that they knew they would never have, because most of them would die in the war."

Empathy and sympathy are different. When Ghantel writes her *Color Purple* interior monologue from the point of view of Mr._____, Celie's uncaring husband, she shows empathy; she tries to imagine how he looks at the world and wonders what experiences made him who he is. But she's not sympathetic; she doesn't approve of his behavior. In fact, she detests him. Interior monologues, by encouraging students to empathize with other people, no matter how despicable, invite kids to probe for the social causes of human behavior. People are not inherently sexist or racist; and while interior monologues are not analytical panaceas, they can be useful tools in nurturing insight about why people think and act as they do.

Points of Departure for Interior Monologues

In our experience, success with interior monologues depends on:

- Drawing on media or readings that are emotionally powerful.

- Brainstorming character and situation choices so most students can find an entry into the assignment.

- Allowing students the freedom to find their own passion — they might want to complete the assignment as a poem, a dialogue poem, or from the point of view of an animal or an object (Minnie Wright's dead bird, for instance).

- Giving students the opportunity to read their pieces to the entire class.

- Using the collective text of students' writing to launch a discussion of the bigger picture.

Writing interior monologues won't necessarily have students hugging each other as they sing "We Shall Overcome," but they are a worthwhile piece in our attempt to construct a critical, multicultural curriculum. Students need opportunities to think deeply about other people — why they do what they do, why they think what they think. They also need chances to care about each other and the world. Interior monologues are a good place to start. ■

Interior monologues, by encouraging students to empathize with other people, no matter how despicable, invite kids to probe for the social causes of human behavior.

JACOB LAWRENCE — THE MIGRATION
By Corinne Rupp

"I wanted to create a work that was very sparse. You'd see it immediately — the dark, the light values, very high in contrast. The warmth in the red."
— Jacob Lawrence, 1992

i saw it immediately—
the starkness
the desperation
the pain
faceless men pounding on
steel with steel
faceless women crying
at the rope on the tree
faceless children writing
numbers on the chalkboard
i saw it immediately —
seven basic colors, each portraying
one emotion
one feeling
one more problem
i saw it immediately
i can't be blind to this part
of my history

The Poetry of Protest: Martín Espada

Tony tossed the Tootsie Roll paper over his shoulder as he entered my room. "I'm not your mama, Tony. Pick up that mess."

"Ms. Christensen, the custodians are paid to clean up. If I didn't leave anything on the floor, they'd lose their jobs."

Ruthie Griffin, the custodian, would disagree. But Ruthie, like Marlene Grieves, the cafeteria worker who serves them lunch, is largely invisible to students. Their brooms or spatulas might as well be held by robots. That's one reason why I teach the poetry of Martín Espada in my classroom.

Martín Espada's poetry is a weapon for justice in a society that oppresses people who aren't white, who don't speak English, whose work as janitors and migrant laborers is exploited. His poetry teaches students about the power of language — both Spanish and English — and he makes "invisible" workers visible. What Espada writes about Pablo Neruda's poetry is also true for his own: "[T]he poet demanded dignity for the commonplace subject, commanding respect for things and people normally denied such respect."

> **I want to introduce students to writers, like Espada, whose art speaks out against injustice, as well as give them the tools to write their own poems of empathy and outrage.**

I want to introduce students to writers, like Espada, whose art speaks out against injustice, as well as give them the tools to write their own poems of empathy and outrage.

A while back, Espada refused Nike's offer to produce a poem for them for TV commercials they planned to air during the 1998 Winter Olympics. *The Progressive* magazine published Espada's letter to an ad agency listing the reasons he refused Nike's poet-for-hire offer:

"I could reject your offer based on the fact that your deadline is ludicrous. . . . A poem is not a pop tart.

"I could reject your offer based on the fact that, to make this offer to me in the first place, you must be totally and insultingly ignorant of my work as a poet, which strives to stand against all that you and your client represent. Whoever referred me to you did you a grave disservice.

"I could reject your offer based on the fact that your client Nike has — through commercials such as these — outrageously manipulated the youth market, so that even low-income adolescents are compelled to buy products they do not need at prices they cannot afford.

"Ultimately, however, I am rejecting your offer as a protest against the brutal labor practices of Nike. I will not associate myself with a company that engages in the well-documented exploitation of workers in sweatshops. . . ."

Espada's public refusal to serve as yet-another-artist-for-sale is reason enough to present his work to students. In my curriculum I want to highlight writers who put their talents at the service of humanity, not profits. Espada is right: Nike must be ignorant of his work, but my students shouldn't be.

I use Espada's poetry, in English and Spanish, to teach students how to use metaphors and how to write a "persona poem," but I also use Espada's poetry because he shows how to make visible the work of those who toil in physical labor.

In *Rethinking Our Classrooms* (1994), the editors write about the need to ground our teaching in our students' lives, equip students to "talk back" to the world, pose essential questions, be multicultural, antiracist, and pro-justice, participatory, joyful, activist, academically rigorous, and culturally sensitive: "A

JORGE THE CHURCH JANITOR FINALLY QUITS

No one asks
where I am from,
I must be
from the country of janitors,
I have always mopped this floor.
Honduras, you are a squatter's camp
outside the city
of their understanding.

No one can speak
my name,
I host the fiesta
of the bathroom,
stirring the toilet
like a punchbowl.
The Spanish music of my name
is lost
when the guests complain
about toilet paper.

What they say
must be true:
I am smart,
but I have a bad attitude.

No one knows
that I quit tonight,
maybe the mop
will push on without me,
sniffing along the floor
like a crazy squid
with stringy gray tentacles.
They will call it Jorge.

POR FIN RENUNCIA JORGE EL CONSERJE DE LA IGLESIA

Nadie me pregunta
de dónde soy,
tendré que ser
de la patria de los conserjes,
siempre he trapeado este piso.
Honduras, eres un campamento
de desamparados
afuera de la ciudad
de su comprensión.

Nadie puede decir
mi nombre,
yo soy el amenizador
de la fiesta en el baño,
meneando el agua en el inodoro
como si fuera una ponchera.
La música española de mi nombre
se pierde
cuando los invitados se quejan
del papel higiénico.

Será verdad
lo que dicen:
soy listo,
pero tengo una mala actitud.

Nadie sabe
que esta noche renuncié al puesto,
quizá el trapero
seguirá adelante sin mí,
husmeando el piso
como un calamar enloquecido
con fibrosos tentáculos grises.
Lo llamarán Jorge.

—Martín Espada
(translated by Camilo Pérez-Bustillo
and the author)

> **Teaching students to respect the custodian who mops their halls, the short order cook who makes their tacos, or the field worker who picks their strawberries should be a part of our critical classrooms.**

social justice curriculum must strive to include the lives of all those in our society, especially the marginalized and dominated." Teaching students to respect the custodian who mops their halls, the short order cook who makes their tacos, or the field worker who picks their strawberries should be a part of our critical classrooms.

Teaching Strategy:

1. Prior to reading Espada's letter, ask students if they would ever turn down money if it compromised their beliefs. What are some examples? Then read Espada's letter and discuss why someone would give up a chance to earn $2,500. Would it really be such a big deal if he let them use his poem? What does he stand to lose by not agreeing to write a poem for them? What does he gain? Why did he make his letter public?

2. Ask students to read the poem in both languages. (This validates students who speak Spanish and also locates writing in the broader linguistic world. I encourage students who speak more than one language to write in either or both languages.)

3. Discuss the poem: Who is the narrator? How do people treat Jorge? What evidence in the poem tells us that? What does he compare the mop to? What does Espada want us to know about Jorge? How do we learn that?

4. After reading and discussing, return to Espada's letter. He wrote, "I could reject your

offer based on the fact that you must be totally and insultingly ignorant of my work as a poet, which strives to stand against all that you and your client represent." Ask students to identify evidence in this poem that might indicate why Espada would turn down Nike's money.

5. Ask students to make a list of "invisible workers" they know whom they could make visible: for example, hotel maids, strawberry harvesters, the seamstress who sewed their shirt or blouse. A few students might share their lists to helped stumped classmates find a topic. (For younger students, I sometimes begin by asking them to write a paragraph or two about the worker or situation. Later, they can underline details and language to arrange into a poem.)

6. Direct students to write for 15 to 20 minutes. I demand silence, so we can all write, but I do allow students to move to more comfortable places in the room.

7. Then we share. I tell students to consider their classmates as teachers and to learn techniques from each other that make powerful writing. So while every student reads, I expect them to listen and take notes on what they like in the piece — specifically, the incident/story, the use of metaphor, the illumination of injustice or a person who is invisible, the use of language, a particular line. I also speak about the importance of positive feedback: We want people to keep writing. If we criticized them instead of praising them, they might not want to write or share again.

We live in a society where it appears that everything is for sale — including movements for social justice. Students need stories about people who work for change, people who refuse to allow their work to be commodified. They need models of people whose work is animated by social justice. They need to know about poets like Martín Espada. ■

Remember Me Poems

In my classroom I attempt to establish new traditions by creating times where students pause to celebrate themselves and each other. One of those occasions is the last day of school. As a going away present to the class, I make a book of their favorite writings from the year. In addition to the poem, story, or essay that students submit to the book, each student writes one "Remember Me" poem about a fellow classmate. As we gather for the last time in our circle, students honor each other in a final read-around. (See page 14 for a full description of read-arounds.)

Each student gets a moment in the spotlight when the poem about him or her is shared aloud. As the final bells rings, many of us are in tears, signing each other's books with pleas to keep writing or to "remember that day when. . . ."

Teaching Strategy:

1. I ask students to write their names on slips of paper and place them in a basket. After everyone's name is included — those who are absent as well as the teacher — each student draws one name out of the bowl. If students draws their own names, they put them back. In some classes, I remind students not to groan, roll their eyes, or say they don't want to write about someone. I create a master list of who is writing about whom.

2. I talk about the necessity of grounding their poems in details about their classmates. I select one student out of the class and talk about some positive things the class will remember about this person. For example, in our class we might remember that Matt sat by the pencil sharpener and was always the first one in the door in the morning. We might remember that he wrote wonderful historical fiction and was passionate about chess. We might talk about how he remained friends with his buddies from Ockley Green Middle School or tell about the day he played Raheem's grandfather in the improvisation. I try to get students beyond the "he was nice" generalities in their poem.

3. I read Jessica Rawlins' poem "Remember Sihaya?" (see page 142). It is playful — evoking Sihaya Buntin's love of dance with the "tap, shuffle, tap" and the "electric angel with the dancer's feet" references. Jessica shares details about Sihaya that we remember: her tardiness, the fact that she was a Jefferson dancer, her constant movement in class.

We also read "Remember Amanda?" (see below). This is a poem Amanda wrote about herself. At one time, I asked students to write a remember me poem about themselves as well as about someone else. As Amanda's poem demonstrates, these poetic self-reflections gave insights into the student's role in the class. We discuss how Amanda included gossip about herself — "The one accused of kissing another girl's boyfriend on prom night." But she also shared positive traits as well: "The person you could count on/to say something positive about your piece,/the passionate big mouth who couldn't be silenced . . . the girl who . . . replaced

---

REMEMBER AMANDA?
By Amanda Wheeler-Kay as remembered by herself

Remember me?
Love struck Lucy who dyed my hair temporarily green.
The one accused of kissing another girl's boyfriend on prom night.
The person you could count on
to say something positive about your piece,
the passionate big mouth who couldn't be silenced,
the girl who killed mistrust with friendship,
healed bitterness with time shared,
and replaced prejudice with knowledge,
the one who tried to bring us all together.

If you need something:
a candy bar,
help with a story or essay,
a hug
or a smile,
just call me
and I'll come:
feet dancing,
green eyes shining,
and equally green hair swingin'.

---

prejudice with knowledge."

4. I start this process several weeks before the end of the year, so students have time to watch their assigned classmate and collect ideas from others before they write. This needn't be a "private" piece of writing. I urge students to ask their classmates or me for details they might include. Also, I make sure that everyone has a poem written about them and that all poems are positive. In my class, students keep the name of their person secret until the last day when the class books are distributed and the poems read.

Students need to learn how to build new traditions — ones that don't involve corporations telling them how to think and feel about death, birth, illness, celebrations, or each other. By creating practices in our classrooms that honor our time together, our work, and our community, we can teach students how to develop meaningful new traditions in their own lives. ■

REMEMBER SIHAYA?
By Jessica Rawlins

I am the electric angel
with dancer's feet,
the slick sister who grins,
strolls into class only ten minutes late,
toting too many bags for a lady.
I am the laughter that echoes.
With a tap, shuffle, tap,
I practice my moves
to the silent beat in my head.
I am the Jefferson Dancer
who loathes Geometry
and classes that I know I won't need later in life.
So I roll
and let it all slide by.
When grades come in,
I'm swimming upstream.
I am the party girl,
who lived for my friends
and thinks hell is getting stuck at home.
I am the fire,
who doesn't wait for details.
I'll catch up sooner or later,
just watch me.
I am Sihaya.

MARY
By Erika Howard

Mary, Mary, child of grace.
Long slim fingers, baby face.
When the boys catch at your skirt,
Do you kiss or court or flirt?
When you marry charming Jim,
how many kisses will you give him?
Two   four   six   eight   ten.
Two   four   six   eight   twenty.
Two   four   six   eight   thirty.
Two   four   six   eight   forty.
Two   four   six   eight…
Did you jump rope when you were a very little girl?
Or did you climb
wild in the branches of the play structure?
Perhaps you sat serenely
on the grass with a friend and a doll,
but I doubt it.
You, with the book of bright colors,
bright pictures,
and your own smooth pen.
You, with the smile that never stops.
Do you have sorrow or is your life
a huge joyous rave?
Sometimes I wonder,
but your smile gives a hand to my limping heart
and your laugh in the silence
nudges my elbow to include me.
You, with the clogs and wild tights.
You, with the red hair to almost match Lulu's.
When you walk in together,
both striding long,
yelling,
"Am I a ho? No. I ain't no ho."
You, who sat in the window,
silhouetted by the rich blue sky.
Mary, I'll always remember you.

A PUBLICATION OF RETHINKING SCHOOLS

Immigration

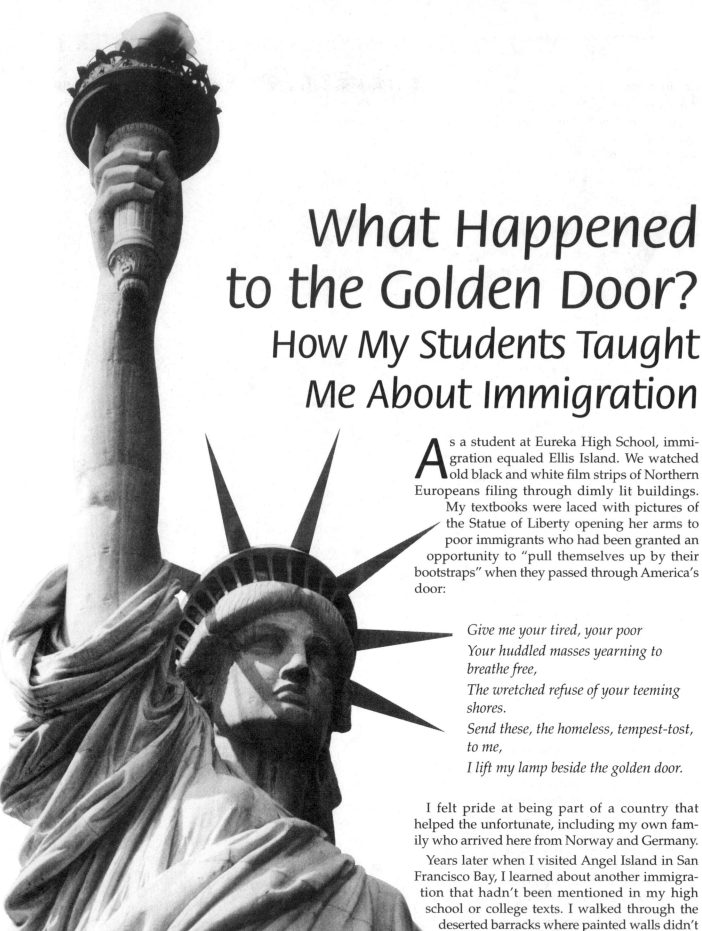

Jean-Claude Lejeune

What Happened to the Golden Door?
How My Students Taught Me About Immigration

A s a student at Eureka High School, immigration equaled Ellis Island. We watched old black and white film strips of Northern Europeans filing through dimly lit buildings. My textbooks were laced with pictures of the Statue of Liberty opening her arms to poor immigrants who had been granted an opportunity to "pull themselves up by their bootstraps" when they passed through America's door:

> *Give me your tired, your poor*
> *Your huddled masses yearning to breathe free,*
> *The wretched refuse of your teeming shores.*
> *Send these, the homeless, tempest-tost, to me,*
> *I lift my lamp beside the golden door.*

I felt pride at being part of a country that helped the unfortunate, including my own family who arrived here from Norway and Germany.

Years later when I visited Angel Island in San Francisco Bay, I learned about another immigration that hadn't been mentioned in my high school or college texts. I walked through the deserted barracks where painted walls didn't quite cover the poems of immigrant Chinese

144

who viewed the "Golden Mountain" through a barbed wire fence. I felt angry that yet another portion of U.S. history had been hidden from me.

Between 1910 and 1940, the "tired, poor, wretched refuse" from Asian shores were imprisoned on Angel Island before being accepted as "resident aliens" or rejected at the "golden door" and returned to their home country. All Europeans were legally eligible to apply for citizenship once they passed through Ellis Island, a right denied to immigrant Asians until the mid-1940s.

As historian Ronald Takaki (1989) notes, "Their quarters were crowded and unsanitary, resembling a slum. 'When we arrived,' said one of them, 'they locked us up like criminals in compartments like the cages in the zoo.'" Turning their anger and frustration into words, the Chinese carved poems on the wooden walls, poems that stood in stark contradiction to the Statue of Liberty's promise:

America has power, but not justice.

In prison, we were victimized as if we were guilty.

Given no opportunity to explain, it was really brutal.

I bow my head in reflection but there is nothing I can do.[1]

Jean-Claude Lejeune

In 1995 California voters passed Proposition 187, which, when implemented, would deprive so-called "illegal" immigrants of health care and schooling. This initiative sparked my decision to teach about immigration — not just the traditional version, but the more dangerous and unspoken version that examines why large numbers of immigrants are discriminated against based on color, nationality, or politics. I wanted my students to read behind the media rhetoric that villified millions of human beings.

As a social justice educator, I consistently ask, "Whose voices are left out of our curriculum? Whose stories are buried? What can we understand about contemporary immigration laws by looking at these historical exclusions?" Ronald Takaki notes in the introduction to *Journey to Gold Mountain* (1994), "[M]any history books have equated 'American' with 'white' or 'European' in origin." I left high school with that equation. I don't want to pass on the same misinformation to my students. To broaden their under-

standing of immigration as well as U.S. policy, they need to investigate how race, class, and gender have shaped immigration policy. If the textbooks don't provide an answer, I must create the space for students to conduct the research.

Beyond these political reasons, I had personal and educational reasons to continue to teach this unit in the days following the passage of Proposition 187. It was the last quarter of the year in Literature in U.S. History, a combined junior level untracked history and English class that met 90 minutes a day for the entire year. The days had warmed up and the students smelled summer. If I said the words essay, interior monologue, or role play, I knew I'd hear a collective moan rise from the circle and settle like stinky fog around my head.

For three academic quarters, my planning book had been filled with lessons attempting to teach students how to become critical readers of history and literature. They'd written essays, critiques, short stories, personal narratives, poems, and interior monologues analyzing their own lives as well as the history and contemporary issues that continue to deprive Native Americans of land and economic opportunities.

---

[1] From Lai, Lim, and Yung. 1986, p. 58. See References.

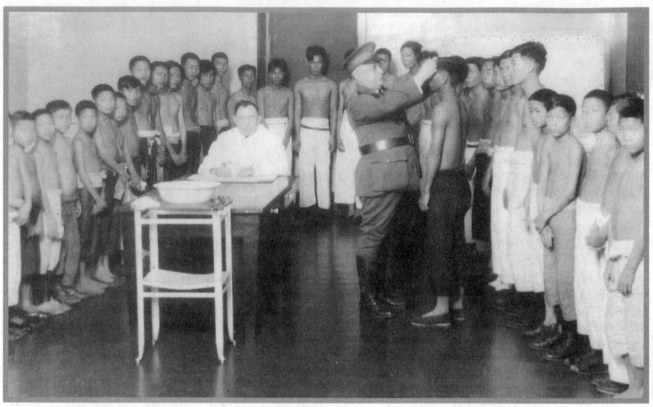

Asian newcomers being examined at a hospital on Angel Island.

They'd also reflected critically on the enslavement of Africans, starting with life in Africa before slavery as well as forced immigration and resistance. We'd examined the literature and history of the Harlem Renaissance, the Civil Rights Movement, and contemporary issues. They'd read and critiqued presidential speeches, historical and contemporary novels, and poems written by people from a variety of backgrounds. They were ready to do their own investigation and teaching — putting into practice their analytical skills.

Fourth quarter I wanted them to conduct "real" research — not the scurry-to-the-library-and-find-the-closest-encyclopedia-and-copy-it-word-for-word kind of research, but research that made them ask questions about immigration policies, quotas, and personal stories that couldn't be lifted from a single text. I wanted them to learn to use the library, search for books, look up alternative sources, find the Ethnic NewsWatch (see references) , search the Oregon Historical Society's clipping files, photo files, and rare documents room. I wanted them to interview people, as well as read novels and poetry that told the immigrant's story in a more personal way. Through this kind of thorough research, I hoped they would continue to hone their ears for what is unsaid in political speeches and newspaper articles, and learn to ask questions when their neighbors or people on the bus began an anti-immigrant rap.

Setting the Stage for Research and Teaching

I started fourth quarter by outlining my goals and expectations. I do this each term, so students know the kinds of pieces that must be in their portfolio, e.g., a literary essay comparing two novels, an essay exploring a historical issue, a poem that includes details from history, etc. As part of the opening-of -the -quarter ceremonies, I passed out an outline of their upcoming project (see page 156). I wanted a lengthy deadline so students would have the opportunity to work the entire quarter on the project.

Before students started their research, I modeled how I wanted the lessons taught by presenting Chinese and Japanese immigration. While students who come through the Jefferson neighborhood network of feeder elementary and middle schools get at least surface background knowledge of Native Americans and African Americans, they appear to know less about Asian or Latino literature and history. In fact, students are often surprised that the Japanese, Chinese, and Mexicans faced any prejudice.[2]

During the lessons on Japanese Americans, students examined Executive Order 9066 signed by President Roosevelt, which gave the military the right to force

---

[2] I have to thank my former student Mira Shimabukuro, who pointed out my own lack of attention to these groups, and Lawson Inada, a professor at Southern Oregon State College, who served as my mentor in these studies.

Japanese Americans from their homes and businesses into camps surrounded by barbed wire and guard towers. Because these Japanese Americans, who included both "resident aliens" and U.S. citizens, were allowed to take only what they could carry to the "camps," they were forced to sell most of their possessions in a short period of time. Students read "Echoes of Pearl Harbor," a chapter from *Nisei Daughter* by Monica Sone (1979) where she describes her family burning their Japanese poetry, kimonos, breaking their Japanese records, destroying anything that could make them look like they cherished their Japanese heritage. Students wrote moving poetry and interior monologues imagining they were forced to leave their homes, businesses, and treasured possessions. "Becoming American" was written by my student Khalilah Joseph:

I looked into the eyes of my Japanese doll
and knew I could not surrender her
to the fury of the fire.
My mother threw out the poetry
she loved;
my brother gave the fire his sword.
We worked hours
to vanish any traces of the Asian world
from our home.
Who could ask us
to destroy
gifts from a world that molded
and shaped us?
If I ate hamburgers
and apple pies,
if I wore jeans,
then would I be American?

I created overheads and slides from the artwork in *Beyond Words: Images from America's Concentration Camps* (Gesensway and Roseman, 1987), a fascinating book of personal testimony and artwork produced in the camps: black and white drawings, watercolors, oil paintings, and pieces of interviews that give students a window into the lives of the imprisoned Japanese Americans. While I showed slides of the artwork, students I prompted ahead of time read aloud "Legends

As a social justice educator, I consistently ask, "Whose voices are left out of our curriculum? Whose stories are buried?"

from Camp" by Lawson Inada (1993), "The Question of Loyalty," by Mitsuye Yamada (1976), and segments of the internees' interviews that matched pictures on the screen. With images and words of the prisoners in their minds, students wrote their own poems. My student Thu Throung's poem is called "Japanese Prisoners":

Guards watch us.
They wrap us around
in barbed wire fences
like an orange's meat
that never grows outside its skin.
If the orange's skin breaks,
the juice drains out.
Just like the Japanese behind the wire fence.

We watched and critiqued the somewhat flawed film *Come See the Paradise*[3] and talked about the laws that forbade Japanese nationals from becoming citizens or owning land.[4] Students read loyalty oaths imprisoned Japanese-American citizens were forced to sign. After learning about the "No No Boys," Japanese-American men in the internment camps who refused to sign the loyalty oath (see Okada, 1957), students argued about whether or not they would have signed the loyalty oath if they'd been interned.

Students also looked at the number of immigrant Chinese allowed to enter the country compared to European immigrants. For example, in 1943 when Congress repealed the Chinese Exclusion Act because of China's war-time alliance with the United States against the Japanese, 105 Chinese were allowed to enter Angel Island, while 66,000 English immigrants passed through Ellis Island. (Lowe, 1988).

The Research Begins

While I presented lessons on Chinese and Japanese immigration during class, students started work on their own projects. They had two 30-minute sessions

---

[3] For example, like many films about an oppressed people, *Come See the Paradise* features a white man in the lead. His Japanese-American wife is interned during the war. The film depicts Japanese Americans who are forced to sell their homes and belongings at unfair prices, and it follows them to the internment camps. *Rabbit in the Moon*, which came out after I completed this unit, is a stronger film on the same topic.

[4] The California Legislature passed the Alien Land Law in 1913. This law barred all "aliens" ineligible for citizenship from holding agricultural land.

INDIAN KITCHEN
By Francis Ram

The sounds and smells
have been with me since birth.
Curries and soups.
Chicken to eggplant.
Cabbage to potatoes
My mom stirring,
a new and better smell
with every stroke.
A whole herbal garden rising
up from the pot.
Curry on the stove and
rice or roti on the other.
The splashing, sizzling sounds of
fresh vegetables as they hit the
bottom of the steaming pan.
The smell of curry powder.
The scent of spicy peppers
punctures the clouds of steam.
The curry presses against my tongue
a hundred different flavors jump
towards me at once.
The last bite leaves me wanting more.

the first week to discuss what they knew, itemize what they needed to find, and list the resources they had (people to interview, books at home, potential videos to use, outside resources like Vietnamese, Russian, or Latino teachers or district-wide coordinators.) During the following weeks while I continued my presentations on Chinese and Japanese immigration, they were given varied amounts of time to conduct research: 45 minutes to prepare for the library, a full day at the library, additional 90-minute periods as we got closer to deadline, etc.

At the end of each period of research/preparation time, students turned their information in to me so I could see if they had made headway, run into a block, needed a push or help. During this research period I moved between groups, listening in, asking questions, making lists of questions they raised but didn't answer, or questioning literary choices when a piece was by a writer from the immigration group but didn't deal with any of the issues we were studying.

During this time it was not unusual to see some of my students gathered around a television in the hallway outside my door or in the library as they watched

and critiqued videos, looking for potential sections to show to the class. Travis, Roman, and Sophia, who conducted individual research projects, could be seen translating notes or cassette tapes for their stories. Sometimes they met to talk over stories or ideas for their presentation.

The group researching Mexican immigration had eight members — too many, really. They watched videos together and then split the rest of the work: Rosa, the only group member fluent in Spanish, talked with recent immigrants in ESL classes and the Latino coordinator to find speakers, videos, and stories to feed to her group; Danica and Komar collected and read books to find a story; Shannon researched César Chávez and wrote a profile to hand out to the class; Heather gathered information for a debate on Proposition 187; Stephanie and Stacey coordinated the group, collecting information from each sub-group, fitting research into a coherent lesson plan, and creating a writing lesson that would pull information together for the class.

Before I end up sounding like a movie starring Michelle Pfeiffer, let me quickly insert into this idyllic classroom picture a word or two about other things you might have seen: kids whining and competing for my attention RIGHT NOW; students gossiping about a fight, or guess-who's-going-out-with, or an upcoming game or a movie they saw last night; a sly student attempting to take advantage of the chaos to catch up on math or Spanish; the slippery students who said they were going to the library or to see an ESL coordinator, but who actually sneaked into the teachers' cafeteria for coffee or outside for a smoke.

There were also two students who attended regularly and might have learned something through other people's work but who produced no work themselves, and a few others who rode the backs of their group work, contributing a little in spurts but not making the sustained efforts of most students. The ESL coordinators and librarians and I developed an easy communication system regarding passes. I called students and parents at home to talk about some students' lack of work. While the calls pushed the back-riding students who made some effort, I failed to bring the "slackers" into the research fold.

Besides the usual chaos a teacher might expect when turning over the curriculum to students, I simultaneously hit another problem. I'd set up immigrant groups that I knew would have some interesting and contradictory stories because I was familiar with their history and literature. While students did accept some of the groups I'd proposed — Mexican, Haitian, Cambodian, Irish, and Vietnamese — others argued vehemently that they be allowed to choose the immigrant group they would study. Our previous les-

Skjold Photographs

sons on resistance and solidarity had certainly taken root within each of the class members, and I was the target of their solidarity.

A few wanted to research their own family's immigration stories: Greek, Jewish, Macedonian, and Russian. Several African-American students wanted to study immigrants from Africa or from the African Diaspora, which we'd studied for an entire quarter earlier in the year. Most were happy to study Haiti, one of my original groups; one student chose to study Eritrea, since Portland has a larger population of Eritreans than Haitians. I agreed: In fact, he made an excellent choice, but sadly, he left school before finishing his project.

We ended our first rounds with the following research groups: Cambodians, Eritreans, Greeks, Haitians, Irish, Jews, Macedonians, Mexicans, Russians, and Vietnamese. This first dialogue marked the end of my control over the history and literature presented in class. And I was nervous because I knew almost nothing about Greek and Macedonian immigration and not much more about the Russians.

Ultimately, the contrast between groups made for great discussion. In my class of 31 students, three had immigrated from Vietnam, one from Russia, one from Cambodia; several students were second-generation Americans from Greece, Ireland, Nicaragua and Mexico; half of the class's ancestors included enslaved

Africans, and one girl's grandmother was the only surviving member of her family after the Holocaust.

But I can imagine a more homogenous classroom where this might not be the case. In my high school English class over 30 years ago, 29 students were white and one was Black. These ratios would have made me demand more diversity in the research if all students wanted to study their own heritage. It is important to negotiate the curriculum with students, and I'm sure some students would be more interested in researching their own past than researching the past of others. But sometimes, in order to surface issues of race and class inequality, it is necessary to move beyond our personal histories.

> **Students became wonderfully devious researchers, using their own connections to gain information.**

Research Problems

Prior to beginning the unit, I spent time in the public library and the Oregon Historical Society (OHS) library, finding sources, articles, books, practicing computer research programs before bringing my students across town. OHS officials were friendly and helpful, but told me that I couldn't bring the entire

Skjold Photographs

class to their library; I'd have to bring one or two at a time after school or on Saturdays. And they closed at 5 PM.

In addition to limited library time, I discovered that easily accessible research materials did not have a critical page in their spines; they just restated the textbook version of history. Because I had initiated this project to scrutinize U.S. immigration practices, I wanted students to learn the "whole truth," not just a watered-down version that left out facts which might complicate the issues. I figured that part of research is getting lots of material and then deciding what is important to present so that others hear a fuller truth. But when I discovered that much of what students were reading only told one side of the immigration story — the same side I learned in high school — I made an effort to put other facts in students' hands as well.

We searched computer files of Ethnic NewsWatch, an online source for news about specific ethnic groups, as well as alternative news and magazine sources. Although many students dutifully read the computer-generated articles, most of these pieces were too academic or required extensive background knowledge to understand. If we relied solely on these sources of information — either textbook or alterna-

> **I discovered that easily accessible research materials did not have a critical page in their spines; they just restated the textbook version of history.**

tive — many students would come away with material that they might be able to cite and copy into a readable paper, but they wouldn't understand much about the underlying political situations their immigrant group faced.

After the library research, I linked students with people or information that might provide facts and stories not available in the library. The Haitian group, for example, read articles, but hadn't comprehended what was going on: Who was Papa Doc? Baby Doc? What was the United States' involvement in Haiti? What was happening with Jean-Bertrand Aristide? I distributed copies of the Network of Educators on the Americas' (NECA) booklet, *Teaching About Haiti* (Sunshine and Menkart, 1994), which gave my students historical and political analysis they needed in order to make sense of the newspaper and magazine articles. The collection of interwoven short stories *Krik? Krak!* by Edwidge Danticat (1991) developed their personal connection; she gave faces and voices to the people on the boats, to those who lived in fear. The names and terms in the newspaper became real: Aristide, Tontons Macoutes, boat people, refugees. (The group's enthusiasm for the novel caught on. I'd purchased five copies, and there were arguments over who got to read *Krik? Krak!* after group members finished.)

Students became wonderfully devious researchers, using their own connections to gain information. They learned to find back doors when the front doors closed, and windows when all the doors were locked. But sometimes these back door, through-the-window type researches posed another problem: What if personal history omitted vital historical facts and perspectives? While I could help students who studied immigrant groups that I knew something about, I had little time to read and research the Macedonians, Greeks, and Russians.

Travis, for example, was thoroughly confused when his research on Macedonians revealed a snarled web of history involving Greece, Bulgaria, and a historic trade route through the mountains. His research took him back to 146 B.C., when Rome conquered the Kingdom of Macedonia, and forward to today. He wanted to know why his grandfather immigrated. Instead of untangling the web of Macedonian history, he spent time with his grandfather, talking, asking questions, going through photo albums, relying on his personal relationships to decode the past. He arranged for a day at the Macedonian lodge where he interviewed men his grandfather's age about their immigration experiences. Because of my own limited knowledge of events in Macedonia, I let him. This was history via personal story — how much or how little of the history was included, I wasn't sure.

Likewise, when Meghan and I met one Saturday at the Oregon Historical Society, we discovered the letters James Mullany, an Irish immigrant, wrote to his sister in Ireland in the mid-1800s. In one letter (1860), he pleaded with his sister not to mention that he was Catholic: "their [sic] is a strong prejudice against them here on account of the people here thinking it was the Priests that caused the Indian war three or four years ago." Interesting. But in another letter (ibid, p. 14) he wrote of the Snake Indians who attacked a train of 45 whites, "only 15 survived but some of them died of starvation. . . . [A] company of soldiers . . . found them living of [sic] the bodyes [sic] of them that were killed by the [I]ndians." Could we count these letters as historic evidence? Whose voices weren't included? What stories might the Snake Indians have told?

Students using voices of immigrants or novels to tell the history created a dilemma for me: What happens when personal narratives exclude the stories of large groups of other people, or neglect important historical facts? When and how do I intervene? If students tell only their own stories or draw on personal testimonies, is that "inaccurate" history? As an English teacher who weaves literature and history together, who values personal stories as eyewitness accounts of events and who encourages students to

HOPELESS IN VIETNAM
By Danny Cang Dao

Blood floats like a river.
Innocent souls are trapped
under the ground.
Dead bodies haven't been buried yet.
The beautiful barn becomes
a cemetery.

It wasn't supposed to be like this.
Sorrow will never stop.
I get a pack of cigarettes
and start smoking.
I feel the pain curl like smoke in my lungs
and wish I could exhale the sorrow.

"tell their stories," I began to question my own assumptions.

The Vietnamese group underscored my history versus personal story dilemma. Their student-told account emphasized a pro-American stance around the Vietnam War, but said nothing, for example, of U.S. support for French colonialism, its creation of "South Vietnam," or its devastating bombardment of the Vietnamese countryside. How could I challenge the story these students grew up hearing from parents and elders in their community?

I worried that the rest of the class would come away without an understanding of the key role the United States played in the Vietnam War, and without that understanding, how would they be able to critique other U.S. interventions?

I talked with Cang, Tri, and Thu and gave them resources: a timeline that reviewed deepening U.S. involvement in Vietnam, and numerous readings from a critical standpoint. I also introduced them to the film *Hearts and Minds*, which features testimony from numerous Vietnamese critics of the war, as well as prominent U.S. anti-war activists like Daniel Ellsberg. (For more on this film see Chapter 5, "Poetry: Reinventing the Past, Rehearsing the Future.") Without a sustained dialogue, this insertion seemed weak and invasive. But I learned a lesson: Personal story does not always equal history. This lingers as a vexing teaching dilemma.

The Presentation

Once presentation deadlines hit, students argued over dates and who got to go first, last, etc. Our biggest struggle came around the issue of time. Students lobbied for longer time slots. The group studying Mexican immigration was especially ardent. They'd found great movies as well as short stories, informational videos, and a guest speaker from PCUN, the local farm workers union, about working conditions and the boycott of Garden Burgers, a national veggie burger sold in stores and restaurants across the country. They figured they needed at least a week, possibly two. We had five weeks left: four for presentations and a last sacred week to finish portfolios and evaluations. Rosa said, "Look how many days you used when you taught us about the Japanese and Chinese. Two weeks on each! Aren't the Latinos as important as the Asians?" They bargained with students who worked alone, like the Russians and Greeks, for part of their time.

A week or so prior to presentations, groups submitted detailed lesson plans. I met formally with each group to make sure all requirements were covered, but also to question their choices. During previous weeks, I'd attempted to read unfamiliar story and novel selections, and see video clips. I also went over writing assignments: I didn't want any surprises on their teaching day.

The power of my students' teaching was not just in the individual presentations, where students provided historical information in a variety of mostly interesting and unique lesson plans, but also in the juxtaposition of these histories and stories. Students created a jazz improvisation, overlaying voices of pain and struggle and triumph with heroic attempts to escape war, poverty, or traditions that pinched women too narrowly into scripted roles. Their historical research and variety of voices taught a more varied history of immigration than I'd ever attempted to teach in the past.

> **Students' historical research and variety of voices taught a more varied history of immigration than I'd ever attempted to teach in the past.**

But the presentations were also like improvisation, in that they were not as tightly connected and controlled as a rehearsed piece I would have conducted. There were off notes and unfinished strands that seemed promising, but didn't deliver an analysis that could have strengthened student understanding of

> **WHEN I WAS SMALL**
> By Jesus Rangel
>
> When I was small
> in Michoacan,
> the streets of Portland had gold.
>
> Now I am here.
> It's not easy.
> There is no gold,
> only feathers
> at Lynden Farms.

immigration. Few students found research on quotas, few had time left in their presentation to engage in a discussion that linked or compared their group to another. The Haitian group, for example, tied our past studies of Columbus and the Taínos to present Haiti, but didn't develop the history of Duvalier or Aristide or U.S. involvement.

Although presentations varied in length and depth, most gave us at least a look at a culture many students weren't familiar with, and at best a strong sense that not only did racial and political background influence who gets into this country, but also how they live once they arrive.

The group studying Cambodian immigration arranged for our student Sokpha's mother to come to class, and for a viewing of the film *The Killing Fields*. Sokpha's mother told of her life in Cambodia, of hiding in the deep tunnels her father built to keep them safe from U.S. bombs, of her fear of snakes at the bottom of the tunnel that scared her almost as much as the bombs. She talked about the Khmer Rouge, the Vietnamese, and the United States. On her father's death bed, he said, "Go to America. Leave Cambodia." She did. Shoeless, nine months pregnant with Sokpha, and carrying a three- year-old on her back, she walked for three days and three nights from Cambodia into Thailand, dodging land mines that killed some of her fellow travelers. She also spoke of difficulties here — how her lack of language skills kept her from finding a good job, her reliance on Sokpha, the erosion of their culture, the Americanization of her children.

The group researching Haitians presented background history tying the modern struggle in Haiti with previous history lessons; their strengths were chilling descriptions of the refugees, their choice of story, their research into Haitian culture, and their writing assignment. Read aloud by a male and a female student, the two-voice story "Children of the

Sea" (Danticat, op.cit.) portrayed a political young man who dared to speak out against the Haitian government, writing to his lover as he rides a sinking boat in search of refuge in the United States. His lover writes of the increased military violence of the Tontons Macoutes, who make parents have sex with their children and who rape and torture suspected supporters of Aristide.

Cang, from the Vietnamese group, recounted Vietnam's history through a timeline. Thu's stories of escape and life in the refugee camps created nightmare scenes for her fellow students of drownings, rapes, and the difficulties of families who got separated. Tri pointed out the geographical settlements of immigrant Vietnamese and their induction into the United States. He talked about the struggle of Vietnamese shrimp fisherman in the Gulf of Mexico, the attempts of the KKK to drive the fishermen out of the region[5], and the creation of Little Saigon in California, a space where Vietnamese have forged a community inside the United States, not unlike many immigrants who came before them.

Skjold Photographs

The student writing assignments generated excellent poems and personal narratives. After Sophia spoke about her mother's experiences, she talked of inheriting her mother's strength to pursue her goals even when she faces opposition. Her assignment for the class: "Write about something you treasure from your family. It might be an heirloom, like a ring, but it can also be a story, a memory, a tradition, a personal trait. Write it as a poem, a personal narrative, or a story." Komar Harvey wrote an essay about his family's love of music:

> *You can hear music on the porch before you enter our house. Tunes climb through those old vinyl windows and mailbox and drift into everybody's ears in the neighborhood. If you came during the holiday season you could hear the Christmas bells chiming through the static of that old crackling phonograph needle. You hear the rumbling voice of Charles Brown as if he were digging a hole up in the living room, "Bells will be ringing. . . ." Nobody graces our door during those Christmas months without a little Charles ringing his bells in their ears. . .*

Travis, the student who researched Macedonians and talked about his grandfather's struggles to get to

[5] See the film *Alamo Bay*, which despite its white-hero-as-main-character flaw does tell some of the story of Vietnamese immigrant fishermen.

the United States, asked each student to write a personal narrative about an obstacle he/she overcame in life. Cang wrote about his difficulty learning English in the face of classmates' ridicule. His narrative had a profound effect on students (I have not changed or corrected his language because it is part of the story):

> *[After he left Vietnam, he was in the Philippines.] In 1989 we came to America. That's when I started to go to school. I went to all of the classes I had, but I felt the blonde and white-skinned people not respected me. They make joke over the way I talk. . . . I'll never give up, I say to myself. One day I'm going to be just like them on talking and writing, but I never get to that part of my life until now. Even if I can understand the word, but still I can't pronounce it, if I do pronounce it, it won't end up right. Truly, I speak Vietnamese at home all the time, that's why I get used to the Vietnamese words more than English, but I'll never give up what I have learned. I will succeed with my second language.*

The group who had researched Mexican immigration did indeed take several days for their presentation. They taught about the theft of Mexican land by the United States during the 1846-48 war with Mexico,

> **I watched students crack through stereotypes they had nurtured about others. Students who sat by their lockers on C-floor were no longer lumped together under the title "Chinese." They became Vietnamese, Cambodian, Laotian. Students no longer mimicked the sound of their speech as a put-down.**

Jean-Claude Lejeune

immigration border patrols, the effects of toxic sprays on migrant workers, the migrants' living conditions in Oregon. The students also initiated a debate on Proposition 187: Should the United States deny health and education services to undocumented immigrants? Then the presenters asked the class to write a persuasive essay taking a point of view on the question.

One day we watched the movie *Mi Familia*, about a "Mexican" family whose original homeland was in California. As we watched, we ate tamales and sweet tacos that Rosa and her mother-in-law lugged up three flights of stairs to our classroom. Then we wrote food poems that tied us to our culture. Sarah LePage's "Matzo Balls" is a tribute to her grandmother:

> *Grandma's hands,*
> *wise, soft, and old,*
> *mold the Matzo meal*
> *between the curves of each palm.*
> *She transforms our heritage*
> *into perfect little spheres.*
> *Like a magician*
> *she shapes our culture*
> *as our people do.*
> *This is her triumph.*
> *She lays the bowl aside*
> *revealing her tired hands,*
> *each wrinkle a time*
> *she sacrificed something for our family.*

Evaluation

On our last day, students overwhelmingly voted that immigration was the unit they both learned the most from and cared the most about. Komar, the first to speak, said, "I never realized that Cambodians were different from Vietnamese. Sokpha's family went through a lot to get here, so did Tri's, Thu's and Cang's." Stacey, a member of the Haitian group, added, "I learned that the United States isn't just Black and white. I learned that my people are not the only ones who have suffered in this country." Khalilah noted that she hadn't realized what research really meant until she struggled to find information about the Haitians. While others added similar points about various groups or presentations they learned from, Travis summed up the conversation by saying, "I didn't know anything about Proposition 187 or the discrimination immigrants have faced because that wasn't part of my family's history. I didn't know that there was discrimination about who got in and who was kept out of the United States, and now I do."

I felt that students learned from each other about immigrants' uneven and unfair treatment. But they had also learned lessons that would alter their interactions with the "Chinese" — actually Korean —

154

storekeeper at the intersection of Martin Luther King Jr. and Fremont. At Jefferson, one of the most offensive scenes I have witnessed in the hallways or classrooms is how U.S.-born students silence immigrant Asian, Russian, and Mexican students as they speak their own languages or struggle to speak English. Throughout the year, Cang, Thu, and Tri's personal testimony during discussions or read-arounds about the pain of that silencing — as well as their stories about fighting with their parents or setting off firecrackers in their school in Vietnam — created much more awareness in our classroom than any lecture could have.

I credit our study of history — for example, the Mexican-American War — as part of that change, but through this student-led unit on immigration, I watched students crack through stereotypes they had nurtured about others. Students who sat by their lockers on C-floor were no longer lumped together under the title "Chinese"; they became Vietnamese, Cambodian, Laotian. Students no longer mimicked the sound of their speech as a put-down. Latino students who spoke Spanish near the door on the west side of the building were no longer seen as outsiders who moved into the neighborhood with loud cars and lots of children, but as political exiles in a land that had once belonged to their ancestors. The Russian students who moved together like a small boat through the halls of Jefferson were no longer odd, but seekers of religious freedom.

Throughout fourth quarter, I tossed and turned at night questioning my judgment about asking students to teach such an important part of history — and the consequence that much history would not be taught. But after hearing their enthusiasm and their changed perceptions about their classmates, the world, and research, I put my critique temporarily on hold. Turning over the classroom circle to my students allowed them to become the "experts" and me to become their student. While I lost control and power over the curriculum and was forced to question some key assumptions of my teaching, I gained an incredible amount of knowledge — and so did they. ∎

References

Danticat, Edwidge. *Krik? Krak!* New York: Vintage Books, 1991.

Ethnic NewsWatch, an electronic database of articles from newspapers, magazines and journals of the ethnic, minority, and native press. Available from SoftLine

On our last day, students overwhelmingly voted that immigration was the unit they both learned the most from and cared the most about.

Information Co., (800) 524-7922, www.slinfo.com.

Gesensway, Deborah, and Roseman, Mindy. *Beyond Words: Images from America's Concentration Camps.* Ithaca, NY: Cornell University Press, 1987.

Houston, Jeanne Wakatsuki, and Houston, James D. *Farewell to Manzanar.* Boston: San Francisco Book Company/Houghton Mifflin, 1973.

Inada, Lawson. *Legends from Camp.* Minneapolis, MN: Coffee House Press, 1993.

Kim, Elaine H. *Asian American Literature.* Philadelphia, PA: Temple University Press, 1982.

Lai, Him Mark, Lim, Genny, and Yung, Judy. *Island: Poetry and History of Chinese Immigrants on Angel Island, 1910-1940.* San Francisco: San Francisco Study Center. (P.O. Box 5646, San Francisco, CA 94101), 1986.

Lowe, Felicia. 1988. *Carved in Silence.* San Francisco, CA: National Asian American Telecommunications Association. (415) 552-9550.

Mullany, James. Letters from James Mullany to his sister Mary Mullany, August 5, 1860. Oregon Historical Society Mss # 2417, p. 10.

Okada, John. *No-No Boy.* Seattle, WA: University of Washington Press, 1980.

Sone, Monica. *Nisei Daughter.* Seattle, WA: University of Washington Press, 1979.

Sunshine, Catherine A., and Menkart, Deborah. *Teaching About Haiti* (3rd. ed.). Washington, D.C: Network of Educators in the Americas, 1993.

Takaki, Ronald. *Strangers from a Different Shore: A History of Asian Americans.* New York: Penguin, 1990.

Takaki, Ronald. *Journey to Gold Mountain.* New York: Chelsea House, 1994.

Yamada, Mitsuye. *Camp Notes.* San Lorenzo, CA: Shameless Hussy Press, 1976.

For Further Reading

Asian Women United of California. *Making Waves: An Anthology of Writings By and About Asian-American Women.* Boston: Beacon, 1989.

Chan, Jeffrey Paul, et al. (Eds.), *The Big Aiiieeeee! An Anthology of Chinese-American and Japanese-American Literature.* New York: Meridian, 1991.

ACTIVITY
IMMIGRATION PROJECT

In this unit, you will work with a self-chosen group to study the history, politics, and stories of a past or contemporary immigrant group. You will conduct research in and out of the library. You will find and read poetry, novels, and short stories, and watch videos in order to understand their lives and circumstances more clearly. During a presentation, your group will teach the history and stories of these immigrants to your classmates. Listed below are the questions your group needs to research, the criteria for your presentation, and a list of related individual tasks to complete on your own during this quarter.

Content Questions to Research:

1. Background history: Why did this group come to the United States? What was happening in their home country that caused them to leave? Famine? War? Poverty? Political disagreements? What was something happening in the United States that encouraged them to come?

2. Treatment in United States: What kind of reception did this group receive in the United States? Any problems entering? Who else was coming at the time? Any quotas on the group? How has this group of immigrants been treated since their arrival in the United States? Give examples, tell stories.

3. Where did these people find work? Did their work pit them against workers of other racial or ethnic backgrounds? Were they able to find work that matched their occupations in their home country?

Lesson plan:
Each lesson plan must include the following:

____**1. Story, movie or speaker:** Bring the "voice" of the group to our class — either as part of the historical background information or as a way of showing us the group's culture and/or living situation.

____**2. Background information:** Present the history of the people and their struggles (as outlined by the three content questions above) as a lecture, a reading, a movie, a timeline, role play, or a series of stories.

____**3. Class discussion:** After your presentation, plan some discussion questions that will explore the subject of immigration more thoroughly — relate it to previous presenters or past units of study or link it to broader social issues.

____**4. Written activity for class:** As a culminating activity for your group, give your classmates a writing assignment that grows out of your presentation.

Individual Tasks:

____**1. Short Story:** Write a short story or play based on the lives of the people you researched. This is required of every student.

    You must include the following in your story:

    A. History — some background to let us know about this group

    B. Dialogue

    C. Blocking — locating the characters in the setting as they speak: Where are they? What are they doing as they speak?

    D. Description of character and place

    E. Flashback — revealing past action to shed light on present situation

    F. Interior monologue — the thoughts and feelings of a character from his/her point of view

____**2. Final Essay for the year:** Write about immigration. Explore the three content questions above using specific examples from your research and/or the presentations of your fellow classmates.

    You may choose to focus your essay on one or more immigrant groups. You may choose to compare the treatment of immigrant groups or you may choose to focus on the issue of immigration. Your essay must be grounded in specific evidence from your research. **See the essay criteria sheet below for details.**

____**3. Profile (Extra Credit):** Was there someone we should know about from this group who displayed extraordinary courage or leadership? Profile this person or people somehow.

ESSAY CRITERIA: ATTACH THIS SHEET TO YOUR ESSAY.

_____1. **Thesis Statement: Stated or implied.** Write it in the space below.

_____2. **Introduction:** What kind of introduction did you use?

- Question
- Quotation
- Anecdote
- Wake up call

_____3. **Evidence:** Prove your point. Check which of the following types of evidence you used below. **ON YOUR ESSAY — MARK EACH TYPE OF EVIDENCE WITH A DIFFERENT COLOR:**

- Personal Experience: Evidence from your daily life
- Anecdotes: Stories you've heard that illustrate your point
- Statistics/Facts
- Examples from the media
- Interviews with immigrants
- Research from historical texts

_____4. **Conclusion:** What kind of conclusion did you use?

- Summary
- Circle back to the beginning
- Possible solution
- Restate and emphasize thesis
- Further questions to think about

_____5. **Tight Writing:**

- Active verbs
- Lean language
- Metaphoric language
- Sentence variety

_____5. **Grammar, Punctuation, Spelling checked and corrected.**

WHAT ARE YOU?
By Robert Smith

What are you if you're not Black and you're not white?
I am both, so how could I choose just one?
No, I am not an "other."
I am not a small box to be filled
with the dark markings of your pen.

I am not a blank space between Black and white.

There is no other like me.
No one holds what I know.

"Then what are you?" you ask.

I am a Black man who has never
touched the sands of Africa.
I am a European looking for riches.
I am a slave stripped away from his home.
I am a lost woman in Egypt, Niger, Cameroon, or Zambia.
I am a merchant who sells fish from his brother's boat.
I am the men and women who died at Plymouth Rock.
I am the Aztec Indian whose blood was spilled for a little
gold.
I am the pregnant women who sits in the icy cold.
I am the red faces who walked the Trail of Tears.
I am my mother's father whose face is covered by a cold
hood.
I am the German soldier who spills my Jewish blood.
I am the South African Republic that beat
my Black grandmother.
I am a being, called human, from the word "humane."
I breathe as a product of marriage.
I am a child of life.
I can't be put into a box and filled up
with cruel ink.
I can't be spoken of as an other or decide
the simple choice of Black or white.

I am a soul, flesh and blood and so much more.
I am history
I am diversity.

A PUBLICATION OF RETHINKING SCHOOLS

Portfolios

Portfolios and Basketball

It was 5:30 on finals day. Most students had left the building at noon, giving teachers a chance to work on their grades before the weekend or prepare for the new classes starting on Monday. They had three hours; the possible uses for their time were endless. I was in the library's prehistoric computer lab with a roomful of students who were still writing, revising, and polishing work for their portfolios.

Lloyd had walked out of the lab and into the adjoining library. At 5:30 college basketball comes on cable. Lloyd slid onto the library table, obviously through with portfolios for the day. "Hey, Linda, why do we have to write these evaluations anyway? You've got all my work in there. You're the teacher. Just read my work and give it a grade. Why do I have to evaluate it?"

His eyes moved back to the TV, where Arizona was playing UCLA.

I looked over at him. Somehow this year he'd moved from his one or two line papers without punctuation to essays, scrappy and sometimes not quite full enough to be called "done," but a big improvement over last year's meager output. He wasn't ready for college writing yet, and our class was ending.

"Do you watch videos after your basketball games?" I asked, knowing that the coach always scheduled mandatory post-game reviews.

"Yeah, every day after our game we got to go watch those videos," he answered without taking his eyes off Damon Stoudamire.

"Why do you think Coach Harris makes you watch

> **The connection between teaching, practicing, performing, reviewing, and critiquing is a common thread between disciplines. It also gives me a way to connect the student's passion with learning to evaluate their own writing.**

your game after you already played it? Couldn't he just tell you what you did?"

"Because then we can see our mistakes — and what plays we're running that work. We look at videos of teams we're going to play, too, so we can see what kind of offense and defense they've got. We can see who to match our players up with. We learn their plays so we can outwit them at the basket." He shifted on the table, still not seeing how his writing portfolio had anything to do with post-game videos. I turned off the TV and we sat and made comparisons between basketball videos and writing portfolios.

With Lloyd it was basketball, with Harold it was wrestling, with Tawni and Aaron it was dance. The connection between teaching, practicing, performing, reviewing, and critiquing is a common thread between disciplines. It also gives me a way to connect the student's passion with learning to evaluate their own writing.

Portfolios: Grading, Evaluation, Assessment?

I've had students make portfolios for years. When I first started keeping writing folders, I called them portfolios, but they were really glorified work folders, where students stored everything from false starts and ugly "I didn't want to write that poem anyway" fragments along with polished pieces. Now I've come to see portfolios as places where students keep the journey of their writing, but also as a place where they analyze both their work and their process, so they can take what they know and apply it to the next piece

160

Skjold Photographs

the student and gives the act of judgement and power to the teacher. Ultimately, students learn a great deal more about their writing if they learn to "watch the post-game video" and critique their "play." But it's hard to get them to that point.

Portfolios are hot items in the educational marketplace today. They abound in education catalogues, teaching and assessment journals, and conference book fairs. Vermont has a statewide portfolio assessment which other states are eyeing, as "authentic assessment" becomes a way to tie "workplace skills" to classroom outcomes.

As a classroom teacher and director of the Portland Writing Project, I'm skeptical of legislators and school bureaucrats mandating portfolios. The ones I've seen designed for English classrooms too often dictate types of writing students must include, and then provide ways to score them so that once again student achievement can be reduced to a single digit number — easily compared across cities, states, and the nation.

I'm not interested in reducing my students to a single digit. I am concerned about their growth in writing and thinking. Frankly, I've never found district or state reading and writing scores to be reliable or useful in my classroom practice. I use portfolios to shape my instruction for individual students, but I also see portfolios as a tool to move students from object to subject in their education. For a critical teacher, portfolios are an evaluation method that pushes students to participate with their teacher in their assessment, rather than being judged by teacher-as-outside-authority.

But let me be clear, I'm not a hands-off kind of teacher. Some of my colleagues believe the portfolio belongs to the student; therefore, the student should be allowed complete freedom to select and control the content. I disagree. There are places and times when students have control; for example, at the end of my class, students make a book of their writing where they can choose the pieces. Jessica, a terrific poet, put poetry and pictures in her book; Aaron made his a collection of fiction writing. With portfolios, I try to establish and negotiate higher expectations. I'm setting the standards. Each grading period in each class, I determine the kinds of writing that students must include in their portfolios.

that comes along — just as my basketball players view their videos to improve their next game.

While most students enjoy rummaging through their folders and don't mind tossing their work from one folder to another, they are resistant to reflection. Lloyd's comment that I'm the teacher, therefore I should just do the evaluation, is common. Most students aren't accustomed to standing back from their work and assessing it. The routine has been write it, turn it in, the teacher grades it, get it back. End of cycle. When the teacher evaluates a piece, it takes an essential part of the learning experience away from

One term in Literature and U.S. History class, they needed a literary analyis, a historical fiction piece, and a research paper on either a resistance movement or a person who worked for change. Students also included poetry, interior monologues, film critiques that we worked on, but unless they completed satisfactory drafts of the requirements, they didn't pass. I provided lots of work time, models, and demonstrations; these tasks were not assigned; they were taught. I spent two to three afternoons a week in the computer lab after school working with students who either needed extra help or who wanted more work time.

Partly, my insistence on variety and standards comes from real world concerns: I'm at the high-stakes end of education; I work mostly with juniors and seniors. Tyrone, a thoughtful rapper, would like to write every assignment — from museum critique to historical fiction — as a rap, but if I allowed that, I wouldn't be providing him a rigorous education. He already knows how to write raps. He doesn't know how to write essays. As more colleges move toward

> **Most students aren't accustomed to standing back from their work and assessing it. The routine has been write it, turn it in, the teacher grades it, get it back. End of cycle.**

portfolios as entrance criteria in addition to SATs, I want my students, who tend to score poorly on these tests, to be able to demonstrate their range.

Beyond the college connection I want to push students to think more deeply about the world, to make connections in their essays between literature and life in their neighborhood. I don't just want pretty words and adept dialogue; I want searing analysis. My students walk out the school door into a social emergency. They are in the center of it. I believe that writing is a basic skill that will help them both understand that emergency and work to change it.

The portfolio in my classroom fulfills several duties: It showcases students' work in a variety of genres; it demonstrates their journey as a writer — from early to polished drafts as well as stumbling first attempts at poetry, fiction, and essays to later, more accomplished pieces. But it also provides a space for student and teacher to reflect on the change and growth in writing and thinking as well as pointing out a trajectory for future work.

Over the years, I've made some discoveries and

fine-tuned my approach to portfolios. Some terms I'd end up with amazing evaluations — where students had obviously internalized discussions on craft and content. Other terms, the analysis was thin — even when I could see remarkable changes in students' writing. Sometimes I knew I'd crammed too much work in at the end of the term; other times, it was obvious that the portfolio prompts were too meticulous or too broad, and still other times it was clear that my teaching was off target. Although I'm still struggling with the evaluation process — as well as the teaching process that precedes it — I've learned some lessons along the way.

Time is important.

Students need enough time between their entry into the class and the analysis of their writing to see change or growth. Often the portfolio evaluation written after the first nine weeks of class is weak. Students are just "finding the basket," learning to dribble. I'm still working at moving them from perfunctory "for-the-teacher writing" to committed writing, from all-rhyming poetry to free verse, from aimless diatribes to essays with support, but after nine weeks, the pathway has not been traveled often enough to see it clearly. Still, it's important to begin the process, so they are critiquing their own work. They also need to begin noting how they work, what they do to move out of a block, how to get a first draft finished. In short, they need to become critics of their own learning.

I used to jump into the writing evaluation at the end of the quarter without giving students time to reread their pieces. Now I devote a 90-minute class period for students to transfer papers from their work folder to their writing portfolio.

Before they begin, I bring in one of my portfolios and talk about pieces I chose to put in and why. Some are samples of my best writing, others are pieces I want to work on, while some show how much my writing has improved. I show them all the drafts of my pieces — including the false starts and comments from my writing friends. I want them to see that most people do not create a perfect draft the first time. This is a noisy 90 minutes, as students read and talk about their writing (mostly, but not always on task). It's when I hear students say, "I didn't realize how much work I completed." Or, "Look, I didn't even know how to line my poetry out." And sometimes, "I wrote better pieces last year."

> **As more colleges move toward portfolios as entrance criteria in addition to SATs, I want my students, who tend to score poorly on these tests, to be able to demonstrate their range.**

I learned that if I expect a thorough analysis of their writing, then I need to give that signal by weighting the evaluation as heavily as I do a major writing assignment. I need to give models, criteria, set standards, and give them adequate time to complete the task.

I also need to practice patience. It takes as much time to teach students how to think about and write a reflection on their writing as it takes to teach them how to write a literary or historical analysis. Older students with more experience tend to write better analyses than younger, less experienced writers.

I have to praise the effort and push them to the next level.

Models & Prompts
For Portfolio Reflection

When I first started asking students to critique or examine their own writing, I underestimated their need for models of self-reflection. I expected them to "do it" without knowing what they were doing. Bobby Harris, Jefferson High School's basketball coach, wouldn't spend two hours watching a game video without telling his players what to look for — or developing the criteria together with them.

"What is self reflection?" Johnny asked, "What do you mean, 'What did I learn from my writing?'" Amber didn't understand how to use examples from her work for support. Students need to see what I want. They need models of past portfolio evaluations so they can gain a sense of how to look at their writing. Just as they needed examples of former students' essays or historical critiques so they could see what embedded and block quotes look like in text.

I discovered that students took their own writing more seriously after they listened to conversations by writers about writing. For this reason, I read selections from William Stafford, Tess Gallagher, Donald Murray, and Toni Morrision writing about their writing. Students are fascinated, for example, to discover that the idea for Toni Morrison's novel *Beloved* came from an old news article explaining how a woman killed her children because she didn't want them to grow up in slavery.

I also save samples from previous years. I provide guidelines to get students started, but leave them loose enough so that students have room to follow their passion. Sometimes inexperienced writers take the model and copy it exactly, substituting examples from their writing, but using the knowledge of the

ODE TO WRITING
By Jessica Rawlins

I screamed
and scribbled
tore words from within
that were never meant to match.
I lived the story,
tortured the page
like life and death.
It was the fear that drove me
somewhere in my stomach
remembering the thought
of spilled words
numbers of them
that didn't make sense.
I yearned to be eloquent,
understood.
Somehow
the writing
bandaged the wounds,
made up for the words
not spoken
on the page.
I became pungent,
invincible,
knowing I could always be better
from the inside.
I spelled out a new name
making myself a face
with paper,
pen, and ink.

A PUBLICATION OF RETHINKING SCHOOLS

model. They are not really thinking deeply — they are mimicking. I've come to see this as a stage in their evolution.

Some students like more specific prompts, while others find them stifling — so I vary them and allow them choice. When a student says he/she can't get excited about this (or any) assignment, I say, "Find your passion." They know they have to write an evaluation of their work. Renesa, for example, couldn't put pen to paper until I showed her an article by a local columnist on writing. She wrote her evaluation as an advice column for writers, and typed it in newspaper format — including her picture and examples from her writing to prove her point. Frank wrote his as a letter to my future students telling them what they could expect to learn about writing, then giving examples from his own writing.

Some terms I ask my class to focus their evaluation on one genre — essays or fiction, perhaps. Using colored pencils or highlighters, they have to identify types of evidence, introduction styles, block and embedded quotes, and they must analyze their content and conclusion in essays (see Chapter 3 for a more detailed discussion of essays). In fiction, they have to point out dialogue, blocking, imagery, flashback, interior monologues (see Chapter 1 for a more detailed discussion of fiction). Aaron discovered that he rarely used dialogue. Shameica realized that she didn't use blocking and wondered if that was why people got confused about who was speaking in her story. Tony saw that he didn't use evidence from Andrew Jackson's speech on the Cherokee removal; in his critique, he had no quotes to support his position that Jackson was a "racist pig." The act of coloring their drafts made the holes concrete.

Sometimes I ask students to draw pictures or write poems that describe themselves as writers, and then write a paragraph explaining the image for me. Gabriella drew a sculptor with a block of clay. She wrote, "I am the potter with clay, molding, shaping, by taking off pieces and discarding pieces until I have a piece of art." Jim wrote that he was a chef and his writing is dough that he pinches and pulls into just

> **The compiled work and the evaluation of it allows both student and teacher to reflect on what worked, on our mistakes, what we can do better next time.**

the right shape. Licy drew a jar full of candy to describe herself as a contributor to the class:

"My writings and contributions are like the taste of candy itself — some sweet, some sour. Like melting bits of chocolate, I melt cultural information to teach the class something about Mexicans. Like the wrinkled wrapper, I make a sound so everyone knows I am aware. I am here."

One obvious lesson I learned was that students should share their insights with the class. At the beginning of the new term, students showed their metaphors and drawings. These became conversation starters about the craft of writing. As students talked about their drawings or poems, they also shared their roadblocks and their detours. Johanna was a planner who ran into difficulty because her drafts never went as she predicted. The information didn't lay itself out as neatly as she initially hoped it would. Lisa needed to doodle to get started. Anthony said that seeing all of my drafts freed him to get started because he knew he didn't have to get it right the first time. Peter taught some classmates his method of outlining , which was flexible enough to allow for surprises, but gave his piece "river banks" to contain the flow. The point of our class discussion wasn't to make students all work the same way through a piece of writing, but rather to encourage them to find alternative strategies, so if they weren't successful they could try someone else's for a spell to see if it helped.

Portfolios are one small part of the total classroom, but an important part, because it's where I "measure" not only the students' success and growth, but my own as well. I can lay the foundation of expectations at the beginning of the grading period and help students meet those criteria. The compiled work and the evaluation of it allows both student and teacher to reflect on what worked, on our mistakes, what we can do better next time. Perhaps because evaluations give us time to pause and look back, they also rehearse us for our next performance — whether it's writing an essay or making a three-point outside shot in the state tournament. ■

Portfolio Evaluation: Pulitzer

1. **Write a list telling what you know about writing.**

   A. Check two items on your list

   B. Elaborate on how you learned this technique/strategy or how you currently use it in your writing.

   C. Tell how knowing this strategy is going to influence the next piece you write.

2. **Select one piece of your writing. Imagine for a moment that you have been recognized as one of your state's outstanding writers and you've been asked to write about this piece.**

   A. Tell how you "got" this piece. Discuss why you wrote it the way you did.

   B. Tell what this piece demonstrates about your ability to write — use of an effective introduction, development of a powerful argument, use of imagery and rhythm, or expansion of character through dialogue.

   C. Note the changes you made during revision. Please mark them on your drafts. Number your drafts. Number your changes so we can both follow what you are writing about. How do these changes reflect new knowledge about writing?

   D. Discuss the role your classmates played in improving your writing.

   E. Write your observations about your writing habits — what you've noticed helps you get started on a piece or helps you revise a piece.

   F. Discuss your observations about what good writing is, by using examples from your work, the work of your peers, or the work of professional writers.

WHERE POEMS HIDE
by Deonica Johnson

Poems can be found
under the bark dust of trees
and can be blown away in the wind
of a rain storm.

Poems ride home on the bus
and keep you company.
Washing dishes,
vacuuming the carpet,
cleaning out the attic,
poems are everywhere.

I found a poem
beneath a blossoming rose bush
in the garden.

I've seen poems drizzle off plump lips
to say beautiful things.
I've seen poems dance with anger
and hide with fear
and laugh when nothing's funny.

Poems can be found
in the sweat of a basketball game,
in the buzz of bee delivering honey to the hive.

Poems can be found
when watching that favorite cartoon character,
even in that teacher that gives you the extra
push to continue.

I've found my poem, now where can you find yours?

Writing Portfolio

Criteria: At least three pages handwritten, or two pages typed (12-point font). This must be thorough and use examples from your work.

Writing can be a process of discovery. When asked about all of his failed experiments Einstein responded, "Those weren't failures. I learned what didn't work each time." Sometimes our writing "works," other times it doesn't. One of the purposes of a portfolio is to give you time to reflect on what you've learned about writing — either through your mistakes or your successes. When you figure out what makes you a successful writer and articulate that on paper or in dialogue, you are more likely to transfer that knowledge to your next writing project. Find your passion in this assignment. Find a way to make it meaningful to you.

Procedure:

___ 1. Look back through your work folder. I want you to begin this portfolio by reading through your papers. As you read, look at the kind of growth you've made over the year. Take some notes on the changes you've witnessed in your writing.

___ 2. Find pieces that you want to put in your portfolio. Remember to find examples for each genre: narrative, expository, persuasive, and poetry. Think about what these pieces will show an audience about your writing talent.

___ 3. Choose either the Pulitzer (See "Portfolio Evaluation — Pulitzer" on page 166) or the Profile style of portfolio. Please note that both of these will use essay criteria — whether you write them as a letter or as a speech:

   A. Introduction
- Question
- Anecdote
- Quote
- Wake-Up Call

   B. Evidence:
- **SPECIFIC EVIDENCE/QUOTES/CITATIONS FROM YOUR WORK**
(This section will vary depending on your topic choice)
- Explanations of how to write a narrative or essay
- Discussion about revision or getting started
- Discussion of your writing strategy

   C. Conclusion

Untracking English

Untracking English:
Creating Quality Education For All Students

Aaron, a dancer in Jefferson High School's elite Jefferson Dancers, tapped his pencil against his desk as he spoke: "Schools are geared towards repeating society's pattern. Some people succeed; some people fail. Tracking makes it seem like the kids are at fault. My father is a doctor. My mother is a voracious reader who read to me and bought me books. What about the kids whose parents didn't have the time or couldn't afford that? I entered school ahead of the race. I ended up in all advanced classes. An 'aha' I came to is that everybody should have all opportunities open to them. Why figure out ahead of time for people what they're going to do with their lives."

Aaron paused and looked around the room at his classmates in this junior Literature and U.S. History class before calling on Jim, who hadn't spoken during our discussion on tracking.

Jim drew a deep breath before speaking. His voice cracked with tears. "What I learned in school is that I'm not good enough. I was never in an advanced class. Schools are set up like beauty pageants — some of us were set up to fail. The way they treat us, they might as well say, 'You suck. Get lost. Get out of here.' Look, I've always been in bonehead English. Why wasn't I good enough to be in top classes? Haven't I written as good papers as you? Can't I talk about things as good as you?"

Jim's statement continues to haunt me years later as I teach a "low-track" class where students gleam like unpolished agates on Moonstone Beach. And Aaron's question, "Why figure out ahead of time for people what they're going to do with their lives?" should be

placed at the top of every course guide that designates the test scores students need before they apply for an honors class.

The classes I taught at Jefferson — Literature and U.S. History, Contemporary Literature and Society, and Writing for Publication — were all untracked. I knew tracking was unjust, and I didn't want to perpetuate the myths about academic ability that tracking imparts. I also wanted to demonstrate that it was possible to teach a wide range of students in one class, to present a model for my school and district. After ten years of teaching remedial English, I also knew I didn't want to teach one more low-tracked class. Even if my seniority allowed me the privilege of teaching advanced classes, morally, I couldn't teach them any longer either.

Tracking helps create and legitimate a social hierarchy within a school based on perceived differences in student ability. Students in higher tracks have access to college preparatory classes: algebra, geometry, calculus, chemistry, physics. But even in English and social studies, students participate in different educational experiences. Students in advanced classes read whole books from the classics or the canon, write papers analyzing literature, and complete library research which prepares them for college, while students in lower track classes typically read "light bites" of literature and history — short stories or adolescent novels. Their writing, if they write, tends to remain in the narrative, personal storytelling mode rather than moving to the analytical.

Jean-Claude Lejeune

Beyond the lack of preparation for academic tasks, the larger problem I witness is the embedded beliefs students carry with them when they leave these classrooms. Students in advanced classes come to believe they "earned" a privilege that is often given them based on race, class, or gender, while students in remedial classes come to feel they are incapable of completing more difficult work.

> **Students in advanced classes come to believe they "earned" a privilege that is often given them based on race, class, or gender, while students in remedial classes come to feel they are incapable of completing more difficult work.**

say, "See, untracking doesn't work." To successfully untrack English classes, teachers must unmask the myths about student ability, redesign the curriculum, and change teaching strategies.

I created untracked classes because of the injustice I saw in students' education. I continued to teach untracked classes as long as I was at Jefferson because they are better classes — for the students and the teacher.

But I wonder what other messages students learn when they see majority white or wealthy students in advanced classes. Do they believe that those students are smarter than students of color or poor and working-class students? When we allow tracking — especially tracking which privileges one race, one class, or one gender over another — we unwittingly allow students to walk away with these and who knows what other assumptions.

Too many good intentions have been undermined by implementing a detracking policy without helping teachers reconstruct their ideas about students and curriculum. Dumping low-tracked students into advanced classes without changing strategies and content harms students and derails the possibility for change. It becomes all too easy to point at the drop-out and failure rates of under-prepared students and

Looking for Each Student's Gifts

After teaching untracked classes for several years, I've come to believe that the notion of great differences in student capacity is false. One of the first obligations of a teacher in an untracked class is to look at student ability in a new light. Teachers must see the gifts that each student brings to class, not the deficits. The teacher must absolutely believe in the potential of the student, but even more essentially, the teacher must believe in the right of the student to have access to a rigorous education. And the teacher must convey those beliefs clearly to the student who may be working off years of failure and poor work habits. Many of the students who come from remedial or regular classes are bright. But the abilities they bring to class often go unrecognized because they aren't the skills traditional education has prized: reading and writ-

To successfully untrack English classes, teachers must unmask the myths about student ability, redesign the curriculum, and change teaching strategies.

ing. I especially found this to be true of many African-American males who had been misplaced in special education. These students had amazing dexterity with verbal language and astute social/political insights, but their literacy skills were underdeveloped.

Because of the variation in students' scholastic histories, they come with distinct sets of skills, but not necessarily different sets of intellectual capacities. The students who typically perform well in class have better reading, writing, geographic, and math skills. They have better school work habits. They know how to study. Sometimes they are voracious readers. They have written more essays and frequently know how to put together a well-organized paper. They are confident of their ability as students. They see teachers as allies and know how to use their teachers, and others, as resources. Often, they have college-educated parents who can help them with homework and who are available in the evenings to make sure their work is completed. They have access to more information and materials — from computers and home libraries to transportation to city and college libraries. Their parents are not intimidated by these institutions and know how to use computer searches, librarians, and the school system to gain information. And because they travel through their school careers being rewarded for their performance, they are generally better behaved.

Whereas many lower-tracked students may still have problems with the basics in punctuation, spelling, sentence structure, and grammar, they may not know where to begin or end a sentence, much less a paragraph or an essay. Some have never read a complete book by their junior or senior year in high school. Some are not accustomed to the practice of homework. They are often intimidated when it comes to advanced class work because they lack the skills necessary to perform the tasks — especially if they are assigned rather than taught. Unlike their high-

achieving peers, they often don't view their teachers as resources and aren't as successful in using the school system for their benefit. Frequently, they are alienated or bored by the material in advanced classes and don't see the immediate relevance to their lives. Their parents may work one or more jobs and may not have the time, expertise, or materials to help or push their children at home. Over the years, I've noticed how much my training as an English teacher is called on with my two daughters' education, and I wonder how children without college educated parents (or with parents who have to work the night shift) can compete.

But often the most creative students in my mixed-ability classes are the students who have not succeeded in school. Many previously low-tracked students have a great ear for dialogue and metaphor because their listening and speaking skills are more finely honed. These students tend to be playful, talkative, adept at role plays, debates, and class discussions. They are the risk-takers. Steven, for example, literally jumped into the middle of a debate. Once, in a unit on men and women in literature and society, he strode to the center of our circle and acted out how he believed women have a shopping mall approach to men. Steven pretended he was a woman inspecting each man as if he were a piece of merchandise, then tossing him aside when someone better came along. Although he had difficulty writing an essay on the topic, his spontaneous "presentation" during discussion was well-argued and gave students a metaphoric framework for many of their debates on the topic.

Each group of students (as well as each individual student) presents its own problems. While most of the "advanced" students complete their class work and homework on time, too often they write "safe" papers. Chris, a potential valedictorian, summed it up when he asked, "What do I have to do to get an A?" Not "what tools must I be capable of using," not "what knowledge will I need to understand literature, writing, society, or history," but "what must I get done." My goal is to shake these students out of their safety, to create a desire to write instead of a desire to complete the work, to awaken some passion for learning, to stop them from slurping up education without examining it. I wanted them to walk around with note pads, ready for their next poem, story, or essay, but I also wanted them to question themselves and the world: In fact, I wanted them to question the privilege that placed them into advanced or honors classes. I wanted the same for my low-skilled students, but additionally, I was challenged to harness their verbal dexterity onto paper and motivate them to work outside of class. And I also wanted to provoke them to examine the inequities that landed many of them in low-skilled classes in the first place.

Changing Misperceptions

One of the biggest lies about ending ability grouping is that "low" students benefit while "advanced" students languish. Parents and educators worry that the behavior of unruly, uninterested students will keep the teacher focused on classroom control rather than on teaching. As my student Ellie said when I discussed untracking with her tracked class, "We couldn't learn if those students were in our class." Chetan Patel wrote one of his college essays for University of Chicago — "A Lesson in Tolerance" — about his view of my class on the first day:

> Rowdy students hung off their seats as I walked into class the first day of my junior year. The desks were arranged in a circle around the classroom, almost every seat was occupied. I looked for a chair next to a friend, but found the only empty seat near a window. I sat and looked around the class. It included dancers, athletes, and the leftovers from Jefferson's dismantled Scholar's program. I was in the Scholar's program until its end, taking advantage of the small classes, countless field trips and advanced curriculum. Because of last year's

> budget cuts, the program was disassembled and students were left to face Jefferson's overcrowded and often crude classes. Outside the 30 students in the scholars program, I thought the rest of Jefferson's thousand students were completely ignorant. They spat in hallways, punched ceiling tiles, smoked on the street curb, and talked in slang. The Literature and U.S. History class I was in was supposed to be the best Jefferson had to offer. From the looks of it, Jefferson's best didn't seem like much.

While I don't want to underplay the challenge to maintain an orderly classroom so that all students can learn, too often the word "rowdy" is a code word for "lots of poor students or students of color" — as can be seen in Chetan's initial portrayal of the students who were not in the Scholar's program. When the expectations are clear and the assignments challenge students to think critically about the world and their place in it, students are not as likely to act out. Because low-track students, in general, have less patience for busy work and value grades less than honors students, they are more likely to complain loudly, criticize the demeaning work and

> **The teacher must absolutely believe in the potential of the student, but even more essentially, the teacher must believe in the right of the student to have access to a rigorous education.**

their teachers. They are more likely to turn their attention to disrupting the class. And they have lots of practice; they're good at it.

I can't entirely dismiss the fact that some classes are more boisterous — especially low-tracked classes where students do not believe that the work has any real meaning for their lives. Yes, untracked classes will probably be louder than honors classes. Yes, more students will arrive more academically unprepared than in an honors class. Yes, if the balance of the class is shifted too heavily in favor of low-track students, "discipline" may remain an issue. But well-balanced untracked classes will also be more inventive, more creative, and more honest. As Chetan wrote, "The following days, I began to talk with my neighbors and my opinion of the class changed entirely. I loved coming to second block and hearing everyone's clever stories. . . . My [former classmates] looked down on other students who I now thought of as equals."

Certainly, untracking honors English is not an easy sell for students — or their parents — who have been offered the privileges of honors programs that Chetan outlined earlier: small classes, frequent field trips, and advanced curriculum. They like their privileges and believe they've earned them, unlike the "rowdy students" Chetan met on the first day of my class. This book has been an argument for a rigorous, untracked curriculum. Every activity I've highlighted here is designed to challenge students who have diverse academic histories.

Parents and educators also worry that top students end up playing teacher to their under-prepared peers in an untracked class — and unfortunately this is sometimes true, but it shouldn't be. Turning advanced students into tutors occurs when the curriculum and methodology of a high-tracked class remain the same. It's the worst-case scenario that proponents of tracking use to scare us into maintaining the status quo. They assume that top students master the material quickly and must either tap their toes or play teacher while remedial students struggle to catch up. This situation places students, like Jim in the opening of this piece, who arrive feeling one-down educationally, at a further disadvantage, but it also takes time away from more skilled students who should be working at the edge of their ability instead of repeating what they already know. Adam, a senior in my untracked Contemporary Literature and Society class, wrote of his experience in this role:

> I was always the one the teacher looked at when someone else needed help. "Oh, Adam can help you." It's not the usual form of discrimination, but I realize now how much it bothered me when I was in grade school. "Well, so-and-so isn't a good student, he needs extra help. We'll make him partners with Adam. Adam won't mind spending his extra time explaining things to so-and-so."

If we turn the practice of students as teachers around and look more carefully at our students' gifts, then we acknowledge that all students can be teachers. As Jessica noted in her class evaluation:

> This is the first English class in three years where I have been around different students. All of us have been tracked into separate little migrating groups, forever stuck with each other. I think that having so many different thinking minds made it rich. All the experiences we shared were exciting and new. It made us debate things because most often we didn't agree with each other. But we listened and we all think a little bit differently now. Don't you wish the whole world could be like our class?

When there is real diversity in the class, students teach each other by sharing their strengths: Steven's

In all of these classes, the mainstay of the curriculum is rigorous reading and writing activities that prepare all students for the university or post-secondary institutions.

improvisation on gender issues helped create a metaphor for students to discuss men and women in society and literature. Jessica's ability to capture the talk of the neighborhood provided her classmates with a model of how to use dialogue to build characters in their own writing. Kanaan's analysis of the teaching of language, and how it affected African-American students as they were learning to read and write, had a profound effect on his fellow students' understanding of how political the nature of reading and writing can be. Curtina's images in her poetry broke the barrier between the academy and the music scene. Joe's insight into how the politics of race reverberate in his neighborhood educated his peers who lived on the other side of town in a way that no traditional book learning could have.

Students teach each other by telling the stories of their lives or debating issues from diverse perspectives. Scott, who drove to Jefferson every day from an almost all-white suburb, thought that racism had disappeared after the '60s. When Suntory wrote about the hour it took for 911 to respond after gunshots were fired into his house, Scott's education about race relations moved up a notch. So did DeShawn's when Alejandro spoke of crossing the border with his grandmother when he was six and acting as a translator for his parents.

Chetan learned quickly that his initial assessment of his peers was flawed and that he had a lot to learn from his classmates:

> The teacher, Ms. Christensen, spent five minutes silencing the side chatter. . . . It took almost an hour for her to go over the class expectations that seemed entirely too high for this group. Amid more side talk, Ms. Christensen expounded on the first assignment, "We're going to write profiles on each other." After a five-minute explanation of what a profile was, the class groaned. She partnered the students up and I got stuck with Ayanna Lashley, a short girl whose growing stomach contrasted with her tiny body... [A]s the bell rang, Ms. Christensen announced, "Bring your finished profile tomorrow."

> That night I wondered how bad the year was going to be. Expecting Ayanna to write a poor profile, I quickly scribbled a few notes on a piece of paper about her.

> The next day Ms. Christensen told us to read what we wrote. She asked for a volunteer and the all-

too-eager Tony started us out. Ten readers later, I couldn't believe what I was hearing. I had never heard writing like this — writing this good. To my surprise, no one used a single slang word. . . . One by one, the class went around the circle, every person painting a perfect picture of their partner. My turn finally came and I nervously read my shameful piece. I slumped into my chair as my partner read hers. I frowned, not because her piece was bad (it was terrific), but because I had let myself and the class down. . . .

The students around me wrote in different, exciting styles instead of the bookish Scholars' type. My writing became dynamic and versatile, something my past efforts had failed to accomplish.

At year's end, I realized how prejudiced I had been. I totally misjudged my fellow students and learned more making and sitting next to new friends. The class turned out to be my favorite at Jefferson, not because everyone suddenly changed their ways, but because I changed mine.

In fact, the writing was rougher, less polished than Chetan remembers. Students began the year with rich lives, not rich writing skills. Chetan wrote his memo-

ries of the class after spending his junior and his senior year — by choice — in untracked classes. But he is right that he learned from the stories of classmates and from their writing styles. This notion of enlisting all students as teachers implies a major shift in the structure, content, and methodology of the class.

Changing the Curriculum

Successfully untracking means re-examining and changing the curriculum. Instead of constructing my curriculum around a parade of novels, I teach thematic units that emphasize the social/political underpinnings of my students' lives: the politics of language, the politics of literacy, men and women in society and literature, the politics of cartoons and mass media. In each unit I attempt to engage students in a dialogue, to teach them to find connections between their lives, literature, and society while at the same time remaining academically rigorous. As I discussed at greater length in Chapter 4, "essential" questions provide the focus for most units. In the politics of literacy section of Sophomore English, I ask, "What is literacy? Can people who don't know how to read and write be literate?" There is no one text that answers those questions.

A variety of readings — essays, poetry, short stories — as well as role plays, discussions, improvisations, writing from our own lives, all serve as "texts." We read excerpts from Frederick Douglass's and Malcolm X's autobiographies (1998 and 1992). We read sections from Joe Kane's *Savages* (1995) where an old man leads Kane through the Amazon jungle, identifying and discussing the properties of each plant. Students conduct interviews with their parents or grandparents about ways they "read the world without words," and return with stories about fishing, hairstyling, and driving diesel trucks. The curriculum becomes a symphony or a church choir. Each text, each student's life, adds a "voice." The texts are interwoven, but the recurring refrain is made up of the students' stories and analyses — their voices, either in discussion or in read-arounds of their own pieces — hold the song together. (See page 14 for a complete discussion of read-arounds.)

But let me state clearly, in case this sounds like all we do is sit around in a cafe-like atmosphere discussing politics and our lives: In all of these classes, the mainstay of the curriculum is rigorous reading and writing activities that prepare all students for the university or post-secondary institutions. The way these activities are taught, the undergirding of preparation for each reading and writing activity, and the follow-up differs from more traditional classes.

Years ago, when I taught my first untracked classes, I eliminated the canon from the curriculum altogether because I wanted students to hear the voices of women and people of color who are not traditionally represented. Students complained that *The Scarlet Letter* and *The Odyssey* weren't relevant to their lives. But I have come to see the value of maintaining some pieces from the canon so that students can understand literary allusions, read and critique the common curriculum, enter conversations that include these classics, and perceive how some themes do reverberate through the years. I also want them to look for the relevance that they might have missed. *Pygmalion* (1914) is the perfect example. On the surface, students may not see how a play set in England could teach them anything about their own lives, but a closer look reveals how the class issue of language that Shaw explored when it was first produced in London in 1914 is as relevant to their lives as it was to Eliza's.

Of course, some classics can also be used to hone students' critical reading skills as they investigate race, class, and gender issues in these books. Students need to ask the question "Whose classics? Why these books and not others?" as anti-racist educator Enid Lee does in her *Rethinking Schools* interview, "Taking Multicultural, Anti-Racist Education Seriously" (1994):

> [W]hen we say classical music, whose classical music are we talking about? European? Japanese? And what items are on the test? Whose culture do they reflect? Who is getting equal access to knowledge in the school? Whose perspective is heard, whose is ignored?

For example, students might ask why teach Shakespeare in an American literature class, but not a play by the Pulitzer prize winning African American, August Wilson? If discussion of the issue of slavery is important, why read Mark Twain and not Toni Morrison or Frederick Douglass? These questions raise important issues as students become "literate."

Also, students who have not been prepared for honors classes must learn to negotiate texts like *Othello* or *The Scarlet Letter* that are not immediately accessible. They must develop the ability to work through frustrations and immediate impulses to dismiss these texts as irrelevant or too hard. They need to learn that all readers get confused, but they must also have enough opportunities to succeed with complex materials to embed the belief that if they struggle long enough they will understand. Sometimes this means developing note-taking systems as well as study strategies, including learning when and where to find help.

The biggest shift in curriculum in most honors classes entails a more inclusive reading list. As my daughter Anna wrote when she was a senior at a school where advanced classes are predominantly white, "What student of color would want to come into a tracked honors class where all the work is by dead white men? The fact that writers of color are not a part of the curriculum pulls the welcome mat out from under their feet."

My explicit focus on the politics of language in my senior class, and on the study of education in my junior class, plays an additional role in untracking my classes. Because tracking has to one degree or another shaped students' academic self-concepts, especially for low-tracked students, taking a critical look at this process helps them rethink their potential. As Bill Bigelow (1994) wrote in an article on untracking the social studies classroom, "[T]he unequal system of education, of which tracking is an important part, needs a critical classroom examination so that students can expose and expel the voices of self-blame, and can overcome whatever doubts they have about their capacity for academic achievement."

> **The real challenge in untracked classes is the difference in students' reading ability. Perhaps the greatest roadblock for those of us who want to untrack classes is our students' inability to read difficult texts.**

Changing Reading Strategies

On the surface, a typical reason for not untracking classes is that lower-tracked students don't have the skills or the desire to work at more advanced levels, and will get left behind or slow down their more capable peers. But given the right strategies, these challenges to classroom success need not become barriers to untracking. Throughout this book I have addressed ways to bring students who lack skills to writing (See "Writing the Word and the World," page 58, and "Essay with an Attitude," page 68). But the real challenge in untracked classes is the difference in students' reading ability. Perhaps the greatest roadblock for those of us who want to untrack classes is our students' inability to read difficult texts.

How do we continue to assign challenging literature when not all of our students are initially capable of reading it? Some of the readings I use with students are difficult — for all students. To "dumb down" the curriculum would deny capable students access to a rigorous curriculum, and to always give different assignments to students based on their reading levels would defeat the purpose of joining students together.

Over the years, I've developed strategies to help readers at various levels engage in the curriculum. For example, I begin the year with my "Unlearning the Myths" unit (see page 40) because I want students to learn how to read for silences in the literature — whose voices are heard? Whose stories are told?

Whose lives are marginalized? Who's the hero and who gets saved? I want students to develop a habit of reading for recurring patterns of domination and exclusion. And I want them to approach these questions with "texts" that feel accessible to all: cartoons and children's literature.

And, I admit we read fewer texts/novels in my class because I choose to read, discuss, and think about each piece more thoroughly. Any text is an investigation into both literature and society, chosen not because it's on some university's reading-for-college-preparation list, but rather because it allows us to examine our society and ourselves more fully. *The Color Purple* (Walker, 1985), for example, permits us to probe the relationships between men and women as well as to explore their roles in the world. In *A Pedagogy for Liberation* (Shor and Freire, 1987), Ira Shor's discussion of the "illuminating" course helped me shape my classes:

> [W]e want the 'illuminating' course to be serious and on the other hand it has to develop the habits of intellectual seriousness in a culture field that discourages students from being critical. . . . The point is not to assign fewer books so that students will have time to memorize more of what they read. Learning is not a memory Olympics! The idea is to make critical reflection on society the fundamental activity. The idea is to avoid flying over the words in an heroic effort to reach the end of the reading list, flying over society also in such a way as to avoid knowing how learning relates to reality. Simply shortening the syllabus is not the same thing as investing the pedagogy with a purpose.

Sometimes that "pedagogy with a purpose" is served best by using literature circles that give students a choice of novels at different reading levels within a thematic unit. Students in my junior class, for example, chose from a list of novels written by African Americans about the conditions of slavery: *Beloved* (Morrison, 1998); *Kindred* (Butler, 1979); *I, Tituba, Black Witch of Salem* (Condé, 1992); *A Narrative of the Life of Frederick Douglass* (Douglass, op. cit.); and *Middle Passage* (Johnson, 1998). Because all students read literature dealing with slavery, they were able to discuss the connected issues, but inform each other with examples from various texts.

Sometimes I insist we all read the same material, especially when I try to teach certain reading, writing, critical literacy, or dialogue strategies. Tea parties, improvisations, dialogue journals, poetry, and interior monologues, as well as other tactics, teach students in any class how to read more critically. But in an untracked class, these methods equalize access to reading as well as push students to discuss content. Not every student in my class completes the readings by the due date, but they can still be involved in the discussion. Often the class talk entices nonreaders to read and provides a meaningful context for them to understand the text.

> *For nonreaders like Marvin, teachers must be willing to overcome years of resistance to reading as well as break well-developed non-reading coping strategies.*

Tea Party

Experienced readers don't balk at slow beginnings of novels. They are like swimmers who dive into cold water knowing there will be a delicious rush when they burst into a breast stroke or Australian crawl. But inexperienced readers panic and drown. There are too many names, the location is unfamiliar, they don't see the point. "What's this got to do with me?" They give up too soon — before the writer has grabbed them.

In a class discussion about reading, I once asked strong readers to talk about their habits. Renesa said, "Even if I don't like the first chapter, I keep reading. I know it will get better." Marvin, a poor reader, said if he didn't like the first few paragraphs, he couldn't keep reading. It tired him out just trying to remember the characters' names and long, descriptive passages bored him. Yet Marvin, like many poor readers, could memorize the lyrics to popular music and knew as much about rap artists as I know about most authors. The capacity was evident; the will and the belief that he could succeed were not. For nonreaders like Marvin, teachers must be willing to overcome years of resistance to reading as well as break well-developed non-reading coping strategies.

I use the Tea Party to entice poor readers into novels (or historical periods). The Tea Party is like a movie preview, presenting brief clips of the story line and characters to draw the audience in. For nonreaders or poor readers, this preview is essential, especially as they approach texts generally reserved for advanced classes. (See page 115 for a fuller description of tea parties and sample roles.)

Dialogue Journals

The method I use most frequently to equalize access to articles, essays, stories, and novels in untracked classes is the dialogue journal. The purpose of the journal is to teach students to read closely. As Shor (op. cit.) emphasized, "The idea is to make critical reflection on society the fundamental activity." Instead of reading to consume the story line or just for literary elements, I encourage students to "talk back" to the author — to engage in a conversation with the book, but also to think about the same kind of questions we asked earlier when examining cartoons. (For more details see Chapter 2, "Unlearning the Myths that Bind Us.")

In the dialogue journal, students become the authors of their own questions about reading, instead of reading merely to answer my questions. Because their dialogue journals are the starting ground for class discussions, students usually bring questions or passages they are really interested in discussing with their classmates.

Depending on the book I might prompt students to keep track of specific kinds of information. For example, in the biographical novel *Thousand Pieces of Gold* (McCunn, 1981) , I wanted to focus our discussion on immigration and history. I asked students to keep track of:

- Laws relating to the Chinese in the United States.

- Roles of women and men.

- Historical evidence — descriptions of camp conditions, what was happening in western states, etc.

- Relationships between racial groups.

- Similarities or differences in treatment of Chinese, Native Americans, African Americans.

- Good jumping off points to write poetry, interior monologues, narratives, essays.

At the beginning of class, I ask students to read over their dialogue journals and circle questions or passages they want the entire class to discuss. After students have assembled their contributions, I divide them into small groups and ask them to talk with each other using their questions/comments to initiate the conversation.

Each student poses a question, an observation, or a quote to the group, which they discuss before moving to the next person. Because small-group work requires students to share passages and questions, all students must continually go back to the text to read and reread for clarification — a technique that helps both the skilled and the unskilled reader.

Jean-Claude Lejeune

Each group posts one or two questions and passages on the board. The class chooses one, and we begin the class talk. In an untracked class, this strategy keeps less-skilled readers involved in the conversation. Once they've rehearsed and reread in the small group, they are ready to jump into a discussion — and usually ready to argue. For some students, it pulls them back in the novel because they like being part of the class debates.

In my Literature and U.S. History class, one group returned to the full class discussion with the following question: Is Craig Lesley [author of the novel *River Song* (1990)] racist, sexist, or homophobic when he makes the Mexican jokes, etc. or is he just trying to develop Danny's character? I took notes while the students discussed the question — the following selections are a partial snapshot of that discussion. My hand wasn't as fast their voices:

Angela: I think he's just trying to show what Danny is like.

Aaron: Okay, but then why does he have to keep bringing [racist remarks] up? Couldn't he just have him make those jokes during the first few chapters, then leave it alone? When he keeps doing it, it's an overkill. It seems like with the Native-American issues there is so much to cover, why

> **Instead of reading to consume the story line or just for literary elements, I encourage students to "talk back" to the author.**

spend time making jokes about Mexicans or male nurses?

Janice: Wouldn't he have to keep doing it if it's a characteristic? I mean he couldn't just do it for a few chapters then stop or else his character wouldn't be consistent.

Aaron: Yeah. I hadn't thought of that.

Sarah: I think he's trying to make a point about the Native-American culture — that since they are consistently being put down —alcoholism, lazy — that they put other people down, other racial groups.

Aiden: I think he's just trying to make it realistic. That's how people talk; they make fun of others.

Jim: Maybe he's trying to make us think about the racism, that's why he puts in so many — and against so many groups.

Aaron: But couldn't he do that and then have someone make a comment about it —like Pudge? When Danny makes a joke, couldn't she say, "Hey, that's not funny. Think about how people talk about Indians"?

Janice: Yeah. Because people do that in real life, too — stop someone when they're telling a racist joke.

READING, WRITING, AND RISING UP

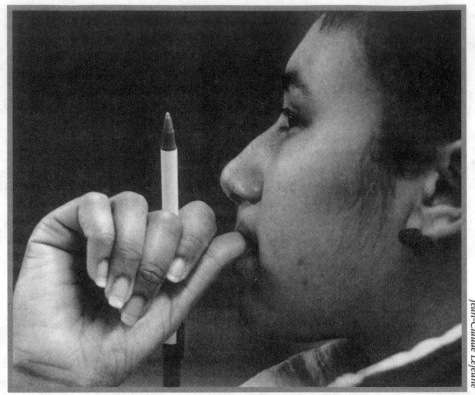

Jean-Claude Lejeune

This questioning method puts students in charge of the discussion rather than the teacher. It validates their questions. This is vital as we work toward a pedagogy of untracking. Sometimes in large group discussions when the teacher discusses symbolism or a well-read student remarks on the imagery in a passage, less-skilled readers are intimidated to ask the simple questions — which may often be more socially relevant. With dialogue journals, these students have an opportunity to figure out confusions with this small group before taking a point to the large group.

Again, students learn from each other by challenging each other's assumptions and listening to other opinions. Writing about the use of dialogue journals and the class discussions that stemmed from them, Claire wrote, "I got ideas I wouldn't have thought of, interpretations I would not have considered. When I really thought about all of it, I acquired some new skills from [my classmates]." Mira said that her notes made it easier to write an essay because she had page numbers and passages to review. And Tracy said, "Writing dialogue journals made me slow down to read."

Improvisations

The tea party sets the stage for the novel and helps students get into the book, and the dialogue journal and group work provide opportunities for rich discussions, but sometimes the story drags or the language is inaccessible for some students. Able readers create images while they are reading, but poor readers often struggle so much with word meanings that they don't visualize the story. In working with untracked students, it is essential to get them to "see" the book and improvisations help do just that. Improvs can also make a "classic" work more relevant by pushing students to create a contemporary version of the scene.

The play *Pygmalion*, for example, has phrasing and vocabulary that leave poor readers confused. I use improvisations to bring the work to life, to make the meaning of the piece clearer by staging it. I divide students into small groups, give each group a provocative part and ask them to create a scene that will help the class understand what took place in that particular section of the play. In small groups, students discuss the scene. As I move from group to group, I catch snatches of questions: What is going on? Who is Freddie? And then moving to higher level discussions: Why does Eliza throw the slipper at Higgins? Why doesn't she fight back when he calls her a "squashed cabbage leaf?"

As the groups reread their scenes, discuss the content, and act out the text, they provide new understandings to confused students. In *Pygmalion*, Goldie and Antonia rewrote the slipper scene in modern Jefferson language. Steffanie and Licy worked with the original script on the bath scene. After performing each scene, students stay in character on "stage," as the class questions them. Although I usually begin by modeling the kinds of questions I want students to ask, they quickly take over. To Higgins, one student asked, "Why do you feel like you can talk about Eliza in that way?" Another student asked Eliza's father, "Don't you care about your daughter? Aren't you just selling her? Isn't that like prostitution?"

Disagreements about the interpretation of a scene lead to engaged dialogue about character motivation, author's intent, and society. Often, students go back to the original text to "prove" their point to the class.

One year Mark's statement, "Henry didn't love Eliza, he considered her a professional equal," kept the class debating for an hour. In another class, Licy questioned whether Eliza's life improved with her new knowledge or brought her misery. Her reading and questioning of the play got at the politics of language. But as she questioned, she also talked about growing up in a Spanish-speaking home, and the difficulty of moving between the English-only world of school and the Spanish-only world of home — offering the class insights that would likely be rare in a more homogenous high-tracked class.

The improvisations help poor and able readers understand the work more deeply and critically. The improvs bring the story to life. We see and hear the story. But additionally, as we question the "actors," we also search for character motivation, for social influence. We read the story from the inside out. For poor readers, improvs provide a pause to bring them back to the table if they've failed to connect with the work or experience difficulty reading the piece on their own.

Interior Monologues and Poetry

When writing interior monologues and poems from a literary or historical character's point of view, students examine why characters act the way they do or capture the character's feelings at a critical moment. The writing puts students inside the literature. My students who come "up" from lower-tracked classes are often quite poetic in their responses. Interior monologues and point of view poems allow all students — regardless of their previous academic levels — to succeed and achieve greater insight.

Prior to writing interior monologues, students brainstorm strong "meditation" points of various characters. I share models from previous years so students understand what I want (see interior monologues, page 134). There is no right answer in these exercises. As I tell students, "The only way you can do this wrong is to not do it." Jenelle Yarbrough wrote from Janie's point of view after she married Joe in Zora Neale Hurston's *Their Eyes Were Watching God* (1991):

> *I am only a vision to them. I am an object. I'm loved by the curious eyes of a man or hated by the envious eyes of a woman. I will never know the love of everyone's caring and generous hearts. I keep silent because I'm told beauty speaks louder than words. Well, if my beauty speaks so loud, why can't anybody hear my heart crying for someone to love me for the reasons God intended them to and not the reasons of a mirror?*

We share the pieces out loud the following day and use the students' monologues as a springboard for our discussion. For example, after Jenelle read her piece, we talked about how Janie's position as the Mayor's wife separates her from the townspeople.

The poetry that students write from literature can generate unusual and important insights. In one exercise, I ask students to draw a metaphor about a character in the book. After students draw, I ask them to explain their drawing to the class, then write a poem which extends the metaphor. Jessica Rawlins drew a bottle of perfume and wrote her poem about Shug Avery from *The Color Purple*:

> **As I tell students, "The only way you can do this wrong is to not do it."**

> *I am Shug,*
> *I am the sweet breath*
> *every man holds onto at night.*
> *I am the lingering scent*
> *that stays*
> *to bring memories*
> *of violets*
> *and lily kisses.*
> *I am the sugar perfume*
> *that comes on strong,*
> *burns the senses,*
> *then vanishes.*
> *Leaving nothing*
> *but the life of a stolen thought.*

These poems sometimes become the raw outline of a metaphorical essay about the character. Again, the poetry balances the fulcrum of achievement in an untracked class because students from lower-track classes sometimes engage in more word play or music. But also, the poetry and the drawing allow for students who process information in different ways to share their strengths.

Filtering reading through improvisations, dialogue journals, interior monologues, poetry, and class discussions "slows" the class down. We don't "cover" as many novels as we did before. But students learn to think more deeply. They discover how to dig beneath the surface, how to make connections between texts, their own lives, and society.

In class evaluations students let me know in no uncertain terms that the units they enjoyed and learned the most from were the units we spent more time on. The units they enjoyed the least were the

> **The common element in each of the reading and writing strategies I've presented in this book is students working together in a community to make meaning and to make change.**

ones where I "bombarded [them] with readings" which I didn't give them time to digest.

The common element in each of the reading and writing strategies I've presented in this book is students working together in a community to make meaning and to make change. Students often mistakenly assume that it's cheating to work in a group. Yet most adults know that the while certain aspects of projects must be completed individually, a community of thoughtful people makes any endeavor stronger. In my own work, the teachers who comprise the local and national Rethinking Schools groups, my Writing Project colleagues, and the teacher-leaders from every high school in our district have been invaluable to my growth as a teacher. Their insights, critiques, reflection, and especially our points of disagreement make my teaching, writing, and community work stronger.

Courage in the Face of Anger

Tracking perpetuates systems of inequality that condemn students not only to unequal education, but to unequal opportunities once they leave school. In examining data regarding the placement of students of color in advanced or honors English classes (and even more drastically in math) in Portland Public Schools, it is clear that inequalities exist.

But untracking schools is not easy. It can be mandated by an administration — but that alone won't ensure success. Teachers must be an integral part of the process; they must have time to meet together, teach each other strategies, and prepare materials for a more diverse audience. Parents — representative of the entire student population — must be involved in creating a successful program to bring quality education to a broader range of students. But without the vision and the experience of a successful untracked class, parents — especially the parents of high-tracked students — might be uneasy partners — as Chetan's initial reaction to the loss of his privileges suggests.

Ten years after my students discussed the social impact of tracking, schools continue to be "beauty pageants" where some students learn they're "not good enough," where they become tracked for life. In addition to making a case against the injustice of tracking, we need to create not only a vision for an education that serves all children, we need models that demonstrate untracked classrooms can work. We can't just wish tracking away. There are too many barriers and too much resistance on too many levels. Now is the time for the language arts community to prove that justice and quality education are possible. ∎

References

Bigelow, Bill. "Getting Off the Track: Stories from an Untracked Classroom," in *Rethinking Our Classrooms: Teaching for Equity and Justice*. Milwaukee, WI: Rethinking Schools, 1994, pp. 58-65.

Butler, Octavia. *Kindred*. Garden City, NY: Doubleday, 1979.

Condé, Maryse. *I, Tituba, Black Witch of Salem*. Charlottesville, VA: University Press of Virginia, 1992.

Douglass, Frederick. *Narrative of the Life of Frederick Douglass: An American Slave*. Cambridge, MA: Belknap Press of Harvard University, 1960.

Hurston, Zora Neale. *Their Eyes Were Watching God*. Urbana, IL: University of Illinois Press, 1991.

Johnson, Charles. *Middle Passage*. New York: Scribner, 1998.

Kane, Joe. *Savages*. New York: Knopf, 1995.

Lee, Enid. "Taking Multicultural, Anti-Racist Education Seriously," in Bigelow, Bill, et al., *Rethinking Our Classrooms: Teaching for Equity and Justice*. Milwaukee, WI: Rethinking Schools, 1994, pp. 19-22.

Lesley, Craig. *River Song*. New York: Dell, 1990.

Malcolm X. *The Autobiography of Malcolm X*. New York: Ballantine, 1992.

McCunn, Ruthanne. *Thousand Pieces of Gold: A Biographical Novel*. San Francisco: Design Enterprises of San Francisco, 1981.

Morrison, Toni. *Beloved*. New York: Penguin, 1998.

Shaw, George Bernard. *Pygmalion: A play in five acts*. Harmondsworth, England: Penguin, 1914.

Shor, Ira & Freire, Paulo. *A Pedagogy for Liberation: Dialogues on Transforming Education*. South Hadley, MA: Bergin & Garvey, 1987.

Walker, Alice. *The Color Purple*. New York: Washington Square, 1982.

For Further Reading

Owen, David. *None of the Above: Behind the Myth of Scholastic Aptitude*. Boston: Houghton Mifflin, 1985.

Rodriguez, Richard. "Achievement of Desire," in *Rereading America: Cultural Contexts for Critical Thinking and Writing*. Boston: Bedford, 1998.

Smitherman, Geneva. *Talkin' and Testifyin': The Language of Black America*. Detroit: Wayne State University Press, 1986.

Tatum, Beverly. *"Why Are All the Black Kids Sitting Together in the Cafeteria?" and Other Conversations About Race*. New York: Basic Books, 1997.

Index

A PUBLICATION OF RETHINKING SCHOOLS

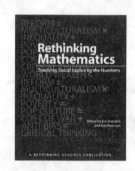

READING, WRITING, AND RISING UP
Teaching About Social Justice and the Power of the Written Word
By Linda Christensen
Essays, lesson plans, and a remarkable collection of student writing, with an unwavering focus on language arts teaching for justice.

Paperback • 196 pages • ISBN 0-942961-25-0
ONLY $12.95!*

RETHINKING OUR CLASSROOMS, Volume 1
Teaching for Equity and Justice
Creative teaching ideas, compelling narratives, and hands-on examples of how teachers can promote values of community, justice, and equality—and build academic skills.

Paperback • 216 pages • ISBN 0-942961-18-8
ONLY $12.95!*

RETHINKING OUR CLASSROOMS, Volume 2
This companion volume to the first *Rethinking Our Classrooms* is packed with more great articles about teaching for social justice, as well as curriculum ideas, lesson plans, and resources.

Paperback • 240 pages • ISBN 0-942961-27-7
ONLY $12.95!*

RETHINKING OUR CLASSROOMS, Volumes 1 and 2 Combined Set
Widely used in teacher education and staff development programs.

ISBN 0-942962-36-6
ONLY $19.95 per set!*
Save 20%!

* Plus shipping and handling.
See order form below for details.